THE ATOMIC BOMB

THE
MAGILL
BIBLIOGRAPHIES

Other Magill Bibliographies:

American Ethnic Literatures—David R. Peck
Biography—Carl Rollyson
Energy—Joseph R. Rudolph, Jr.
Environmental Studies—Diane M. Fortner
The History of Science—Gordon L. Miller
Human Genetics—Jean Helgeson
The Origin and Evolution of Life on Earth—David W. Hollar, Jr.
Poverty in America—Steven Pressman
Shakespeare—Joseph Rosenblum
The Vietnam War in Literature—Philip K. Jason

THE ATOMIC BOMB

An Annotated Bibliography

Hans G. Graetzer
and
Larry M. Browning

South Dakota State University

SALEM PRESS

Pasadena, California   Englewood Cliffs, New Jersey

Library of Congress Cataloging-in-Publication Data

Graetzer, Hans G., 1930-
    The atomic bomb / Hans G. Graetzer
        p.   cm.—(Magill bibliographies)
    Includes bibliographic references and index
    ISBN 0-89356-677-2
    1. Atomic bomb—Bibliography. I. Browning, Larry
M. II. Title. III. Series.
Z6724.A9G73   1992
[UG1282.A8]   92-29628
016.3558'25119—dc20   CIP

"Why do the nations so furiously rage together?"

Psalm 2:1

"Rest peacefully, for the error shall not be repeated."

Hiroshima Park of Peace inscription

This book is dedicated to past and future participants in the search for peace and justice.

EDITORIAL STAFF

CONTENTS

page

Introduction 1
    The Nuclear Arms Race, 1940-1990 1
    Nuclear Physics Background 1
    The Manhattan Project 2
    Hiroshima and Nagasaki 2
    Start of the U.S.-Soviet Arms Race 2
    Bomb Tests and Radioactive Fallout 3
    Strategic Arms Limitation Talks (SALT I) and Détente 3
    The Second Cold War (1980-1986) 3
    Breakup of the Soviet Union 4
    How Books Were Selected for This Bibliography 4
    Movies and Documentaries 5
    How to Use This Bibliography 6
  The Nuclear Arms Race: A Chronology 6

Chapter 1: General Background about Radioactivity, Fission,
    and Fusion 9

Chapter 2: Biographies of Atomic Scientists 14

Chapter 3: Atomic Bomb Development in the United States 25
    The Manhattan Project 25
    Soviet Espionage 30

Chapter 4: Hiroshima and Nagasaki 34

Chapter 5: Bomb Development Outside the United States 42

Chapter 6: Weapons Testing and Radioactive Fallout 55

Chapter 7: The H-bomb and the Nuclear Arms Race 63

Chapter 8: The Peace Movement 111

Chapter 9: Videocassettes, Documentaries, and Movies 128

Chapter 10: The Atomic Bomb in Literature 142

Index 161

THE ATOMIC BOMB

INTRODUCTION

The Nuclear Arms Race, 1940-1990

This bibliography is intended to be accessible to readers who are not specialists in science. As an introduction to the nuclear arms race, some key experiments in the history of nuclear physics will be reviewed here to provide general background for understanding the technology of bomb development. A chronology follows this introduction.

Nuclear Physics Background

Nuclear physics had its beginning in 1897 when Antoine-Henri Becquerel in France observed that uranium ore emits a penetrating, new kind of radiation. The rays were able to pass through black paper wrapped around photographic film and to produce a self-image of the uranium rock on the film. Marie Curie, a graduate student under Becquerel, showed in her Ph.D. thesis that there were actually three distinct types of radiation, which she designated alpha, beta, and gamma radioactivity.

In 1911, Ernest Rutherford in England scattered alpha particles from various metal targets and established the nuclear atom model, in which a small but massive nucleus is surrounded by electrons in orbit, like a tiny solar system. Rutherford also performed the first artificial nuclear reaction. He showed in 1919 that nitrogen can be transmuted into its neighboring element on the periodic table, oxygen.

During the 1920's, a link was established between radioactivity and cancer. Workers had been hired to paint radium on watch dials to make them glow in the dark. Their habit of licking the brushes to point the tips was eventually recognized to be a hazard when a number of them died from cancer of the tongue, jaw, and lungs.

In 1931, the first cyclotron nuclear accelerator was built by Ernest Lawrence at the University of California at Berkeley. With accelerators it became possible to produce new radioactive materials that were useful as tracers in biology, medicine, and nutrition. Enrico Fermi in Italy, using neutral particles called neutrons, extended the technique to make radioactive isotopes for almost all the elements known to chemists at that time.

When the element uranium was bombarded by neutrons, a unique type of reaction occurred, splitting the nucleus into two pieces with a large release of energy. This process, called fission, was first identified in 1938 by Otto Hahn and coworkers in Germany. Some notable European scientists who had fled to the United States as refugees from Nazi persecution pointed out the possibility that fission energy might be used to create a powerful explosive. They warned of a military disaster if Germany succeeded in building a bomb first.

The Manhattan Project

In order to make an atomic bomb from uranium, it is essential to produce a chain reaction. The fission process should produce not only energy but also some extra neutrons, which can then bombard more uranium and release more neutrons to continue the energy production. Fermi created the first successful chain reaction in 1942, using about six tons of uranium metal assembled in a pile of graphite blocks located in a squash court at the University of Chicago.

General Leslie R. Groves was put in charge of the project to convert the basic uranium fission experiment into a usable military weapon. Three major laboratories were built under wartime conditions of urgency and secrecy. Oak Ridge, Tennessee, became the site for purifying and separating the fissionable isotope uranium 235 from the nonfissioning remainder. At Hanford, Washington, four reactors were built to produce another possible bomb material, plutonium. At Los Alamos, New Mexico, the actual work of bomb design was started in 1943 under the leadership of J. Robert Oppenheimer.

In the spring of 1945, President Franklin D. Roosevelt died and Germany surrendered, but the war against Japan continued. The Trinity test explosion, with its awesome mushroom cloud, took place in the New Mexico desert on July 16. Some scientists petitioned to stop the bomb from being used in the war, but it was too late. Hiroshima and Nagasaki were destroyed on August 6 and 9 respectively, and Japan surrendered a few days later.

Hiroshima and Nagasaki

More than 100,000 people in these two cities were killed almost immediately by blast and incineration. Many others died soon afterward from extensive skin burns and a disease previously unknown to doctors, radiation sickness. Photographs of destroyed buildings do not adequately tell the story of the traumatic suffering of survivors. Reading the interviews and stories written by *hibakusha*, the bomb-affected victims, will arouse a deeper understanding among outside observers for the human tragedy of the bomb.

Start of the U.S.-Soviet Arms Race

In 1945, the United States had a monopoly on atomic bombs, but it lasted only for four years. The establishment of the Warsaw Pact in Eastern Europe and the North Atlantic Treaty Organization (NATO) Alliance in the West, as well as the division of Germany, led British prime minister Winston Churchill to state that an "Iron Curtain" had descended across central Europe. The first Soviet atomic bomb test in 1949, the fall of China to Communism, and the start of the Korean War in 1950 brought on an anti-Communist hysteria in the United States. The hydrogen bomb was developed by both superpowers and tested almost simultaneously in 1953. Intercontinental ballistic missiles (ICBMs) and nuclear submarines were being deployed to augment the Strategic Air Command's long-range bombers. The Cold War stimulated an escalation of weapons leading toward a military confrontation.

Bomb Tests and Radioactive Fallout

In 1954, a 10-megaton hydrogen bomb (equal to 500 Hiroshima-size atom bombs) was detonated by the United States in the South Pacific. A Japanese fishing boat, the *Lucky Dragon*, was seriously contaminated by fallout one hundred miles away. Unfortunately, contaminated fish were sold·at market in Japan before the problem was recognized, and public demonstrations against testing took place. In the 1950's, the Atomic Energy Commission also established a bomb testing site in Nevada, not far from Las Vegas, which sometimes produced heavy fallout downwind, in western Utah.

Nobel Prize winners Linus Pauling and Albert Schweitzer, together with other distinguished scientists, made public appeals for an end to testing. Nevil Shute's novel *On the Beach*, published in 1957, further aroused world opinion against fallout. A voluntary moratorium on nuclear testing lasted from 1958 to 1961, but then the explosions were resumed. One huge Soviet blast was equivalent to about 60 million tons of trinitrotoluene (TNT), intended perhaps only to intimidate the United States; there is no suitable target for such a weapon. During his first year in office, President John F. Kennedy recommended the construction of civilian fallout shelters. The Berlin Crisis in 1961, followed by the Cuban Missile Crisis in 1962, brought the two superpowers to the brink of war. Eventually, the fear of mutual annihilation led to genuine negotiations, culminating in a ban on atmospheric testing in 1963.

The nuclear arsenal of strategic weapons grew rapidly, from about 5,000 in 1957 to more than 25,000 in 1965 for the United States. More weapons than that becomes redundant because the number of enemy targets is limited. The older, liquid-fuel Titan missiles were replaced by the solid-fuel Minuteman, which could be launched from its underground silo with less than a two-minute warning.

Strategic Arms Limitation Talks (SALT I) and Détente

Under presidents Lyndon B. Johnson and Richard M. Nixon, the United States became preoccupied with war in Vietnam (and political protest at home), the Civil Rights movement, and the Watergate scandal. In the nuclear arms race, the U.S. position had gradually shifted from monopoly to superiority to parity with the Soviets. Henry Kissinger helped to negotiate the SALT I agreement in 1972, in which the superpowers mutually agreed not to build a defensive antiballistic missile system. Such a defense shield probably would have escalated the production of more offensive missiles on both sides and therefore would have brought no increase in national security. The late 1970's was a period of lessened belligerence between the superpowers, commonly called détente.

The Second Cold War (1980-1986)

American frustration over the long-lasting Iranian hostage crisis and the Soviet invasion of Afghanistan helped President Ronald Reagan to be elected in 1980 on a strong promilitary platform. Large appropriations for building up both conventional and nuclear forces were approved by Congress. Some officials in the Reagan Administration stated openly that nuclear war against the Soviets, the "evil empire," was winnable. In Third World conflicts such as those in Central America and Grenada, the United States relied on military force to attain its political objectives.

In the United States, the Nuclear Freeze movement attracted many supporters and peace organizations. Groups of lawyers, doctors, teachers, and religious leaders spoke out against growing militarism. In Europe, widespread opposition to placing U.S. missiles in NATO countries stimulated a strong disarmament movement. Also in the early 1980's, scientific studies by Carl Sagan and others aroused fears of a "nuclear winter" resulting from dirt and soot in the atmosphere if a nuclear war took place.

In 1983, President Reagan gave a televised speech advocating a protective shield of laser beams and satellite weapons that would shoot down enemy missiles before they reached U.S. targets. This Strategic Defense Initiative (SDI), commonly called Star Wars, drew widespread criticism from scientists. First of all, there were many questions about the reliability of such a system. Secondly, SDI would place reliance on another high-tech superweapon rather than trying to solve political controversies by negotiation.

Breakup of the Soviet Union

When Mikhail Gorbachev became president of the Soviet Union in 1985, he advocated greater freedom of expression and a basic restructuring of Communist society. Unrest about lack of consumer goods and deteriorating social conditions led to protest demonstrations in the occupied countries of Eastern Europe. The Chernobyl nuclear accident in 1986, with its release of radioactivity, showed that such technological problems cannot be confined by national boundaries.

The Soviet political upheaval of the late 1980's was unanticipated and almost unbelievable. The reunification of East and West Germany, the disintegration of the Soviet Union into separate republics, and the fall of the Communist Party would have been unthinkable a few years earlier. In the United States, the end of the Cold War has brought an opportunity to redirect military spending toward neglected social and environmental problems.

New questions are being asked about nuclear weapons. Who has control of the remaining Soviet arsenal of missiles? If weapons are dismantled, what will be done with the warheads? What security measures are needed to prevent weapons from falling into the hands of Third World dictators or terrorist groups?

How Books Were Selected for This Bibliography

Every book selected for inclusion was individually obtained from a library and is reviewed firsthand by the authors of this compilation. Interested readers should be able to find any of these books through college or public libraries or by interlibrary loan.

The primary focus of this bibliography is the atomic bomb and the nuclear arms race. In order to keep the number of entries to a manageable length for general readers, it is necessary to exclude some related topics that have an extensive literature of their own. For example, the subject of nuclear power plants, although indirectly associated with nuclear weapons, is not covered in this compilation.

Other excluded topics are the following: histories of the Cold War and various crises in international relations; professional scientific books on the technology of weapons and missiles; general studies of military strategy; and literature of the pacifist movement.

Only books are included in this bibliography, not magazine articles (unless they were reprinted in book form). Also, government documents are not surveyed. In the chapter on the atomic bomb in literature, short stories from science-fiction magazines are excluded; however, an excellent book by Paul Brians, *Nuclear Holocausts* (see chapter 10), gives interested readers more than a thousand references to this more specialized subject.

Movies and Documentaries

All movies and documentaries listed, like the books, are obtainable, mostly in the form of videotapes, and are reviewed firsthand by the authors. Unfortunately, many significant movies are difficult or impossible to obtain and consequently are omitted. The *1984 National Directory of Audiovisual Resources on Nuclear War and the Arms Race*, edited by Karen Sayer and John Dowling, provides an extensive catalog of atomic bomb movies and documentaries up to 1984. Unfortunately, this source has never been updated and is currently out of print; however, it is available through interlibrary loan.

The MacArthur Library, sponsored by The John D. and Catherine T. MacArthur Foundation, has made available to more than two thousand libraries, at no charge, a set of five movies and supplementary material on "Peace and International Cooperation." Four of the five films are relevant to nuclear war and are included in this review. Additional information and support, including distributor lists and "Discussion and Teaching Guides," may be obtained free of charge from The John D. and Catherine T. MacArthur Foundation, Library Video Classics Project, P.O. Box 409113, Chicago, Illinois, 60640, telephone (800) 346-5383. Copies of the teaching guides may be made and distributed under very broad guidelines.

The authors urge anyone wishing to use a film for other than personal viewing to preview the film and to abide by the copyright laws for that film. The reviews presented here are intended to help find suitable materials but may not be thorough enough for all situations. Only by careful previewing may a user determine the suitability of a film or segment for an intended audience. The authors strongly discourage illegal duplication or viewing of materials. If a user has questions concerning the fair use of any of the listed movies, he or she should contact the distributor.

How to Use This Bibliography
   The intended audience for this bibliography is high school and college students, adult discussion groups, and general readers. Someone who has a particular interest in the topic of radioactive fallout, weapons proliferation, literature written by Hiroshima survivors, or the peace movement, for example, will find numerous entries given in the pertinent chapters.
   Some books are designated as "highly recommended" according to the annotator's best judgment. A college teacher who wants to select an appropriate text for a course on the arms race may find these evaluations helpful.

The Nuclear Arms Race: A Chronology

1938 Discovery of uranium fission by Otto Hahn and Fritz Strassman in Germany

1939 Albert Einstein writes letter to President Roosevelt warning of uranium bomb potential

1941 Bombing of Pearl Harbor; United States enters the war

1942 Manhattan Project organized under General Leslie R. Groves
     First successful chain reaction experiment

1944 Nuclear reactors at Hanford start producing plutonium
     Los Alamos Laboratory set up under Oppenheimer

1945 April 12, Roosevelt dies; Harry S. Truman becomes president
     July 16, Trinity test explosion in New Mexico
     August 6 and 9, Hiroshima and Nagasaki bombed

1946 Two test explosions at Bikini atoll, South Pacific
     John Hersey's book *Hiroshima* is published

1947 Atomic Energy Commission established by Congress

1949 Communists defeat Chiang Kai-shek in China
     First Soviet atomic bomb explosion

1950 Klaus Fuchs, Soviet spy, is arrested
     Truman orders development of hydrogen bomb
     Start of the Korean War

1951 Julius and Ethel Rosenberg espionage trial

1951 United States starts atomic test explosions in Nevada

1952 First British atomic bomb explosion, Australia
First U.S. H-bomb test at Eniwetok atoll, South Pacific

1953 President Dwight D. Eisenhower agrees to Korean armistice
Secretary of State John Foster Dulles warns Soviets of "massive retaliation"
First Soviet H-bomb test

1954 First nuclear submarine USS *Nautilus* is launched
Japanese fishing boat contaminated by fallout
Oppenheimer loses security clearance

1955 Geneva Conference on peaceful uses of atomic energy
Bomb tests continue; worldwide protest against fallout

1957 Sputnik 1, first earth satellite, launched
The novel *On The Beach* is published

1958 Minuteman missile contract awarded to the Boeing Company

1960 First French atomic explosion, Sahara desert

1961 Berlin blockade and airlift; the Berlin Wall is built
President Kennedy urges building fallout shelters

1962 Cuban Missile Crisis
The film *Dr. Strangelove: Or, How I learned to Stop Worrying and Love the Bomb* is released

1963 Limited test ban treaty is signed; underground testing continues

1963-1973 Vietnam War

1964 First Chinese atomic explosion

1966 B-52 accident over Spain; four H-bombs fall

1967 Outer Space Treaty is signed

1968 Assassinations of Martin Luther King, Jr., and Robert F. Kennedy
Race riots in U.S. cities
Solid-fuel rockets developed for Minuteman missiles

1969 First Apollo moon landing

1971 Multiple warhead technology developed

1972 Strategic Arms Limitation Talks (SALT I) lead to ban on antiballistic missiles

1973 Secretary of State Kissinger develops policy of détente

1974 First atomic explosion by India
    President Nixon is forced to resign

1975 Trident submarine program started, each sub carrying 120 megatons
    Soviet physicist Andrei Sakharov awarded Nobel Peace Prize

1976 Neutron bomb production authorized, later canceled

1979 Soviet troops invade Afghanistan; SALT II withdrawn
    Trident I submarine missile deployed

1981 President Reagan inaugurated; military buildup accelerates
    Anti-NATO demonstrations in Europe

1982 Nuclear freeze rally in New York draws almost a million people

1983 U.S. cruise missiles deployed in Europe
    President Reagan gives Strategic Defense Initiative (SDI) speech, urging space
    weapons
    Nuclear winter scenario described by Sagan
    U.S. film *The Day After* shown on television

1985 Gorbachev becomes Soviet president

1986 Chernobyl accident; widespread radioactivity

1987 U.S.-Soviet Union nuclear weapons reduction agreements

1989 Berlin Wall taken down

1990 The Soviet-U.S. Cold War ends
    Political reunification of Germany

1990-1995 Deactivation of Minuteman missiles from silos

Chapter 1
GENERAL BACKGROUND ABOUT RADIOACTIVITY, FISSION, AND FUSION

Burns, Grant. *The Atomic Papers: A Citizen's Guide to Selected Books and Articles on the Bomb, the Arms Race, Nuclear Power, the Peace Movement, and Related Issues*. Metuchen, N.J.: Scarecrow Press, 1984.
An index, with annotations, listing more than a thousand books and journal articles concerning different aspects of nuclear weapons and power plants. The entries are categorized into subtopics such as civil defense, Soviet spies, weapons proliferation, the Cuban Missile Crisis, the Atomic Energy Commission, the peace movement, and so forth. The author feels that the younger generation urgently needs to be better informed about the threat of nuclear weapons. He gives some well-chosen quotations, such as the words spoken by Martin Luther King, Jr., in 1967: "We still have a choice today: nonviolent coexistence or violent coannihilation."

Calder, Ritchie. *Living With the Atom*. Chicago: University of Chicago Press, 1962.
In 1960, the University of Chicago organized two international symposia in which science writers and scientists were brought together to discuss how to present information on atomic energy more effectively for the general public. Calder, a British science editor, served as a session moderator. In this informative book, he describes how people have become apprehensive about radioactivity in the environment, especially from nuclear weapons testing and from storage of radioactive wastes. How can society evaluate technological hazards without magnifying a real risk out of proportion? Fear of radioactivity should not be exaggerated, but neither should it be ridiculed. Public attitudes about other hazards such as food additives or lead in gasoline are discussed for comparison. A well-balanced presentation. Photographs of several nuclear facilities are included.

Campbell, John W. *The Atomic Story*. New York: Henry Holt, 1947.
A popularization of the development of the atomic bomb, written by a well-known author and editor of science-fiction stories. He begins with a historical overview of atomic knowledge: chemical elements, the electron, X rays, radioactivity, the cyclotron, the discovery of uranium fission. In the next section, he explains the basic principles of the chain reaction, plutonium production, isotope separation and bomb design. Finally, he describes the effects of the nuclear weapons used on Nagasaki and Hiroshima, including fallout. Explanations are clearly stated and scientifically correct. Some picturesque analogies are used; for example, Geiger counters "rattled like castanets." The danger of a postwar

nuclear arms race is anticipated with the accurate warning that it would be "all offense and no defense." Strongly recommended for a general audience.

Cantelon, Philip, Richard G. Hewlett, and Robert C. Williams, eds. *The American Atom: A Documentary History of Nuclear Policies from the Discovery of Fission to the Present*. 2d ed. Philadelphia: University of Pennsylvania Press, 1991.
A compilation of letters, memoranda, papers, reports, and so on, dealing with every aspect of nuclear energy. The nine main sections each begin with an elucidating summary by the editors and then reproduce a number of major documents from primary sources. Everything from H. G. Wells's prediction of atomic bombs through the Manhattan Project, the Baruch plan, hydrogen bomb development, Oppenheimer's security hearing, the nuclear test ban, deterrence, arms control, and nuclear power is referenced. A useful collection of primary material is reprinted, such as eyewitness accounts of the Trinity test, President Reagan's views on deterrence, and copies of treaties or agreements. A valuable resource book, updated in the second edition with recently declassified documents.

Graetzer, Hans G., and David L. Anderson. *The Discovery of Nuclear Fission: A Documentary History*. New York: Van Nostrand Reinhold, 1971. Reprint. New York: Arno Press, 1981.
Provides excerpts from the original articles that led up to the discovery of uranium fission in 1939. Publications by Enrico Fermi, Otto Hahn, Irene Curie, Niels Bohr, and others have been translated into English, with introductory comments to provide background material for the reader. The last chapter gives reprints of some historic documents: Einstein's 1939 letter to President Roosevelt; the Franck Report of June, 1945, stating scientists' objections to using the bomb; and Henry L. Stimson's article from *Harper's Magazine* in 1947 justifying his decision. The appendix gives a brief selection of books for further reading.

Glasstone, Samuel. *Sourcebook on Atomic Energy*. New York, Toronto, and London: D. Van Nostrand, 1950.
As an introduction and overview of nuclear physics, this book has become a classic. It was originally intended for journalists, authors, and editors who needed a reliable source of information on atomic energy. A list of topics includes the following: atomic structure, types of radioactivity, isotopes, accelerators, fission, mass-energy conversion, the Geiger counter and other detectors, artificial elements beyond uranium, uses of radioactivity in medicine and agriculture, and hazards of radiation. Clear verbal explanations and helpful diagrams are provided. The book was widely used in college classes and is probably obtainable through a library.

Glasstone, Samuel, and Philip J. Dolan, eds. *The Effects of Nuclear Weapons*. 3d
ed. Washington, D.C.: U.S. Department of Defense and Department of Energy,
1977.
The most comprehensive and authoritative information about all aspects of
nuclear explosions is assembled in this 650-page treatise. Earlier editions were
published in 1950 and 1962. Each chapter starts with a descriptive overview,
followed by a more technical analysis with graphs and equations. The following
topics are included: explosions in the atmosphere, underwater, and underground;
air blast and resulting damage to buildings (with many photos); thermal radiation
from the fireball; immediate nuclear radiation; disruption of radar and of radio
communication; biological effects of blast, burns, and radiation; delayed fallout
of radioactive iodine and strontium; and genetic effects of radiation. This book
provides the scientific basis for predicting how much damage would be produced
by a 1-megaton explosion over Boston, for example. Good reference.

Hecht, Selig. *Explaining the Atom*. New York: Viking Press, 1947, rev. ed., 1954.
A classic of popular scientific writing about the history of the atomic bomb. The
book was kept short and free of scholarly jargon, with simple but precise
explanations. The following topics are discussed: development of the periodic
table of elements before 1900; discovery of radioactivity; structure of the atom;
uranium fission and the first chain reaction; wartime construction of plutonium
production reactors; uranium isotope separation; bomb design and test explosion
in New Mexico; postwar efforts to ban nuclear weapons; the first Soviet bomb
in 1949; the hydrogen bomb and the start of the arms race; and the menace of
total destruction from a nuclear war. Still suitable as an excellent overview for
modern readers.

Lapp, Ralph E. *Roads to Discovery*. New York: Harper & Brothers, 1960.
An elementary introduction to modern physics, suitable for a reader with little
scientific background. The author draws an appealing picture of scientists as
explorers on a quest for new knowledge, adding their contributions toward a
better understanding of the laws of nature. The most important discoveries of
atomic physics are described in their historical context: Roentgen's discovery of
X rays; the early investigations of radioactivity by Marie Curie and others;
Rutherford's nuclear atom model; the invention of the cyclotron by Ernest
Lawrence; the discovery of uranium fission and the first chain reaction; ongoing
research on hydrogen fusion energy and subatomic particles. Clear explanations
of scientific ideas, with helpful diagrams.

Laurence, William L. *Men and Atoms: The Discovery, the Uses, and the Future of
Atomic Energy*. New York: Simon & Schuster, 1959.
The author was a well-known science writer for *The New York Times*, where he
had won the Pulitzer Prize and other awards. In this book, he relates the story

of the atomic bomb, from the discovery of fission to the destruction of Hiroshima and Nagasaki. He was chosen by General Groves as the official journalist to explain the Manhattan Project to the general public. He was given access to the various nuclear laboratories, he viewed the Trinity test explosion in New Mexico, and he accompanied the bombing mission over Nagasaki. He provides interesting anecdotes about the leading scientists. Postwar benefits of atomic energy are optimistically portrayed, including electric power plants, medical breakthroughs, and the hydrogen bomb to maintain peace.

Office of Technology Assessment. *The Effects of Nuclear War*. Washington, D.C.: U.S. Government Printing Office, 1979. Reprint with additions. Detroit, Mich.: Gale Research Company, 1984.
This comprehensive study was prepared as background information for congressional debate on the second round of Strategic Arms Limitation Talks (SALT II) in 1979. Several scenarios were analyzed, ranging from a single nuclear explosion over Detroit or Leningrad to an all-out nationwide attack on military and civilian targets. Direct effects of blast, fire, and radiation were considered, as well as the indirect effects of social, economic, and political disruption. Long-term ecological damage and problems of recuperation were assessed, but large uncertainties were recognized in trying to make quantitative estimates. One chapter deals with the controversial issue of civil defense. Maps, graphs, and casualty estimates from this study have been widely reprinted elsewhere. An executive summary and an interview with Dr. Peter Sharfman, the project director, are included.

Wagner, Henry N., and Linda E. Ketchum. *Living with Radiation: The Risk, The Promise*. Baltimore, Md.: The Johns Hopkins University Press, 1989.
The authors are, respectively, a medical doctor and a science writer. They present a balanced, informative account of both the hazards and the benefits of nuclear radiation. After reviewing important discoveries in the history of radioactivity, they give a summary of atomic bomb development and the decision to use the bomb. A chapter on nuclear medicine gives examples of how radiation is used for detection and treatment of tumors. They provide a good overview of natural radioactivity in the environment, and tell what happened at Three Mile Island and Chernobyl. They express the view that the general public underestimates the dangers of a nuclear war but overestimates the risks of peaceful uses for nuclear radiation. Well written; for a general audience.

Weart, Spencer R. *Nuclear Fear: A History of Images*. Cambridge, Mass.: Harvard University Press, 1988.
The author is the director of the Center for History of Physics at the American Institute of Physics. He has made a scholarly study of common symbols and fantasies about nuclear power, using source material from science fiction,

political debates, comic book representations, and popular journalism. On the one hand, there is an exaggerated hope for a technological utopia with all the wonders of modern civilization, evident, for example, in Walt Disney's Epcot Center. On the other hand, there is Frankenstein's monster, the mushroom cloud, the world ending as one vast Hiroshima. The author argues that both the fears and hopes are frequently naïve, that popular attitudes are based on emotional imagery more than facts. Many examples are given, documented by an extensive bibliography in the appendix.

Wolfson, Richard. *Nuclear Choices: A Citizen's Guide to Nuclear Technology.* Cambridge, Mass.: MIT Press, 1991.
An excellent introduction to nuclear technology for nonscientists. Part 1 gives an overview of atomic structure, radioactivity, fission energy, and radiation hazards. Part 2 explains the operation of reactors and presents both sides of the controversy about nuclear power plants. Part 3 describes the development of nuclear weapons and the arms race, including the ongoing problem of nuclear proliferation. Photographs, cartoons, and quotations from news articles are included in the book, providing a historical context for the reader. Each chapter also gives references for further investigation and a glossary of terminology. This book was written for a college course; readers are invited to form their own opinions on controversial issues. Informative; highly recommended.

Chapter 2
BIOGRAPHIES OF ATOMIC SCIENTISTS

Alsop, Joseph, and Stewart Alsop. *We Accuse!: The Story of the Miscarriage of American Justice in the Case of J. Robert Oppenheimer*. New York: Simon & Schuster, 1954.

The Alsop brothers were well-known journalists who wrote a syndicated column on political issues that appeared in nearly two hundred newspapers. This short book on the Oppenheimer security hearing contains a vehement indictment of the politically motivated charges against him. Oppenheimer's opposition to building the hydrogen bomb in 1949 and other controversial advice had made some important enemies for him. The background of personal antagonism by Admiral Lewis Strauss, chairman of the Atomic Energy Commission, and by Edward Teller are described in the chapter on "Oppenheimer Haters." The fall of Oppenheimer is viewed as part of the power struggle in the 1950's to squash political opposition. Selected testimony from the hearing is reprinted in the appendix.

Bernstein, Jeremy. *Hans Bethe: Prophet of Energy*. New York: Basic Books, 1979.

Hans Bethe (1906-   ) won the Nobel Prize in Physics in 1937 for his work on energy production in stars. This biography is written like an extended conversation, giving Bethe's responses to the interviewer's questions. The middle part of the book, entitled "Working on the Bomb," records Bethe's recollections of his role as head of the Theoretical Physics Division at Los Alamos. After the war, he spoke out on many controversial issues such as antiballistic missiles, the test ban treaty, and the nuclear arms race. He explains his views in support of nuclear power plants while opposing nuclear weapons production. The author of this biography is known for his skill as a writer of science for the general public.

Blumberg, Stanley A., and Louis G. Panos. *Edward Teller: Giant of the Golden Age of Physics*. New York: Charles Scribner's Sons, 1990.

In the public mind, Edward Teller's name is identified with the phrase "father of the H-bomb." This biography is based on personal interviews with Teller, his family, and his scientific colleagues. He was born in Hungary in 1908. His childhood and education in Europe are described. At Los Alamos, he was characterized as a maverick who insisted on working out his own ideas for an H-bomb, instead of cooperating on the main project. He became a frequent spokesman for right-wing politicians in Congress in support of large military appropriations. He antagonized many scientific colleagues by testifying against Oppenheimer in 1954, by opposing the nuclear test ban treaty in 1963, and by supporting the Strategic Defense Initiative (SDI) in 1983. A sympathetic biography of a controversial figure.

Boorse, Henry A., Lloyd Motz and Jefferson H. Weaver. *The Atomic Scientists: A Biographical History*. New York: John Wiley & Sons, 1989.
Contains short biographical sketches of atomic scientists, with summaries of their main scientific contributions. Included among the nineteenth century pioneers of atomic physics are John Dalton, Amadeo Avogadro, James Maxwell, and Dmitri Mendeleev. Early in the twentieth century, significant discoveries were made by Henri Becquerel, Pierre and Marie Curie, Ernest Rutherford, Albert Einstein, and Niels Bohr. The next generation of outstanding physicists included Enrico Fermi, Ernest Lawrence, Werner Heisenberg, and Hans Bethe. The authors also describe the life and work of many less well-known scientists, such as Robert Van de Graaff, Lise Meitner, and Isidor I. Rabi. The style of this book is similar to an earlier two-volume publication by the same authors, *The World of the Atom* (Basic Books, 1966).

Chevalier, Haakon. *Oppenheimer: The Story of a Friendship*. New York: George Braziller, 1965.
The author was a professor of French at the University of California at Berkeley and became a close personal friend of Oppenheimer there. After Oppenheimer was appointed to head the Los Alamos Laboratory in 1943, he told a security officer a false story that Chevalier had approached him about sharing atomic information with the Soviets. Chevalier tells how stunned he was when the Atomic Energy Commission in 1954 released the transcript of the Oppenheimer security hearing, in which the "Chevalier incident" played a prominent role. He felt betrayed. He concludes that Oppenheimer's need to be preeminent was so strong that "he sold his soul to the atom bomb" and tragically destroyed his friend's reputation in the process.

Childs, Herbert. *An American Genius: The Life of Ernest Orlando Lawrence*. New York: E. P. Dutton, 1968.
Ernest O. Lawrence (1901-1958) was the inventor of the cyclotron particle accelerator, for which he won the Nobel Prize in Physics in 1938. This is the most complete biography of his life, covering more than five hundred pages. The author had access to Lawrence's voluminous correspondence files at the University of California and conducted several hundred personal interviews to gather information. Lawrence's family background and upbringing in South Dakota are described in a lively narrative style. His main contribution to the atomic bomb project was the construction of magnetic separators to produce enriched uranium at the Oak Ridge Laboratory. His controversial role in promoting the building of a new weapons laboratory in 1952 to develop the hydrogen bomb is told with many interesting details.

Davis, Nuell Pharr. *Lawrence and Oppenheimer*. New York: Simon & Schuster, 1968.

Ernest O. Lawrence, an experimental physicist, and J. Robert Oppenheimer, a theoretician, both received their Ph.D.'s in 1927. The author conducted interviews with nearly one hundred of their scientific colleagues to obtain firsthand information for this authoritative account. Of special interest is the description of Oppenheimer's role at Los Alamos to inspire, unify, and coordinate the project. His style of obtaining cooperation from strongly conflicting personalities was called "harmonious anarchy." Lawrence is portrayed as someone who appealed to political power to support funding for his accelerators even when his scientific peers advised against it. The dramatic interplay of personalities provides fascinating reading.

Drell, Sidney, et al. *Physics Today* (August, 1990). A special issue devoted to Andrei Sakharov (1921-1989).
Andrei Sakharov is often called the "father of the Soviet hydrogen bomb," his role being comparable to Edward Teller's in the United States. His contributions to basic physics as well as his fearless support of human rights are memorialized by four articles in this special issue. In contrast to Teller, Sakharov spoke out repeatedly on the need for arms control to prevent a nuclear holocaust. He opposed space weapons and the Soviet invasion of Afghanistan. He was awarded the Nobel Peace Prize in 1975 but was not permitted to accept it in person. In 1980, he was exiled from Moscow to the city of Gorky until Gorbachev rescinded the order seven years later.

Fermi, Laura. *Atoms in the Family: My Life with Enrico Fermi*. Chicago: University of Chicago Press, 1954.
Enrico Fermi (1901-1954) was one of the "illustrious immigrants" from Europe who made major contributions to the American atomic bomb project. This book gives a wife's perspective through personal anecdotes. The reader is given a picture of the difficult conditions in Italy under fascism. The exciting story of the exodus from Italy is told. The family was permitted to go to Sweden in 1938 so that Enrico could receive the Nobel Prize, but instead of returning to Italy, they went directly on to the United States as refugees. Mrs. Fermi presents perceptive personality sketches of her husband's scientific colleagues in the Manhattan Project and makes interesting observations about the gradual process of Americanization among the refugee families.

Forsee, Aylesa. *Albert Einstein: Theoretical Physicist*. New York: Macmillan, 1963.
There are many biographies of Einstein; this small book is particularly recommended for a reader who wants to understand the human qualities of this scientific genius. Einstein's family background, his education in Switzerland, and his first job in a patent office are described. His technical publications brought fame, including the Nobel Prize in 1921. He became a distinguished professor in Berlin until forced out by the Nazis in 1933, when he emigrated to Princeton.

He became a popular lecturer and spoke out frequently against militarism. After 1945, he campaigned for world government and a ban on atomic weapons. Many small incidents are recounted that show Einstein's appealing humility and simple life-style. Suitable for younger readers. Photographs and a chronology are provided.

Goodchild, Peter. *J. Robert Oppenheimer: Shatterer of Worlds*. Boston: Houghton Mifflin, 1981.
This book was published in conjunction with a seven-part television series on Oppenheimer that Mr. Goodchild produced. The primary focus is on Oppenheimer's personality development. Intimate incidents from his adolescence and college years are revealed. As a young professor at Berkeley, his involvement with left-wing organizations and friends is described. At Los Alamos, he is portrayed as a rather awkward administrator in dealing with personnel and security problems. A good description is given of the anxiety preceding the Trinity test explosion, because the bomb really might have been a dud. Oppenheimer's great prestige after the war as science advisor to the government and his "fall from grace" at the security hearings are told in dramatic style.

Hahn, Otto. *My Life: The Autobiography of a Scientist*. Translated by Ernst Kaiser and Eithne Wilkins. New York: Herder & Herder, 1970.
Otto Hahn (1879-1968) was the codiscoverer of uranium fission in 1938. He received the Nobel Prize in Chemistry in 1944 but was unable to attend the award ceremony until 1946, after the end of World War II. He describes his childhood and education with a good sampling of humorous anecdotes. He comments on the difficult relationship of German scientists to the Nazi regime. After the war, reporters asked Hahn how it felt to know that his discovery had made atomic weapons possible. His frank personal response and his devotion to humanitarian concerns provide worthwhile reading.

Heims, Steve J. *John Von Neumann and Norbert Wiener: From Mathematics to the Technologies of Life and Death*. Cambridge, Mass.: MIT Press, 1980.
This dual biography traces the life history and contrasting attitudes of two leading mathematicians of the twentieth century. John Von Neumann (1904-1957), a refugee from Hungary in the 1930's, contributed to the atomic bomb project at Los Alamos by creating the first electronic computer. He supported development of the hydrogen bomb and later was appointed to the Atomic Energy Commission. Norbert Wiener (1894-1964) was at the MIT Radiation Lab during the war. After the "massacre at Nagasaki," he had a crisis of conscience about further work on weapons. He developed the science of cybernetics and wrote about human implications of modern technology. The author agrees with Wiener that the idea of separating basic research from technological applications is an illusion. Many interesting details are given.

Heisenberg, Werner. *Physics and Beyond: Encounters and Conversations*. World
Perspectives 42. Translated by Arnold J. Pomerans. New York: Harper & Row,
1971.
Werner Heisenberg (1901-1976) won the Nobel Prize in Physics in 1932 for his
invention of quantum mechanics, which is a powerful mathematical procedure
to describe the structure of atoms. This book contains twenty essays by Heisenberg on a wide range of topics. His view of the Nazi regime is expressed in an
article entitled "Individual Behavior in the Face of Political Disaster (1937-
1941)." Other thoughtful articles deal with "The Responsibility of the Scientist
(1945-1950)," and "Scientific and Political Disputes (1956-1957)," in which he
describes his opposition to atomic armament for postwar Germany. His informal
style of writing recounts many conversations with world-famous personalities in
science and politics. Informative and readable.

Jungk, Robert. *Brighter Than a Thousand Suns: A Personal History of the Atomic
Scientists*. Translated from German by James Clerigh. New York: Harcourt,
Brace & World, 1958.
This book presents a history of the atomic bomb starting from scientific developments in the 1920's and ending with the arms race in 1955. Jungk provides
interesting personality sketches of the leading scientists, with his own rather
controversial interpretations. For example, he writes that Heisenberg and his
colleagues in Germany "obeyed the voice of conscience" and deliberately tried
to distract Nazi attention away from the possibility of an atomic bomb. In
contrast, Oppenheimer is described as someone with no ethical concerns about
the bomb, whose driving ambition was to win worldwide recognition. He
condemns scientists for their "macabre joy" after viewing the first successful
bomb explosion. He finds cause for hope in the postwar crusade against nuclear
weapons by some of the scientists who felt a sense of guilt.

Kunetka, James W. *Oppenheimer: The Years of Risk*. Englewood Cliffs, N.J.:
Prentice-Hall, 1982.
The primary focus of this biography is Oppenheimer's years of public service,
from 1942 to 1954. His successful leadership of the bomb design work at Los
Alamos is summarized. After the end of World War II, he became a frequent
advisor to congressional committees and government leaders. His role in bringing
control of nuclear research under a new civilian agency, the Atomic Energy
Commission, is described. Oppenheimer's opposition to developing a hydrogen
bomb brought him into conflict with Senator McCarthy and other anticommunist
hawks. The controversial hearing in which his security clearance was revoked
in 1954 is told with extensive quotations.

Latil, Pierre de. *Enrico Fermi: The Man and His Theories*. New York: Paul S.
Erickson, 1966.

A brief but well-written biography requiring little technical background from the reader. Fermi's family environment and education are described. He is portrayed as a prodigy whose exceptional talent for scientific work led to a Ph.D. at age twenty-one and the Nobel Prize in Physics at age thirty-seven. His contributions to the atomic bomb project are explained in elementary terms. After Fermi's death from cancer at age fifty-three, the name "Fermium" was given to one of the new artificial elements in his honor. Some selected writings by and about Fermi as well as photographs and a short bibliography conclude this book.

Libby, Leona Marshall. *The Uranium People*. New York: Crane, Russak, 1979.
A collection of reminiscences and rather trivial anecdotes about people connected with the Manhattan Project. The author knew many of the scientists with first-name familiarity. Unfortunately, the bulk of the book is filled with insignificant incidents. Is it important to know that Szilard was a difficult house guest or that the Fermi's son Guilio liked to eat eggplant? Some interesting episodes and conversations are quoted but without any historical documentation, such as a postwar meeting between President Truman and Oppenheimer at the White House. Some of the stories are primarily in the nature of gossip about world-famous scientists. The last chapter contains a polemical defense of nuclear power plant technology. A disappointing book.

MacPherson, Malcolm C. *Time Bomb: Fermi, Heisenberg, and the Race for the Atomic Bomb*. New York: E. P. Dutton, 1986.
An interesting retelling of the atomic bomb project, juxtaposing the American and German uranium research efforts from the early 1940's. The author contrasts the work style of Enrico Fermi, the pragmatist, with Werner Heisenberg, the theoretical thinker. He has selected historically accurate conversations from the published writings of Laura Fermi, Heisenberg, General Groves, Otto Hahn, Arthur Compton, and others to reveal the personalities of the leading scientists. Of special interest are the meeting between Heisenberg and Fermi in 1939 and the dialogue between Heisenberg and Bohr in 1941. Photographs, explanatory notes, and a selected bibliography are given in the appendix.

Major, John. *The Oppenheimer Hearing*. New York: Stein & Day, 1971.
The author is a British historian who has made a thorough study of the Oppenheimer security hearing of April, 1954. The role of the leading personalities in the case is described in detail. The atmosphere of the hearing is portrayed as similar to that of a trial, with an aggressive prosecuting attorney. The author interprets the hearing to be part of the larger political struggle by the armed forces and their supporters to muzzle criticism of a large postwar military buildup. By discrediting Oppenheimer, they sent a warning to other scientists with liberal or left-wing attitudes. Extensive references to books, journals, and newspaper articles are given in the appendix.

Moore, Ruth. *Niels Bohr: The Man, His Science, and the World They Changed.*
New York: Alfred A. Knopf, 1966. Cambridge, Mass.: MIT Press, 1985.
Niels Bohr (1885-1962) originated the well-known model for the structure of the
atom: a nucleus in the center surrounded by shells of electrons. He was awarded
the Nobel Prize in 1922 for his work. This excellent biography documents Bohr's
scientific contributions as well as his involvement in the broader social issues of
the day. It tells how he founded the now-famous Institute for Theoretical Physics
in Copenhagen, which brought together the leading physicists of the time. He
foresaw the likelihood of a nuclear arms race after the war unless international
control of atomic energy could be achieved, with Soviet participation. His direct
appeal to Roosevelt and Churchill failed, but it is worthwhile to know that he
made the effort.

Oppenheimer, J. Robert. *The Open Mind.* New York: Simon & Schuster, 1955.
A reprinting of eight lectures given by Oppenheimer to various audiences between
1946 and 1954. "Atomic Weapons and American Policy" contains the oft-quoted
simile that the nuclear stalemate is like "two scorpions in a bottle, each capable
of killing the other, but only at the risk of his own life." He argues for more
government openness in releasing information about the United States' weapons
capability so that widespread citizen participation in national security issues can
take place. He also suggests that it would be better for world peace if the enemy
knew more about American military capability, so there would be less chance
for miscalculation. One lecture, addressed to the Westinghouse Science Talent
Search winners of 1950, describes his optimistic vision for the peaceful benefits
of technology.

Pfau, Richard. *No Sacrifice Too Great: The Life of Lewis L. Strauss.* Charlottesville:
University Press of Virginia, 1984.
Lewis L. Strauss (1896-1974) played a dominant role in determining postwar
nuclear policy as a member and later chairman of the Atomic Energy
Commission (AEC). The author of this book is a historian who has made a
thorough study of the voluminous private papers of Strauss in Washington, D.C.,
as well as pertinent archive material in several presidential libraries. Strauss grew
up in Richmond, Virginia, worked with Herbert Hoover, became a successful
banker, was appointed assistant to Secretary of the Navy James Vincent Forrestal
during World War II, and served on the AEC for eight years. He was a strong
advocate for building the hydrogen bomb, for weapons testing in the atmosphere,
and for dismissing Oppenheimer as a security risk. A well-written and
authoritative biography.

Rabi, Isidor I., Robert Serber, Victor F. Weisskopf, Abraham Pais, and Glenn T.
Seaborg. *Oppenheimer.* New York: Charles Scribner's Sons, 1969.
These five essays originally were given as public lectures at the Oppenheimer

Memorial Session of the American Physical Society in 1967, shortly after his death. Each author draws on personal recollections to portray Oppenheimer's varied contributions. His charismatic leadership as wartime director at Los Alamos and his role as science adviser to the government are described. A chronology of Oppenheimer's life, a selected bibliography of his writings, and sixteen pages of photographs are included.

Rigden, John S. *Rabi: Scientist and Citizen.* New York: Basic Books, 1987.
Isidor I. Rabi (1898-   ) was one of the leading American physicists of the twentieth century. This informative biography tells the story of his education at Cornell, Columbia, and several European universities, his personal acquaintance with many world-famous physicists, and his contributions during World War II as associate director of the Radiation Laboratory at MIT. Three chapters of special interest deal with Los Alamos and Rabi's role (along with Niels Bohr) as senior advisor to Oppenheimer. Rabi received the Nobel Prize in Physics in 1944, having been nominated by Einstein and Fermi. His postwar opposition to building the hydrogen bomb and his concern for peaceful uses of atomic energy are described with many interesting details and quotations.

Rozental, Stefan, ed. *Niels Bohr: His Life and Work As Seen By His Friends and Colleagues.* Amsterdam: North-Holland, 1967.
A collection of twenty-one essays expressing appreciation of Niels Bohr for his wide-ranging contributions, by people who knew him well. The authors include scientists, politicians, artists, and family members. Of particular interest for this bibliography is an essay on the war years by Aage Bohr (Niels's son) and one on international scientific collaboration by Victor Weisskopf. Also, Bohr's letter of 1950 to the United Nations, expressing his deep concern for international control of atomic energy in order to avoid a dangerous arms race, is reprinted in full.

Sakharov, Andrei. *Memoirs.* New York: Alfred A. Knopf, 1990.
This autobiography of more than seven hundred pages was written by Sakharov during his seven-year exile from Moscow after 1980. He begins with his family history, his education, and his early interest in physics. Ten chapters are devoted to his work on the Soviet nuclear weapons program at a secret laboratory that is identified only as "The Installation." As he rose in the Soviet hierarchy, he became aware of plans for nuclear warfare that could only bring about mutual destruction. Starting in 1968, he began to write on the need for peaceful coexistence. His advocacy of human rights and freedom of expression brought him into frequent conflict with the Soviet authorities. His extensive correspondence with world leaders makes fascinating reading.

Sayen, Jamie. *Einstein in America: The Scientist's Conscience in the Age of Hitler and Hiroshima*. New York: Crown, 1985.
The primary focus of this biography is on the nonscientific aspects of Einstein's life during his years at Princeton, from 1933 to 1955. The author describes Einstein's active role in supporting humanitarian causes, such as helping Jewish refugees in the 1930's and speaking out against nuclear weapons testing in the 1950's. Einstein's letter to President Roosevelt initiated the atomic bomb project, but after Hiroshima he described it as the "most tragic experience of his life." One chapter in the book recalls the harassment of liberal thinkers such as Einstein during the McCarthy anticommunist mania. Incidents from Einstein's private life and his personal kindness to many individuals are recounted, with careful documentation provided in the appendix. Authoritative and readable; highly recommended.

Segre, Emilio. *Enrico Fermi: Physicist*. Chicago: University of Chicago Press, 1970.
Tells the story of Fermi's life from the viewpoint of a colleague and personal friend. The main emphasis in this biography is on Fermi's scientific accomplishments, his truly unique ability to contribute to both theoretical and experimental physics. Of special interest is the chapter on the war years. Fermi was the "greatest living expert on neutron experiments" at the time, and his role in the Manhattan Project is described. The author is very complimentary to General Groves for his skill in coordinating the whole bomb project. The appendix contains Fermi's last public lecture, given at Columbia University in 1954, describing his recollections of the early days of uranium fission.

Smith, Alice Kimball, and Charles Weiner, eds. *Robert Oppenheimer: Letters and Recollections*. Cambridge, Mass.: Harvard University Press, 1980.
Contains a collection of 167 letters written by Oppenheimer between 1922 and 1945, with annotations by the editors. The letters were obtained from family members, personal friends, and scientific colleagues. Oppenheimer is pictured as a precocious eighteen-year-old who received his B.A. from Harvard University in three years and his Ph.D. from the University of Göttingen two years later, at age twenty-three. Some letters that he wrote in 1943 to recruit scientists to work at Los Alamos are reprinted, as well as his famous farewell speech of November 2, 1945, when he spoke to an audience of more than five hundred people at the laboratory. The letters will be useful to scholars and historians who want to work with primary source material on the life of Oppenheimer.

Strout, Cushing, ed. *Conscience, Science, and Security: The Case of Dr. J. Robert Oppenheimer*. Chicago: Rand McNally, 1963.
This pamphlet of sixty pages is part of the Berkeley Series in American History. It contains extensive verbatim quotations from the official transcript of the

Oppenheimer hearing of 1954 before the Personnel Security Board. The editor has supplied a chronology and helpful introductory comments to identify various witnesses. He also addresses questions to the reader to focus on the most significant issues raised at the hearing. The hysteria at that time about possible Communist espionage and the humiliation suffered by Oppenheimer become evident as one reads the quoted testimony.

Weart, Spencer R., and Gertrude Weiss Szilard, eds. *Leo Szilard; His Version of the Facts: Selected Recollections and Correspondence.* Cambridge, Mass.: MIT Press, 1978.
Leo Szilard (1898-1964) was born in Hungary and came to the United States as a refugee physicist in 1938. He is best known for writing the letter that Einstein signed and sent to President Roosevelt in 1939, advising him about a new type of uranium bomb. This book is a collection of 122 documents from Szilard's personal files that show his wide-ranging concerns and remarkable foresight. Szilard describes how the idea of obtaining nuclear energy from a neutron chain reaction occurred to him as early as 1933. In 1939, his correspondence was dominated by efforts to mobilize scientific resources for work on the bomb. In 1945, he played a leading role in trying to prevent its use against Japan. The editors provide helpful annotations.

Weisskopf, Victor F. *The Joy of Insight: Passions of a Physicist.* New York: Basic Books, 1961.
This volume is one of the Sloane Foundation Series of books to develop greater understanding for science among the general public. The author speaks for many scientists when he identifies the "joy of insight" as the essential experience that attracts people into scientific careers. In this autobiography, he describes his family background in Vienna and his education as a physicist in Germany. He relates many personal anecdotes about leading European physicists of the 1930's, whom he met at Berlin, Cambridge, Copenhagen, and elsewhere. In 1937, he emigrated to the United States and was recruited by Oppenheimer to work at Los Alamos in 1943. The chapter entitled "Working on the Bomb" illustrates the intense fascination of scientific research without much concern about long-range consequences. His postwar activities included working for peace through the Federation of American Scientists and other efforts in international cooperation.

Wilson, Jane, ed. *All in Our Time: The Reminiscences of Twelve Nuclear Pioneers.* Chicago: Educational Foundation for Nuclear Science, 1975.
Twelve scientists who worked on the Manhattan Project share their personal recollections in these articles that were originally published in the *Bulletin of the Atomic Scientists*. Luis W. Alvarez gives a firsthand account of nuclear physics research in the 1930's at Berkeley under the leadership of Ernest Lawrence. Herbert L. Anderson tells of his work with Enrico Fermi in assembling the first

chain reaction in 1942. J. H. Manley describes the camaraderie at Los Alamos and the transformation of J. Robert Oppenheimer from theoretical physicist to effective administrator. Kenneth T. Bainbridge gives a vivid description of his role in the Trinity test explosion in New Mexico. Each author contributes a piece of authentic history from his memory album to fascinate the reader. Highly recommended.

York, Herbert F. *Making Weapons, Talking Peace: A Physicist's Odyssey from Hiroshima to Geneva.* New York: Basic Books, 1987.

An autobiographical account of the author's involvement in weapons development and arms negotiations. As a young graduate student in physics in 1942, he was recruited to work on the atomic bomb project. Regarding Hiroshima, he recalls, "I was thrilled and my heart sank at the same time." He describes his developing career as an administrator, from the H-bomb laboratory at Livermore, to the Department of Defense under President Eisenhower, to the University of California at San Diego. Under President Jimmy Carter, he was the chief U.S. negotiator at Geneva for a comprehensive test ban. He has come to believe that the dilemma of increasing military power but decreasing national security cannot be solved through better technology; diplomatic efforts are essential. Interesting inside commentary about notable scientific, military, and political leaders.

Chapter 3
ATOMIC BOMB DEVELOPMENT
IN THE UNITED STATES

The Manhattan Project

Blow, Michael. *The History of the Atomic Bomb*. New York: American Heritage, 1968 Distributed by Harper & Row.
A well-written overview of the atomic bomb project summarized in 150 pages. Almost every page has a photograph or explanatory diagram with an informative caption. The science background, the main personalities, the various laboratories that made up the Manhattan Project, the progress of the war, and the eventual use of the bomb are sketched out briefly. One memorable photograph shows Japanese schoolchildren playing in a park in Hiroshima, with the ruins of a building in the background that was left standing as a reminder of the bomb. A short but well-chosen bibliography of books for further reading is given.

Brown, Anthony Cave, and Charles B. MacDonald, eds. *The Secret History of the Atomic Bomb*. New York: Dell Books, 1977.
The first part of this book is a reprint of the 1945 Smyth report, "Atomic Energy for Military Purposes," with minor deletions (see entry in this bibliography under Henry D. Smyth). The next two hundred pages are selections from the massive thirty-five volumes of the official *Manhattan Engineer District History*, prepared under the direction of General Leslie Groves and now available at the National Archives in Washington, D.C. The next nearly two hundred pages are selections from the history of Los Alamos Laboratory by David Hawkins (see entry in this bibliography), and short reprints about the bombing of Hiroshima and Nagasaki. Unfortunately, no index is supplied, no volume and page numbers are given for reprinted material, and no introductory commentary was provided by the editors. Of limited interest.

Church, Peggy Pond. *The House at Otowi Bridge: The Story of Edith Warner and Los Alamos*. Albuquerque: University of New Mexico Press, 1959.
The author was the wife of the headmaster of the Los Alamos School for Boys, which was requisitioned by the Army in 1942 to build the weapons laboratory. This is the unusual story of Edith Warner (1892-1951), who lived in a small house by the bridge that provided the only access road to Los Alamos. She had come in the 1920's to this semi-wilderness area, where she learned to love the mountains and the nearby Indians. Her house became a frequent gathering place for famous scientists from the laboratory, where they could relax over a simple meal. Niels Bohr in particular expressed his appreciation for the haven of tranquillity that she represented. Quotations from her journal and from letters reveal her remarkable personality.

Compton, Arthur H. *Atomic Quest: A Personal Narrative.* New York: Oxford University Press, 1956.

This is the best account of the Manhattan Project written for a nontechnical audience. From 1941 to 1945, the author was the director of the "Metallurgical Laboratory," a code name for all bomb-related research. He was responsible for coordinating the efforts of several thousand research workers at Oak Ridge, Hanford, Los Alamos, and various universities. He knew all the leading scientists in the project personally and tells the story of their work through conversations and anecdotes. Of particular interest is a long chapter entitled "Choice," which describes how the difficult decision to use the bomb against Japan was made. The last chapter, entitled "Hope," gives his view about the future of nuclear energy from a religious perspective.

Groves, Leslie R. *Now It Can Be Told: The Story of the Manhattan Project.* New York: Harper & Brothers, 1962.

General Groves was the chief military officer for all aspects of the atomic bomb project from 1942 to 1946. He describes his wide-ranging responsibilities: procurement of land and the construction of nuclear laboratories at Oak Ridge, Hanford, and Los Alamos; obtaining uranium ore from the Belgian Congo; negotiating with Du Pont and other industrial suppliers for scientific equipment; selecting Oppenheimer to head Los Alamos; arranging security clearance for many foreign-born scientists; setting up a Military Intelligence mission to interrogate the leading scientists in Germany; coordinating the bombing mission against Japan; and preparing appropriate press releases. The appendix contains his firsthand report on the Trinity test explosion that was delivered to President Truman at Potsdam. A fascinating book, with many anecdotes and personal observations.

Hawkins, David. *Inception Until August, 1945.* Vol. 1 in *Manhattan District History: Project Y, The Los Alamos Project.* Report 2532. Los Angeles: Tomash, 1983.

This report describes the technical accomplishments and the evolving administrative structure of the Los Alamos Laboratory from 1943 to 1945. The report was written in 1947 but not released to the public until 1961. The author had responsibility at the Laboratory for nontechnical matters, such as housing, salaries, and draft deferments. He presents an overview of the organization of the Laboratory into its various divisions: Theoretical, Experimental Physics, Explosives, Chemistry and Metallurgy, and so forth. Scientific personnel lists are given for each division, along with their assigned mission. Primarily a recital of factual information, with no attempt to explore the human drama or to provide historical evaluation.

Hewlett, Richard G., and Oscar E. Anderson, Jr. *A History of the United States Atomic Energy Commission.* Vol 1. in *The New World, 1939/1946.* University

Park: Pennsylvania State University Press, 1962.
This book of more than 750 pages gives a thoroughly documented and detailed account of the atomic bomb project. The authors are two professional historians who were given access to the complete files of the Manhattan Project. Their sources of information include scientific research reports, correspondence, many personal interviews, and site visits. Difficult administrative decisions about funding, personnel problems, and political disputes are described in detail, including frequent clashes of opinion involving General Groves, Secretary Stimson, project leader Arthur Compton, and others. In spite of the book's overall length, any section can be recommended for its historical accuracy and lively style of writing. The book ends with the political battle over military versus civilian control of atomic energy.

Knebel, Fletcher, and Charles W. Bailey. *No High Ground*. New York: Harper & Row, 1960.
The opening chapter of this book shows President Truman on August 6, 1945, receiving word of the bombing of Hiroshima while returning from the Potsdam Conference aboard the USS *Augusta*. After extensive study of declassified government documents and other sources, the authors have recreated the story of the atomic bomb development and the detailed military preparations for using it against Japan. Of special interest is the documentation of opposition to the use of the bomb, expressed by a petition of scientists as well as by military leaders such as Admiral Leahy. The arguments in support of the bomb given by General Groves, Secretary of War Stimson, and members of the B-29 crew are also presented, for the reader to judge in retrospect.

Kurzman, Dan. *Day of the Bomb: Countdown to Hiroshima*. New York: McGraw-Hill, 1986.
Retells the story of the atomic bomb through biographical sketches and anecdotes about the leading actors in the drama. The chapter titles identify the roles of the main characters: "The Initiator" is Leo Szilard; "The Maker" is Oppenheimer; "The Whipcracker" is General Leslie R. Groves; "The Traitor" is Klaus Fuchs; "The Inheritor" is President Truman; "The Warrior" is General Anami, Japanese Minister of War; "The Puppet" is Emperor Hirohito; "The Dissenter" is Admiral Leahy (who opposed the use of the bomb); "The Bluffers" are Stalin and Truman at the Potsdam Conference. The author's information was gathered from previously published material plus an extensive list of interviews, including numerous Japanese sources.

Lamont, Lansing. *Day of Trinity*. New York: Atheneum, 1965. New York: New American Library, 1966.
Tells the story of the Manhattan Project, documented by many personal interviews, Atomic Energy Commission files, and other publications. Brief biographi-

cal sketches are given for a very large cast of characters. The author has a dramatic style of writing that combines trivial incidents of human interest with an overview of the big picture. The story of Klaus Fuchs, the Soviet spy, is told in detail, based on his later confession. The mixed emotions of the people who witnessed the Trinity test explosion is described. Highly recommended for factual accuracy and readability.

Laurence, William L. *Dawn over Zero: The Story of the Atomic Bomb*. New York: Alfred A. Knopf, 1946.

William Laurence was a science reporter for *The New York Times* who was selected to write the story of the atom bomb for the general public. He was the only journalist permitted to observe the test explosion in New Mexico and to fly along in the observation plane that accompanied the bombing mission over Nagasaki. He explains the scientific ideas of nuclear fission and chain reaction in simple language. He gives many details about the work that was done at Oak Ridge, Hanford, and Los Alamos Laboratory. The incredible destruction at Hiroshima is described. His own attitude toward the use of the bomb was clearly favorable: "Thousands of young Americans owe their lives to the theory of relativity." An authoritative account with a distinct promilitary bias.

Lewis, Richard S., Jane Wilson, and Eugene Rabinowitch, eds. *Alamogordo Plus Twenty-five Years: The Impact of Atomic Energy on Science, Technology, and World Politics*. New York: Viking Press, 1971.

The articles in this book were originally published in the twenty-fifth anniversary issue of the *Bulletin of the Atomic Scientists*, a monthly journal of issues involving science and society. Of special interest here are the following selections: "Some Recollections of July 16, 1945," by General Leslie R. Groves; "The Conscience of a Physicist," by Robert R. Wilson; "Disarmament Problems," by Hans Bethe; "Nuclear Weapons, Past and Present," by Ralph E. Lapp; "Scientists and the Decision to Bomb Japan," by David H. Frisch. Several other articles deal with medical and industrial uses for nuclear energy, particularly the production of electricity from nuclear power plants. The editor's introduction discusses the misgivings of young people at that time toward careers in science and technology.

Smyth, Henry D. *A General Account of the Development of Methods of Using Atomic Energy for Military Purposes Under the Auspices of the United States Government, 1940-1945*. Washington, D.C.: Government Printing Office, 1945. Reprint. Princeton, N.J.: Princeton University Press, 1945.

This small pamphlet of 182 pages was issued a few days after the atomic bomb was used against Japan and provided the first authorized public account of the secret Manhattan Project. The author was a professor of physics at Princeton University who participated in bomb research and later served on the Atomic

Energy Commission. He provides an overview of uranium isotope separation at Oak Ridge, plutonium production at Hanford, and bomb design work at Los Alamos. The names of leading scientists and their contributions are acknowledged. Some information could not be revealed yet at this time; for example, the Trinity test explosion in New Mexico is not mentioned at all. An informative and historically important document.

Szasz, Ferenc M. *The Day the Sun Rose Twice: The Story of the Trinity Site Nuclear Explosion, July 16, 1945*. Albuquerque: University of New Mexico Press, 1984.
The author is a historian from New Mexico. He has collected extensive information about the Trinity bomb test based on personal interviews with participants, diaries, oral history recordings, declassified reports from the Manhattan Project, and numerous books and articles. Photographs, maps, and a forty-page bibliography are included. Construction of the test site in the New Mexico desert, reactions of various observers who saw the explosion, and concern about fallout are described in considerable detail. One scientist is quoted for his suggestion that all heads of state in the United Nations should be forced to witness a nuclear explosion once a year, to remind them of the awesome power of the bomb.

Truslow, Edith C., and Ralph Carlisle Smith. *August, 1945, through December, 1946*. Vol. 2 in *Manhattan District History: Project Y, The Los Alamos Project*. Report 2532. Los Angeles: Tomash, 1983.
Continuation of Volume 1 (authored by David Hawkins), describing the evolution of Los Alamos Laboratory from the end of World War II until the newly formed Atomic Energy Commission assumed control in 1947. Oppenheimer resigned as director in October, 1945, and was replaced by Dr. N. E. Bradbury. Many scientists left Los Alamos to return to academic employment. During the transition period, Dr. Bradbury suggested some possible functions that Los Alamos might have in the future: to continue weapons development; to work on peacetime applications; to cooperate with universities on basic research, with graduate thesis projects done at the lab; to compile a library of technical reports. Preparations for the first series of bomb tests at Bikini in the Pacific, called "Operation Crossroads," are described briefly.

Wyden, Peter. *Day One: Before Hiroshima and After*. New York: Simon & Schuster, 1984.
Retells the story of the Manhattan Project and the decision to use the bomb, as viewed from a historical perspective forty years later. The author gives extensive references to the library collections of original material located at Los Alamos, Hiroshima, and elsewhere. He also conducted more than one hundred personal interviews. He gives a very negative assessment of Oppenheimer, accusing him of deliberately covering up growing opposition to the use of the bomb. He asks the scientists to recall whether they had any qualms about working on the bomb

or any regrets after its use. The author visited the Hiroshima Peace Museum and Los Alamos Laboratory and gives his reactions to the continuing arms race.

Soviet Espionage

Fineberg, S. Andhil. *The Rosenberg Case: Fact and Fiction*. New York: Oceana, 1953.

Julius and Ethel Rosenberg were convicted and sentenced to death in 1951 as Russian spies, but the execution did not take place until 1953. The author vigorously attacks the two-year effort to win clemency for the Rosenbergs as a systematic Communist propaganda campaign. The Rosenbergs are described as fanatical enemy agents who were being made into political martyrs in order to divert attention from Soviet outrages in East Germany and other Kremlin-dominated countries. Scientists and lawyers who wrote letters in defense of the Rosenbergs, as well as protest rallies in New York, Paris, and elsewhere, are characterized as a "Big Lie," trying to discredit the American system of justice in the eyes of world opinion. An emotional, anticommunist polemic.

Goldstein, Alvin H. *The Unquiet Death of Julius and Ethel Rosenberg*. New York: Lawrence Hill, 1975.

In 1976, a documentary television program on the Rosenberg case was produced by Alvin Goldstein, funded by the Corporation for Public Broadcasting. This small book contains many photographs from the program, with brief explanatory captions. Pictures of the judge, members of the jury, lawyers for the prosecution and defense, key witnesses in the trial, and the two Rosenberg children are shown. The Rosenberg case is portrayed as a political trial in which government prosecutors exploited fears about the "Communist menace" to obtain a conviction. Some parallels are suggested to the Watergate break-in and coverup, where abuse of power and deception at the highest levels of government also were present.

Hirsch, Richard. *The Soviet Spies: The Story of Russian Espionage in North America*. London: Nicholas Kaye, 1947.

The author served during World War II with the Military Intelligence Division of the U.S. War Department. He tells the story of the gradual unraveling of the Soviet spy network in Canada. It was first brought to light by an employee of the Soviet Embassy, Igor Gouzenko, who defected in 1945 with secret documents that he gave to the Canadian authorities. Eventually, these revelations led to the arrest of Dr. Nunn May, a nuclear scientist who had transmitted information and even some samples of enriched uranium. Of particular interest in this book is a chapter entitled "Motives of the Betrayers." Dr. May stated that his hope for international control of atomic energy was the reason why he allowed himself to be recruited as a spy.

Hyde, H. Montgomery. *The Atom Bomb Spies*. New York: Atheneum, 1980.
An account of Soviet espionage during and after World War II. The author worked for British intelligence during the war and has published more than fifty books on various topics. He tells the life story of Klaus Fuchs, a respected scientist in the Theoretical Physics Division at Los Alamos who sent regular secret progress reports to the Soviet Union, according to his later confession. Another notable Communist informer was Bruno Pontecorvo, who defected to the Soviet Union in 1950. The famous case of Julius and Ethel Rosenberg is described with extensive quotations from their trial in 1951. The questionable evidence against them, the controversial judge who sentenced them, and the public outcry against the death penalty are portrayed in the highly emotional political climate of the time.

Nizer, Louis. *The Implosion Controversy*. Garden City, N.Y.: Doubleday, 1973.
A detailed account of the dramatic Rosenberg spy trial, written by a well-known lawyer and author twenty years after the defendants had been executed. The facts of the case are objectively presented, including the personal backgrounds of the accused, the judge, the lawyers, and the individual jury members. The progress of the trial is portrayed through extensive direct quotations of witnesses, with commentary about courtroom strategy. The verdict, sentencing, appeals for clemency, and eventual electrocution are described. The author concludes that the evidence was sufficient for conviction but that capital punishment was not justified. Nizer wrote the script for an Otto Preminger film based on the trial.

Philby, Kim. *My Silent War*. New York: Grove Press, 1968.
This story could be subtitled, "I Was a Soviet Spy." Kim Philby gives a first-person account of his espionage activities from 1933, when he became a Soviet agent, to 1963, when he fled to Moscow and was granted political asylum. He describes his career, beginning as a correspondent for the *London Times*, later hired by the British Secret Intelligence Service and eventually rising to become head of anti-Soviet counterintelligence. He was clearly proud of his role in transmitting secret information to the Soviets. In 1949 he was assigned to Washington, D.C., where he became the British liaison with the Federal Bureau of Investigation (FBI) at the time of the atomic spy cases. An interesting view of espionage from the inside.

Pilat, Oliver. *The Atom Spies*. New York: G. P. Putnam's Sons, 1952.
The author has collected numerous incidents of alleged Soviet espionage in the British-American atomic bomb project. He describes the Canadian spy ring that was first revealed by Igor Gouzenko in 1945. He tells the life story of Klaus

Fuchs, a trusted scientist at Los Alamos who later confessed his role as a spy. Bruno Pontecorvo, another Communist scientist, managed to escape to the Soviet Union in 1950 shortly before his imminent arrest. Finally comes the controversial trial of Julius and Ethel Rosenberg, who were convicted of espionage to commit treason in 1951. The author cites incriminating private conversations as if he had been present to hear them. Fact and speculation are not clearly separated in this book of foreboding warnings against Communist infiltration.

Radosh, Ronald, and Joyce Milton. *The Rosenberg File: A Search for the Truth.* New York: Holt, Rinehart and Winston, 1983.
Were the Rosenbergs innocent victims of Cold War hysteria or were they Soviet agents engaged in atomic bomb espionage? The authors of this book have made use of FBI and Central Intelligence Agency (CIA) files that were not released until 1980 through the Freedom of Information Act, along with other very extensive documentation and personal interviews. This historical study provides an in-depth review of the trial, subsequent appeals to the U.S. Supreme Court and to President Eisenhower, and the international propaganda campaign that followed the Rosenberg's execution. The key testimony presented by prosecution and defense witnesses is carefully analyzed to establish historical authenticity. A well-written, scholarly assessment of the evidence.

Root, Jonathan. *The Betrayers: The Rosenberg Case—A Reappraisal of an American Crisis.* New York: Coward, McCann, 1963.
Julius and Ethel Rosenberg were executed in 1953 for their alleged role in transmitting atomic bomb information to the Russians during World War II. The author has done considerable research to give many details of the couple's family background. During the Depression of the 1930's, the Rosenbergs became involved with Communist organizations that seemed to offer help for the laboring class. The author's viewpoint is that economic frustration caused a hatred for American society that led the Rosenbergs into espionage for the Soviets. The drama of the trial itself is depicted day by day. Widespread public protests against the eventual death sentence and appeals for clemency are described. The author expresses his satisfaction that the trial was fair and the penalty was justified.

Sharp, Malcolm P. *Was Justice Done? The Rosenberg-Sobell Case.* New York: Monthly Review Press, 1956.
This book was written shortly after the Rosenbergs were executed for atomic espionage. The author was a professor of law at the University of Chicago who made a careful study of the trial. He gives a detailed analysis of weaknesses in the case against the Rosenbergs. In particular, one of the key prosecution witnesses had previously been convicted of spying and was offered a more lenient sentence if he would testify against the Rosenbergs. Also, some of the

circumstantial evidence lacked confirmation. The Rosenbergs are viewed as scapegoats in the Cold War era of fear and hatred toward Communism, attitudes that were intensified by the Korean War.

Williams, Robert Chadwell. *Klaus Fuchs, Atomic Spy*. Cambridge, Mass.: Harvard University Press, 1987.

Contains a detailed study of the espionage activities of Klaus Fuchs, a respected physicist who acted as a Soviet spy at Los Alamos. The author uses documents that were not available until recently under the Freedom of Information Act. The appendix contains Fuchs's signed confession of 1950, obtained from declassified FBI files. A twenty-eight-page statement gives the testimony of Harry Gold, who describes in detail the occasions when Fuchs gave him information to be transmitted to Soviet contacts. The author provides interesting background about Fuchs's family, his motivation for helping the Soviets, and his reasons for later voluntarily making a confession. A general overview of Soviet espionage is given and the extent of Fuchs's contribution to the Soviet atomic bomb program is evaluated.

Chapter 4
HIROSHIMA AND NAGASAKI

Amrine, Michael. *The Great Decision: The Secret History of the Atomic Bomb*. New York: G. P. Putnam's Sons, 1959.
Gives a chronological account of the events from April to August, 1945, which influenced the decision to use the bomb against Japan. The primary decision makers are identified as Truman, Secretary of War Stimson, and General Groves. It is remarkable that the atomic bomb project had been kept secret from Generals MacArthur and Eisenhower, from the president's cabinet, and even from Truman until after Roosevelt's death. Most of the information comes from published memoirs of Truman, Churchill, and Stimson. The last chapter discusses a number of searching questions: Was the Nagasaki bomb necessary? Did the scientists' petition opposing the use of the bomb receive any consideration?

Baker, Paul R., ed. *The Atomic Bomb: The Great Decision*. New York: Holt, Rinehart and Winston, 1968.
A reprinting of fifteen excerpts from various authors, expressing support or condemnation for the decision to use the atomic bomb on Japan. Among the authors are Secretary of War Henry L. Stimson, *The New York Times* analyst Hanson Baldwin, British physicist P. M. S. Blackett, and American historian Herbert Feis. The selections are well chosen to show a diversity of viewpoints. The editor provides a helpful introduction, a chronology of events, and a guide for further reading. Highly recommended for stimulating interest in further historical research on a controversial subject.

Bernstein, Barton J., ed. *The Atomic Bomb: The Critical Issues*. Boston: Little, Brown, 1976.
Contains a collection of seventeen excerpts from books and articles written between 1945 and 1975, all dealing with the controversial decision to use the atomic bomb against Japan. Among the authors are political leaders such as Henry L. Stimson and James F. Byrnes, and historians such as Gar Alperovitz and Herbert Feis. Supporters of the bomb claim that it shortened the war and saved lives. Opponents argue that its use was inhumane since Japan was close to surrender, and also that the bomb had an ulterior motive: to intimidate the Soviets into making postwar concessions. The editor provides helpful introductions and commentary on the clashing viewpoints presented in these selections. A well-chosen list of books and articles for further reading is given in the appendix.

Chinnock, Frank W. *Nagasaki: The Forgotten Bomb*. New York: World Publishing, 1969.

The author was a journalist and editor with *Reader's Digest*. He gathered extensive information for this book by personal interviews with the crew of the B-29 plane that dropped the bomb on Nagasaki and with Japanese survivors from the blast. The format of the book is an hour-by-hour timetable for August 9, 1945, switching back and forth from Captain Sweeney and his crew to the scene on the ground. Events of everyday life in the city before and after the explosion are told through the lives of individual people. The description of destruction and human agony in Nagasaki duplicates the impact that John Hersey's book *Hiroshima* had in 1946.

Craig, William. *The Fall of Japan*. New York: Dial Press, 1967.
Describes the military and political developments from the summer of 1944 up to the Japanese surrender and the arrival of occupation troops in September of 1945. The story of the emotional Japanese cabinet meetings during which surrender was being debated is told in great detail. The author gives an extensive list of sources for his information, including books, newspapers, and diaries written in Japanese. He has consulated the Atomic Energy Commission files and interviewed or consulted with numerous scientists, military leaders, and individual American soldiers. The result is a readable narrative with many significant details based on thorough scholarship.

Eatherly, Claude. *Burning Conscience: The Case of the Hiroshima Pilot, Claude Eatherly, Told in His Letters to Günther Anders*. Preface by Bertrand Russell. Foreword by Robert Jungk. New York: Monthly Review Press, 1962.
Claude Eatherly grew up in Texas and volunteered for service in the Air Force during World War II. He was the pilot of the plane that flew over Hiroshima for the final weather check about an hour before the atom bomb was dropped. This book is a collection of seventy-one letters, mostly correspondence between Eatherly and an Austrian journalist, written while Eatherly was confined to a mental hospital in Waco, Texas. Günther Anders depicts Eatherly as a person who was overcome by guilt feelings and mental anguish. (See the entry in this bibliography by Huie, *The Hiroshima Pilot*, for a very different interpretation of Eatherly's character.)

Feis, Herbert. *The Atomic Bomb and the End of World War II*. Princeton, N.J.: Princeton University Press, 1961. Rev. ed., 1966.
An authoritative history of the last four months of the war against Japan, based on official documents and the published memoirs of political, military, and scientific leaders. Part 1 discusses three options for bringing about Japan's surrender: invasion, negotiation, and the atomic bomb. Part 2 gives a day-by-day account of the Potsdam Conference (July 16 to August 2, 1945) between Truman, Churchill, and Joseph Stalin. Part 3 describes the power struggle within the Japanese cabinet over whether to surrender or not, finally resolved by Emperor

Hirohito's personal intervention. Part 4 gives the author's thoughtful reflections on what might have happened if the atomic bomb had not been used, or if an effective warning could have been issued without demanding unconditional surrender. An informative combination of factual history and analysis.

Fogelman, Edwin. *Hiroshima: The Decision to Use the A-Bomb*. New York: Charles Scribner's Sons, 1964.
A well-chosen collection of reprinted material from original sources, giving a variety of viewpoints that either criticized or defended the use of the atomic bomb against Japan. Among the eighteen selections are quotations from the writings of President Truman, Secretary of War Henry L. Stimson, Secretary of State James F. Byrnes, General Leslie Groves, Leo Szilard, Arthur H. Compton, Japanese Foreign Minister Togo, science writer Hanson W. Baldwin, and others. Each selection is introduced with a brief biography. The book provides convenient access to original source material for a college student writing a term paper or for anyone else who is interested in this controversial topic.

Giovannitti, Len, and Fred Freed. *The Decision to Drop the Bomb*. New York: Coward, McCann, 1965.
This book grew out of an earlier NBC television documentary program with the same title. It describes the historic developments from April 12, 1945, when President Roosevelt died, until September 2, when Japan signed the terms of surrender. Almost every page contains substantial direct quotations from published writings, personal diaries, and interviews with the leading political figures and scientists. Attempts within the Japanese government to bring the war to an end before Hiroshima are documented. Of special interest is the appendix, which gives reactions to the bomb use as expressed by Truman, General Marshall, Churchill, Oppenheimer, Teller, and others, as well as by Japanese cabinet members, military leaders, and scientists.

Guillain, Robert. *I Saw Tokyo Burning: An Eyewitness Narrative from Pearl Harbor to Hiroshima*. Translated by William Byron. New York: Doubleday, 1981. Originally published in France, 1946.
The author was a French journalist assigned to Tokyo in 1938. After Pearl Harbor, he was forbidden to leave and thus had a unique opportunity to observe the course of the war from inside Japan. At first he describes the triumphs of Japanese troops at Hong Kong, Singapore, and Java. Then came losses at Midway, Guadalcanal, Manila, and Okinawa. He recounts the firebombing of Tokyo in March, 1945, and the annihilation of Hiroshima and Nagasaki. He expresses his strong opposition to the use of the atom bomb against civilians: "Atrocity in warfare crossed another threshold." He makes many interesting observations about Japanese militarism, the internal propaganda that misled the people, and the role of the emperor.

Hachiya, Michihiko. *Hiroshima Diary: The Journal of a Japanese Physician, August 6-September 30, 1945*. Translated from Japanese. Chapel Hill: University of North Carolina Press, 1955.

The author was director of the Hiroshima Communications Hospital, a 120-bed facility located about two miles from the center of the bomb explosion. In this daily diary, he recorded his firsthand observations of the destruction and carnage. The hospital was swamped with burn victims begging for water, some with "sheets of skin coming loose." He tells of the exhausted medical staff trying to deal with the effects of radiation sickness, something they had never encountered before. The diary was a personal record originally not intended for publication, but the translator convinced Hachiya that his observations and thoughts should be shared.

Hersey, John. *Hiroshima*. New York: Alfred A. Knopf, 1946. New edition with an added chapter published in 1985.

The human tragedy of the Hiroshima bombing is told through the experiences of six survivors. One is a Jesuit priest, another a young woman factory worker, another a physician. One can begin to know them as real people, as the daily routine of their lives is described. On the day of the bombing, the lack of medical help for burn victims was particularly traumatic. The effects of radiation sickness are explained in personal terms, not in abstract medical jargon. A new chapter was added by the author forty years after the original publication, telling what happened to each of the six individuals.

Huie, William Bradford. *The Hiroshima Pilot*. New York: G. P. Putnam's Sons, 1964.

This is the story of Claude Eatherly, the pilot who flew over Hiroshima to check on weather conditions shortly before the atom bomb was dropped. An earlier book called *Burning Conscience* (see Eatherly entry in this bibliography), portrayed an image of Eatherly as a person with a severe guilt complex that led to his mental illness and attempted suicide. Mr. Huie presents convincing evidence that *Burning Conscience* contains many factual errors and distortions. Huie searched out and interviewed Eatherly's wartime flight crew, his psychiatrist, members of his family, and Eatherly himself. It becomes evident that Eatherly thrived on overdramatized publicity about himself in the media and helped to fabricate the exaggerated image of his supposed remorse.

Jungk, Robert. *Children of the Ashes: The Story of a Rebirth*. Translated by Constantine Fitzgibbon. New York: Harcourt, Brace & World, 1961.

The author is a noted journalist who traveled to Hiroshima in the 1950's to see for himself what traces of the atomic bomb catastrophe remained. The stories of people's lives that he relates are set against the background of postwar reconstruction. He describes how quickly people returned to the devastated city to dig through the rubble and build temporary shacks. Food shortages brought a black market, and orphaned children turned to robbery and prostitution to survive. In 1950, the Korean War was an economic windfall for Japan. Many newcomers moved to Hiroshima so that by 1959 the city had more houses than before the bombing. The incidents described by the author are all true and cannot fail to arouse the sympathy of the reader.

Lifton, Betty Jean, with photographs by Eikoh Hosoe. *A Place Called Hiroshima.* New York: Harper & Row, 1985.
A 150-page collection of photographs and text, showing the modern city of Hiroshima and the legacy of its bombing. The Atomic Dome, Peace Park, and exhibits from the Peace Museum are displayed. One story tells about Sadako Sasaki, who was two years old when the bomb exploded near her home and who died of leukemia at age twelve. In her memory, a Children's Monument was erected, where colorful paper cranes made by children are collected. Another memorable vignette tells about Kiyoshi Kikkawa, whose back was severely burned; he later ran a souvenir shop and let tourists photograph the grotesque pattern of his wounds. Through words and pictures, this book conveys the message that the victims of Hiroshima should not be forgotten.

Lifton, Robert Jay. *Survivors of Hiroshima: Death in Life.* New York: Random House, 1967.
The author is a psychologist who lived in Japan for several years and undertook a study of the psychological aftereffects of the atomic bomb on Hiroshima survivors. He tape-recorded individual interviews in the early 1960's, from which he quotes extensive excerpts along with his interpretation. Right after the bombing, the survivors experienced "psychic numbing" as a result of the emotional shock of the massive human suffering. The annual commemoration on August 6 brings back vivid memories that are difficult to deal with. The author compares the Hiroshima experience to the trauma of Nazi concentration camps. One chapter summarizes the artistic response of Japanese novelists, poets, filmmakers, and songwriters to the bomb. Feelings of anger, guilt, and depression are given an outlet for dramatic expression.

Maruki, Toshi. *Hiroshima No Pika.* New York: Lothrop, Lee & Shepard, 1980.
A picture book about the Hiroshima bombing, with a few sentences of text on each page that an adult could read to a young child. The story tells of a seven-year-old girl and her parents who survive the "Flash" and walk to a river to escape from the fire. The color illustrations are drawn in a surrealistic style, to portray for a child how so many people died and the city became a wasteland of rubble. The book is dedicated to "the fervent hope that the Flash will never happen again, anywhere."

Marx, Joseph L. *Nagasaki: The Necessary Bomb?* New York: Macmillan, 1971.
On August 9, 1945, Nagasaki became the second Japanese city to be obliterated
by an atomic bomb, three days after Hiroshima. The author gives a suspenseful
account of the B-29 bomber and its crew of thirteen men as they made preparations for their mission. The main drama in this book is provided, however, by
a detailed account of the Japanese cabinet meetings at which the Potsdam
Declaration for unconditional surrender was being strenuously debated. The
important role of Emperor Hirohito is portrayed in breaking the deadlock between
the opposing military and political leaders. He decided to speak directly to the
people of Japan by radio, to explain that surrender was the only alternative to
complete destruction. The text of his speech is reprinted, and the emotional
impact it had on his people is described.

Minear, Richard H., ed. *Hiroshima: Three Witnesses*. Translation. Princeton, N.J.:
Princeton University Press, 1990.
Contains English translations of writings by three notable Japanese authors who
experienced the Hiroshima bombing firsthand. *Summer Flowers*, by Hara Tamiki
(1905-1951), was written within four months after August 6, 1945. It describes
the utter destruction and the painful burns and unforgettable dazed faces of
survivors. *City of Corpses*, by Ota Yoko (1903-1963), also written in 1945, was
published in 1949 after censorship by American occupation authorities. It relates
individual stories about the tragic victims of radiation sickness. *Poems of the
Atomic Bomb*, by Toge Sankichi (1917-1953), expresses a mixture of grief and
anger. Like concentration camp survivors in Europe, these writers needed to bear
witness to what they had seen. Other translated Japanese atomic bomb literature
is listed in the appendix.

Morimoto, Junko. *My Hiroshima*. New York: Penguin Books, 1987.
A picture book intended to be read to young children, with large drawings and
one or two sentences on each page. The author grew up in Hiroshima, having
just entered the fourth grade when the war started. Some of the drawings show
her family, the school that she attended, and other childhood recollections.
August 6, 1945, the day of the bomb, is portrayed in pictures of half-clothed
survivors fleeing from the fire and destruction. The author graduated from Kyoto
University of Fine Arts. She has taught as well as exhibited her artwork. She
addresses a concluding note to parents and teachers, expressing her hope that "we
shall not repeat the evil."

Osada, Arata, ed. *Children of the A-Bomb: The Testament of the Boys and Girls of
Hiroshima*. Translated by Jean Dam and Ruth Sieben-Morgen. New York: G.
P. Putnam's Sons, 1963.
The author was president of the University of Hiroshima. On the sixth
anniversary of the atom bomb, he asked schoolchildren who had survived "the

flash" to write down their recollections. Out of two thousand compositions, he selected sixty-seven for this book, grouped by ages from grammar school to college. The children describe their unforgettable memories of seeing a baby brother die, of people searching for relatives among the corpses. Some children escaped the holocaust by having been evacuated to the countryside, but their families perished. One child tells how lonely she feels now when she sees a classmate and mother together. A boy writes, "I hate war! I hate war!" The stories of innocent victims of war is preserved here for all to read.

Oughterson, Ashley W., and Shields Warren, eds. *Medical Effects of the Atomic Bomb in Japan*. New York: McGraw-Hill, 1956.
The authors were doctors in the U.S. Medical Corps who served on the Joint Commission for the Investigation of the Effects of the Atomic Bomb in Japan. The commission made a careful study to determine the number of casualties at Hiroshima and Nagasaki. This book gives a technical report of their results. Injuries were divided into three categories: blast injuries (flying glass, falling beams), burns (blisters, charred skin), and radiation sickness (vomiting, diarrhea, blood cell damage). Abnormal bone marrow, brain tissue, and other body cells were studied microscopically. Many tables of data, graphs, and photographs of victims are reproduced. The lack of physicians, nurses, hospital facilities, and medicines is documented. A factual, scientific report on a grim topic.

Selden, Kyoko, and Mark Selden, eds. *The Atomic Bomb: Voices from Hiroshima and Nagasaki*. Armonk, N.Y.: M. E. Sharpe, 1989.
An introductory essay describes how the distinction between military and civilian targets gradually disappeared during World War II. The destruction of Dresden, Germany, in February and the firebombing of Tokyo in March of 1945 are cited. The agony and terror of the atomic bomb explosions are portrayed here in the vivid personal recollections of survivors. Through poems, short stories, drawings, and photographs, the human tragedy is documented. The aftereffects of radiation sickness and psychological trauma continue to cause suffering for its victims. A powerful cry for "Never again!"

Steinberg, Rafael. *Postscript from Hiroshima*. New York: Random House, 1966.
The author is a journalist who has written for major news magazines and knows the Japanese language and culture from personal experience. He visited Hiroshima on the twentieth anniversary of the bombing and writes about his conversations with various people there: a salesman, elementary school teacher, taxi driver, high school boy, and others. He describes the Park of Peace with the Hiroshima motto carved in granite: "Rest peacefully, for the error shall not be repeated." He visits the Peace Memorial Museum with its grim collection of relics. Hiroshima is a remarkably clean and prosperous city after its reconstruction. He expresses sympathy for the *hibakusha*, the radiation victims

with scarred skin tissue who now have difficulty finding a job or a marriage partner. Well-written human interest stories.

Thomas, Gordon, and Max Morgan Witts. *Enola Gay.* New York: Stein & Day, 1977.
Tells about the year of preparation and training leading up to the Hiroshima bombing. The selection of Colonel Paul Tibbets as commanding officer, the training of the flight crew, and many other factual details are described. The author has a dramatic style of writing in which he switches rapidly from one location to another. For example, the scene shifts from General Groves's office in Los Alamos to the control room of a Japanese submarine in the Pacific to a meeting between President Truman and an advisor. Among the interesting details is Colonel Tibbets' visit to the airplane assembly line in Omaha to select personally the B-29 that was used for the mission.

Trumbull, Robert. *Nine Who Survived Hiroshima and Nagasaki: Personal Experiences of Nine Men Who Lived Through the Atomic Bombings.* New York: E. P. Dutton, 1957.
The nine men who were interviewed for this book are called "double survivors" because they witnessed the first atomic bombing at Hiroshima, and three days later they were in Nagasaki when the tragedy was repeated. One man was an accountant, another was a dockyard worker, two were engineers at the Mitsubishi Shipbuilding Company, one was a newspaper publisher, and four men worked on barrage balloons. They provide heart-rending accounts of the human carnage similar to other eyewitnesses: burned and blinded victims, dead bodies floating in the river, the search for missing family members. By chance circumstances, these men had the misfortune to see it happen twice. The author briefly describes the role of the Atomic Bomb Casualty Commission and the remarkably rapid rebuilding of the destroyed cities.

Wheeler, Keith. *The Fall of Japan.* Vol. 37 in *World War II.* Alexandria, Va.: Time-Life Books, 1983.
Keith Wheeler is a journalist who had previously authored three other volumes of this World War II series. Selecting from the large library of photographs at Time-Life, he tells the story of Japan's surrender in words and pictures. There is a condensed overview of the Manhattan Project, followed by a pictorial biography of President Truman and his wartime advisors. The victims of Hiroshima are portrayed. Then comes a series of expressionistic color drawings done by Japanese civilians, who were far enough from the blast to survive but close enough to see the horrible effects. The final section shows the first American troops landing at Japanese airfields after the official surrender.

Chapter 5
BOMB DEVELOPMENT OUTSIDE
THE UNITED STATES

Aron, Raymond. *The Great Debate: Theories of Nuclear Strategy.* Translated from the French by Ernst Pawel. Garden City, N.Y.: Doubleday, 1965.
The author presents a European view of the strategy of deterrence. One chapter describes the French development of an independent nuclear force, which was strongly opposed by the United States because proliferation was seen as dangerous. On the other hand, Europeans were apprehensive about the reliability of American commitments to come to their defense when U.S. cities were threatened by Soviet intercontinental missiles. Political strains in the Atlantic alliance are enumerated. The future stability of nuclear deterrence could be affected by several factors: further proliferation of nuclear weapons to other countries; development of new armament or delivery systems; political realignments, especially in central Europe or Asia; changes in strategic doctrine by the two superpowers. Knowledgeable analysis, clearly stated arguments.

Bader, William B. *The United States and the Spread of Nuclear Weapons.* New York: Western, 1968.
A scholarly discussion about the prospects for halting the spread of nuclear weapons, sponsored by the Center for International Studies at Princeton University. The shifts in United States policy in regard to sharing nuclear technology with allies are described. After China exploded its first bomb in 1964, India reacted with a call for developing its own bomb in self-defense, which the United States was unable to prevent. The technical capabilities of West Germany, Israel, Australia, and Japan to join the "nuclear club" are assessed. The appendix includes the complete text of the proposed nonproliferation treaty and a selected listing of pertinent government documents, speeches, and published articles.

Beaton, Leonard. *Must the Bomb Spread?* Baltimore: Penguin Books, 1966.
This well-written book of 150 pages is based on a 1965 conference at the Institute for Strategic Studies in London, to examine the problem of nuclear weapons proliferation. What would the world be like if ten or twenty nations possessed nuclear bombs? Since China had just exploded its first one in 1964, India will want one, but if India gets the bomb, then Pakistan may soon follow. Similar possibilities for escalation at other world trouble spots are discussed. Some suggestions for preventing weapons proliferation are presented: Uranium producers should not sell nuclear materials without strict safeguards; the test ban should be extended to underground tests; and, finally, the nuclear powers have to provide binding guarantees to protect nonnuclear nations if they are threatened.

Beyerchen, Alan D. *Scientists Under Hitler: Politics and the Physics Community in the Third Reich.* New Haven, Conn.: Yale University Press, 1977.
This book provides an authoritative account of what happened to German science, especially physics, under Hitler. The author's information was obtained from private correspondence, tape-recorded interviews, and previously published material, all listed in the appendix. Individual case studies of prominent physicists are presented. Among those who emigrated from Germany in the 1930's were James Franck, Edward Teller, Albert Einstein, and Max Born. Those who stayed included Max Planck, Werner Heisenberg, Otto Hahn, and Max VonLaue. Their reluctance to participate in war research for the Nazi government is termed an "inner emigration." The interesting story of "German Physics" is told through the lives of Johannes Stark and Philipp Lenard, who used Nazi ideology to purge non-Aryan contributions to science.

Bhatia, Shyam. *India's Nuclear Bomb.* Bombay: Vikas Publishing, 1979.
This book was written shortly after India's first and only nuclear explosion in 1974. The author reviews the political history of India beginning with independence from British rule in 1947. Prime Minister Nehru developed a policy of neutralism and strongly opposed Soviet and U.S. nuclear tests. The Indian Atomic Energy Commission was started in 1948 under the chairmanship of Dr. Homi Bhabha. India needed trained scientists to develop nuclear power for industrialization because resources of coal and oil were insufficient. The author argues that two events in 1964—the Chinese nuclear explosion and the death of Nehru—caused India to decide to build and test a plutonium bomb. The close connection between nuclear power and nuclear weapons technology is analyzed, and the need for stronger safeguards is suggested.

Boskey, Bennett, and Mason Willrich, eds. *Nuclear Proliferation: Prospects for Control.* New York: Dunellen, 1970.
A collection of eleven essays by a panel of distinguished writers with varied backgrounds in law, political science, physics, and international relations. The essays respond to different aspects of the Treaty on Non-Proliferation of Nuclear Weapons, which had just gone into effect in March 1970. Some issues of concern at the time were the military potential of nuclear power plants, on-site inspection of nuclear facilities, and safeguarding nuclear fuel against theft or terrorism. The appendix gives the full text of the treaty and other pertinent documents. The editors express the hope that the treaty will receive broad support through greater public understanding of its content.

Buchan, Alastair, ed. *A World of Nuclear Powers?* Englewood Cliffs, N.J.: Prentice-Hall, 1966.
A collection of nine short essays on nuclear proliferation, prepared as background reading for the participants at a 1966 conference in Ontario, Canada. Four essays

discuss the respective situations of West Germany, India, Sweden, and Japan, where the technical capability for nuclear weapons exists but the governments have opposed their development so far. Other essays consider the threat to world security if unstable governments in Africa, the Middle-East, or South America should acquire a few nuclear bombs, either illegally or by purchase.

Dunn, Lewis A. *Controlling the Bomb: Nuclear Proliferation in the 1980's*. New Haven, Conn: Yale University Press, 1982.
This book deals with the increasing risk of nuclear weapons proliferation. The author is particularly concerned with unstable regional rivalries such as those between Pakistan and India, Israel and the Arab states, or Brazil and Argentina. He discusses the early history of weapons development among the major powers and the spread of nuclear technology to the Third World. He examines some ways to reduce the likelihood of proliferation: stricter export controls on nuclear equipment, an improved inspection system, political sanctions against violators, guarantee of national security through conventional arms sales, establishment of nuclear-free zones. Authoritative, clearly written analysis, with detailed citations of references in the appendix.

Gallagher, Thomas. *Assault in Norway: Sabotaging the Nazi Nuclear Bomb*. New York: Harcourt Brace Jovanovich, 1975.
Tells the story of a commando raid against a hydroelectric power plant in Nazi-occupied Norway in 1942. This was a target of the highest priority because it produced heavy water, a vital ingredient for the German atomic bomb project. The author was able to locate and interview all the surviving members of the raid thirty years later. He also had access to official documents from the British War Office. The result of this careful research is a true story of great daring.

Gowing, Margaret. *Britain and Atomic Energy, 1939-1945*. London: Macmillan, 1964.
Presents the official history of Britain's role in the atomic bomb project. The author is a historian who was employed by the British Atomic Energy Authority and was given access to its official documents. Important contributions were the MAUD Committee report of 1941 (which outlined the essential steps to build a bomb) and the work of the "Tube Alloy" Committee (a code name for uranium enrichment). Britain was treated like a junior partner in the Manhattan Project. Strained relations between American and British colleagues are described in detail. The writing style is scholarly and factual in seeking to attain historical accuracy, which limits its appeal for the general reader.

Greenwood, Ted, Harold A. Feiverson, and Theodore B. Taylor. *Nuclear Proliferation: Motivations, Capabilities, and Strategies for Control*. New York: McGraw-Hill, 1977.

A careful analysis of the main factors that would either impede or promote the spread of nuclear weapons. The authors first consider the matter of motivation for nuclear proliferation, such as the desire for national prestige, security against aggression by neighboring states, Third World resentment against the superpowers, economic incentives by industrial states to export nuclear technology. The second part of the book considers the capability of nations to acquire a nuclear arsenal, based on availability of weapons-grade material from a civilian nuclear power industry. Safeguards against plutonium diversion and against theft by revolutionary or terrorist groups are evaluated. The authors advocate no reprocessing of reactor fuel rods in order to stop plutonium production, a policy that President Carter later put into effect.

Ha, Young-Sun. *Nuclear Proliferation, World Order, and Korea*. Seoul: Seoul National University Press, 1983.
The countries that possess nuclear weapons, based on known test explosions, are the United States, the Soviet Union, Great Britain, France, China, and India. This book discusses the incentives for "near-nuclear" countries such as South Korea, Pakistan, Israel, and South Africa to develop their own nuclear weapons. If neighboring countries are a threat to national security, the motivation to acquire nuclear capability is strong. The author gives interesting tables of information, such as a chronology of political crises since 1945, a listing of nuclear power plants, and so forth. The issue of nuclear weapons proliferation is viewed from the perspective of a developing nation such as Korea.

Halperin, Morton H. *China and the Bomb*. New York: Praeger, 1965.
The first Chinese nuclear test explosion took place in October, 1964. The author presents a scholarly analysis of Chinese-American political relations and how they might change as a result of the bomb. He reviews the background of mutual hostility since the Korean War and the continuous tension over Taiwan. He gives the Chinese scientists full credit for building their own bomb, with no Soviet technical assistance after 1960. Several possible American reactions to the Chinese bomb are discussed, including a preemptive military strike with Polaris missiles. He cites examples of the aggressive rhetoric used by Chairman Mao, which remind a modern reader that the threat of nuclear annihilation was very real.

Harkavy, Robert E. *Spectre of a Middle East Holocaust: The Strategic and Diplomatic Implications of the Israeli Nuclear Weapons Program*. Denver, Colo.: University of Denver, 1977.
The author is a political science professor with a special interest in international relations and arms control issues. He has carefully sifted through the available information about Israeli nuclear weapons development. The Dimona reactor, with technology supplied by France, started operating in 1964, and a plutonium

separation plant was completed in 1969. By 1976, the U.S. Central Intelligence Agency estimated the Israeli stockpile to contain between ten and twenty nuclear bombs. The Jericho missile, with a 280-mile range, could reach all the major cities of the neighboring Arab countries. The author speculates about various scenarios in which Israel might use its bombs, presumably as a last resort to prevent annihilation. If the Arabs also acquire nuclear weapons, the outlook for effective deterrence is very precarious.

Hart, David. *Nuclear Power in India: A Comparative Analysis*. London: Allen & Unwin, 1983.
This book primarily focuses on nuclear power plants for producing electricity, but India's single nuclear test explosion of 1974 is also described in considerable detail. The history of nuclear research under the leadership of the eminent Indian physicist Homi Bhabha is summarized. The Tarapur Atomic Power Station, located near Bombay, went into operation in 1969 with a nearby reprocessing facility to separate fissionable plutonium. India has repeatedly emphasized that its underground explosion was intended only to study applications for possible peaceful excavation projects, not for military weapons. Nevertheless, the author concludes that the one successful explosion boosted India's prestige, demonstrating its technological superiority to Pakistan and parity with China. No stockpile of nuclear weapons is believed to exist in India at this time. Informative and concise.

Irving, David. *The German Atomic Bomb: A History of Nuclear Research in Nazi Germany*. New York: Simon & Schuster, 1967.
A well-written account of the German equivalent of the Manhattan Project. The author is seeking an answer to the question, Why did their atomic bomb project fail? He has made a thorough study of the captured documents from the German uranium project, which were stored in a warehouse at Oak Ridge, Tennessee, after World War II. A memo written by the physicist Heisenberg in 1939 is reprinted, showing that even then they were clearly aware of the steps that would lead to a bomb. The ensuing lack of progress is attributed to several factors: disorganization among the German nuclear scientists, disruption of the heavy water supply from Norway by sabotage, damage to research laboratories by Allied bombing and competition for scarce resources with other war projects of higher priority.

Imai, Ryukichi, and Henry S. Rowen. *Nuclear Energy and Nuclear Proliferation: Japanese and American Views*: Boulder, Colo.: Westview Press, 1980.
The first author is manager of engineering for Japan Atomic Power Company. He presents the Japanese viewpoint that nuclear electric power plants are essential for economic development in a nation that otherwise must import almost all of its oil and coal. The second author is a professor at Stanford University, former

president of the RAND Corporation, and frequent government adviser. He defends President Carter's policy of restricting plutonium processing technology in order to prevent nuclear weapons proliferation. Specific differences between Japanese and U.S. concerns regarding fuel supply, radioactive waste storage, and other issues are presented in a debate format, with an opportunity for rebuttal by each author. Knowledgeable and informative, with suggestions for improved safeguards.

Jabber, Fuad. *Israel and Nuclear Weapons: Present Option and Future Strategies.* London: Chatto & Windus, 1971.
The author presents an evaluation of the military potential for Israel's nuclear research program. Numerous public statements by political and military leaders are cited, along with United Nations documents and international news reports. Part 1 of the book describes the Israeli nuclear establishment: its facilities, trained personnel, and policy-making organization. The Dimona reactor, capable of producing plutonium, is described in detail. Part 2 analyzes the problems of weapons production, from fuel procurement to delivery systems. Part 3 discusses political and strategic issues. Israel has deliberately created a climate of uncertainty as to whether it possesses nuclear bombs or not. The author suggests that this policy is designed to impress the Arab nations that the Jewish state can protect itself, without alienating world opinion for being overly militant.

Kapur, Ashok. *India's Nuclear Option: Atomic Diplomacy and Decision Making.* New York: Praeger, 1976.
A scholarly study of India's nuclear development and the decisions leading up to the underground test explosion in 1974. Quotations from Prime Minister Nehru are used to explain and justify India's postwar policy of nonalignment, rejecting alliances with the superpowers. Border clashes with China, Pakistan, and Bangladesh are reviewed. India refused to sign the Non-Proliferation Treaty of 1972 because it restricts the nonnuclear weapons states while allowing the U.S.-Soviet arms buildup to continue. Indira Gandhi, with the support of a few close advisers, made the decision to proceed with a single bomb test. The author credits India with an innovative policy of publicizing its nuclear option to the world while renouncing a military weapons program. Well-documented analysis, expressing India's point of view.

_____. *Pakistan's Nuclear Development.* London: Croom Helm, 1987.
A carefully documented analysis of Pakistan's nuclear program. Pakistan established an Atomic Energy Commission in 1959. A small power reactor, built near Karachi with foreign assistance, started operation in 1972. When Bhutto became Prime Minister in the 1970's, he authorized a military program to develop a bomb using plutonium. The official reason was to counter India's nuclear threat, but the author suggests that internal politics were the dominant concern. A

military coup in 1977 brought about General Zia's rise to power and Bhutto's execution. The nuclear program was reoriented to develop uranium enrichment for weapons production. Pakistan, like Israel, maintains a deliberate nuclear ambiguity, with capability for bombs but no test explosions. The erratic history of nuclear technology exports to Pakistan by Western nations is reviewed.

Kemp, Geoffrey, Robert L. Pfaltzgraff, Jr., and Uri Ra'anan, eds. *The Superpowers in a Multinuclear World*. Lexington, Mass.: D. C. Heath, 1974.
Contains ten essays, four short technical papers, and a summary of discussions from a 1973 conference with international participants, organized by the Fletcher School of Law and Diplomacy at Tufts University, Boston, Massachusetts. At the time of this conference, the SALT I agreement had just been concluded without placing effective limitations on U.S. and Soviet strategic weapons, while India's nuclear test explosion was imminent. Four essays discuss the changing strategic balance. European nations were particularly concerned about regional security in view of NATO's exclusion from the bilateral Strategic Arms Limitation Talks. Three essays describe future nuclear weapons options in China, Japan, and India, respectively. The authors try to envision international relations in a multinuclear world, where decision making would no longer be dominated by the two superpowers.

Kramish, Arnold. *Atomic Energy in the Soviet Union*. Stanford, Calif.: Stanford University Press, and London: Oxford University Press, 1959.
Traces the development of the Soviet nuclear research program starting in the 1930's. Sources of information at the time of this book were still very restricted by secrecy. Based on political speeches, newspaper articles, and technical journals, the first Soviet reactor probably began to operate in early 1947, followed by the first nuclear test explosion in September, 1949. Igor V. Kurchatov is mentioned prominently as the key scientist who was in charge of bomb development, his role comparable to Oppenheimer's in the United States. The status of nuclear power plants and nuclear propulsion for submarines is discussed within the limitations of publicly available information.

Lewis, John Wilson, and Xue Litai. *China Builds the Bomb*. Stanford, Calif.: Stanford University Press, 1988.
The first detailed description of the Chinese nuclear weapons program available in English. Sources of information are the memoirs of Marshall Nie Rongzhen, senior director of the program, which were published in 1984, and an authoritative history of China's nuclear industry published in 1987. Also, numerous Chinese-language articles and speeches are acknowledged in a lengthy appendix. Many parallels to the American bomb development are noted. China had to recruit its most talented scientists to build a uranium enrichment facility and a plutonium production reactor, to solve the implosion problem and to test a bomb

at an isolated location. The coalition of governmental leaders, scientists, and the military is described against the background of political events and economic problems of the time.

Markey, Edward J. *Nuclear Peril: The Politics of Proliferation.* Cambridge, Mass: Ballinger, 1982.
The author has been a member of the Congressional delegation from Massachusetts since 1976. He describes the political battle that took place in 1980 to block the sale of 38 tons of uranium for a nuclear reactor in India. The Nuclear Regulatory Commission had voted unanimously to disapprove of the shipment, but President Carter overrode the NRC in order not to alienate the government of India. The intense lobbying efforts for and against the uranium shipment are described in detail, culminating in the Senate's approval by a majority of only two votes. Markey is hoping to forge a political alliance between the nuclear weapons freeze groups and anti-nuclear power protestors.

Mendl, Wolf. *Deterrence and Persuasion: French Nuclear Armament in the Context of National Policy, 1945-1969.* New York: Praeger, 1970.
The author provides a well-documented twenty-five-year history of the French atomic energy program, with emphasis on the military aspect. Various setbacks for France's role in world affairs are reviewed: losses in Indochina (1954), the Suez Canal (1956), and Algeria (1962). Furthermore, the French government was concerned about possible German rearmament and was distrustful about the reliability of the U.S. nuclear umbrella to protect Europe from Soviet domination. An independent nuclear force became a symbol for national security and world status under President de Gaulle. The first test explosion was in 1960, supported by bombers, land-based missiles, and three submarines to provide a credible deterrent. An extensive list of references to pertinent books and articles written in French is given after each chapter.

Newby-Fraser, A. R. *Chain Reaction: Twenty Years of Nuclear Research and Development in South Africa.* Pretoria: Atomic Energy Board, 1979.
South Africa's first involvement with fission energy dates back to 1944, when the Manhattan Project in the United States was searching the world for uranium ore deposits. This book provides an authoritative review of the first twenty years of nuclear research and development in South Africa. Progress in prospecting and mining is described, along with some new technology for uranium extraction and isotope enrichment. The first research reactor, named SAFARI-1, was imported from the United States and started operation in 1966. Medical applications, food irradiation, new industrial uses, and training of technical workers are discussed. The first electric power reactor is to be completed in 1982. No mention of a South African nuclear weapons program is made, even though the advanced technological infrastructure is available there.

O'Heffernan, Patrick, Amory B. Lovins, and L. Hunter Lovins. *The First Nuclear World War: A Strategy for Preventing Nuclear Wars and the Spread of Nuclear Weapons*. New York: Morrow, 1983.

A mixture of fact and fiction about the problem of nuclear proliferation. Part 1 gives some fictional scenarios in which a reactor in California is blown up by sabotage; Libya, Iraq, and Pakistan possess a stockpile of nuclear bombs; nuclear war erupts against Israel; and Palestinian terrorists threaten the U.S. government. Other Third World countries with nuclear power plants, such as South Korea, Brazil, and South Africa, are presumed to be imminently capable of manufacturing bombs using plutonium from reactor fuel rods. The United States, France and Germany are criticized for exporting nuclear technology, driven by the profit motive for private industry. The authors are strongly opposed to nuclear power plants and suggest alternative "soft energy" paths that would be ecologically sustainable.

Overholt, William H., ed. *Asia's Nuclear Future*. Boulder, Colo.: Westview Press, 1977.

Contains seven articles on nuclear developments in Asia. The first wave of nuclear weapons proliferation took place in the Soviet Union, Great Britain, France, and China. The authors are concerned about a possible second wave of proliferation following India's bomb detonation in 1974. Separate chapters deal with China, Japan, Eastern Asia (Taiwan, Korea, Indonesia), India and Pakistan. General conditions that might encourage a country to go nuclear are regional antagonisms, domestic politics, nuclearization of other countries, national prestige considerations, and availability of technical expertise with foreign assistance. The case of Japan is of particular interest: Public opinion presently is opposed to nuclear weapons, but some scenarios are suggested (such as Korea going nuclear, or withdrawal of U.S. forces) that could drastically change current attitudes.

Palit, D. K., and P. K. S. Namboodiri. *Pakistan's Islamic Bomb*. New Delhi: Vikas Publishing, 1979.

A well-written, understandable summary of India's objections to the Non-Proliferation Treaty (NPT). If Pakistan has the bomb and India does not, Pakistan would probably use it in a border clash over Kashmir, for example, because deterrence, which is based on fear of nuclear retaliation, is lacking. From India's viewpoint, NPT did not help the security of non-nuclear weapons states, since U.S. and Soviet nuclear arsenals have continued to grow without restriction. Furthermore, the NPT would retain the commercial monopoly by Western powers in selling nuclear technology. Also, lax safeguards have allowed Israel to develop nuclear weapons capability; in response, Pakistan has mobilized Arab support for an Islamic bomb, but its eventual target may be to intimidate India rather than Israel. Thus, the NPT is rejected.

Perlmutter, Amos, Michael Handel, and Uri Bar-Joseph. *Two Minutes Over Baghdad*. London: Transworld Publishers, 1982.
Tells the story of a bombing mission by sixteen Israeli war planes on June 7, 1981, to destroy the Iraqi nuclear reactor near Baghdad. With pinpoint accuracy, bombs first demolished the containment building, with its thick concrete shell, and then the reactor inside. The authors describe the confusing background of political rivalries and alliances in the Near East. Starting in 1975, under the leadership of Saddam Hussein, Iraq had contracted with France to build the reactor. The Israeli government, under Menachim Begin, saw the growing threat of a potential nuclear bomb in Arab hands. The decision to make a preemptive strike against the reactor is told here from the Israeli point of view.

Pierre, Andrew J. *Nuclear Politics: The British Experience with an Independent Strategic Force, 1939-1970*. London: Oxford University Press, 1972.
A detailed, chronological account of atomic bomb development and nuclear weapons policy in Great Britain. Part 1 describes British contributions to the wartime Manhattan Project, including the original feasibility report of 1940 and the secret Quebec Agreement of 1943. Part 2 covers the period from 1945 to 1957, when Britain developed its independent nuclear deterrent. A British test explosion was carried out in Australia in 1952, only three years after the first Soviet test. Part 3 summarizes the events from 1957 to 1964, including the Skybolt missile crisis, the political debate over renouncing nuclear weapons, and the eventual acquisition of four Polaris submarines from the United States. Difficulties in British-American collaboration and the evolution of NATO nuclear strategy are described. Authoritative and readable.

Pranger, Robert J., and Dale R. Tahtinen. *Nuclear Threat in the Middle East*. Washington, D.C.: American Enterprise Institute for Public Policy Research, 1975.
This small pamphlet of fifty-seven pages provides a good overview of the potential for nuclear weapons use in the Middle East. The authors remind the reader that Arab-Israeli relations have been marked by four major wars in twenty-five years and that a new conflict constantly threatens to break out. The evidence for an Israeli nuclear weapons capability (without a test explosion, however) is summarized. Delivery systems are described, including aircraft, artillery, and short-range missiles (the Soviet SCUD and the U.S. Lancer) with mobile launchers. To prevent a Middle East nuclear war that would spread worldwide, the authors urge bilateral superpower negotiations, to place a mutual embargo on the sale of sophisticated weapons technology to their respective client states.

Pringle, Peter, and James Spigelman. *The Nuclear Barons*. New York: Holt, Rinehart and Winston, 1981.
The authors are a journalist and a lawyer who present an extensive social

criticism of both nuclear weapons and nuclear power. The nuclear "barons" are the elite scientists, military leaders, politicians, and corporation presidents, who prefer to make decisions without exposing themselves to public debate. The U.S. Atomic Energy Commission is given a very negative evaluation for suppressing information about radioactive fallout while hiding behind the cloak of national security. The authors describe nuclear developments in France, India, Israel, and elsewhere, depicting the same pattern of decision making by a small clique of self-styled experts. A large bibliography of original source material is given in the appendix.

Reiss, Mitchell. *Without the Bomb: The Politics of Nuclear Nonproliferation*. New York: Columbia University Press, 1988.
China in 1964 became the fifth country to explode a nuclear bomb, causing worldwide concern about further proliferation. The author provides an informative analysis to explain why the feared proliferation did not take place. He gives individual case studies of six countries that have the technological capability to build nuclear weapons: Sweden, South Korea, Japan, Israel, South Africa, and India. The author identifies several reasons why it was politically undesirable for these countries to build a nuclear arsenal: internal opposition or economic problems, international nonproliferation agreements and treaties, the danger of provoking an arms race with neighboring countries, and the restraining influence of world public opinion. The appendix gives extensive references to news publications, government reports, and interviews by the author with public officials.

Scheinman, Lawrence. *Atomic Energy Policy in France Under the Fourth Republic*. Princeton, N.J.: Princeton University Press, 1965.
France exploded its first atomic bomb in 1960 in the Sahara Desert. The author traces the history of the French nuclear program, starting with the formation of an Atomic Energy Commission (the CEA) in 1945. Under the forceful leadership of Nobel laureate Frederick Joliot-Curie, a nuclear research center was built at Saclay, near Paris. In 1952, a five-year plan to construct reactors for electricity production was initiated. The French defeat in Indochina in 1954 and the Suez crisis of 1956 generated political support for a military weapons program to regain the world's respect. According to the author's analysis, the decision to build the bomb was initiated by scientific administrators within the CEA, outside the mainstream of public political debate. An interesting appraisal, based on thorough scholarship.

Spector, Leonard S. *Nuclear Proliferation Today*. New York: Random House, 1984.
This paperback book, published by the Carnegie Endowment for International Peace, provides the most thoroughgoing examination of the potential for nuclear

bomb production worldwide. Detailed information is given in separate chapters on each of the eight "emergent" nuclear weapons state: Argentina, Brazil, India, Pakistan, Israel, Iraq, Libya, and South Africa. Each chapter contains a map showing the nuclear installations in that country. Numerous references to the most authoritative sources are cited: newspaper articles, interviews, government documents, and other publications. The role of the International Atomic Energy Commission to inspect suspected weapons production sites is described. The author served as chief counsel of the U.S. Senate committee that drafted the Nuclear Non-Proliferation Act of 1978, which governs American policy to the present time.

Weissman, Steve, and Herbert Krosney. *The Islamic Bomb: The Nuclear Threat to Israel and the Middle East*. New York: Quadrangle Books, 1981.
A detailed exposé of the efforts made by the leaders of Iraq (Saddam Hussein), Libya (Colonel Qadaffi) and Pakistan (Ali Bhutto, and later General Zia) to obtain nuclear weapons. The key scientists in these countries and the construction status of nuclear facilities are disclosed. The authors criticize those nations that export nuclear technology for commercial gain, especially France, Italy, and Japan. They tell the story of the 1981 bombing of the Osirak reactor in Baghdad by Israeli pilots, and the sabotage of two completed reactor cores while being shipped from France to Iraq in 1979. Meanwhile, the Israelis claim to have nuclear capability without having conducted a test explosion, following a policy of "deliberate ambiguity" to keep their Islamic antagonists guessing.

Wilcox, Robert K. *Japan's Secret War*. New York: William Morrow, 1985.
How far did Japanese scientists progress in building an atomic bomb during World War II? Robert Wilcox tells an incredible story about a secret Japanese laboratory at Hungnam, in Northern Korea, where bomb materials were manufactured and a successful atomic explosion supposedly was carried out on August 12, 1945. Soon after the test, Soviet troops captured the area and took the equipment, scientific records, and technical staff away. The author bases his story on formerly secret intelligence reports, magazine articles, and some Japanese references. He has accumulated circumstantial evidence about possible uranium shipments and isotope separation experiments. The story is fascinating but speculative, somewhat like the claims for UFO sightings.

Williams, Shelton L. *The U.S., India, and the Bomb*. Baltimore: The Johns Hopkins University Press, 1969.
At the time of this book, the Non-Proliferation Treaty had been signed by seventy-five nations, but not by India or China. The focus of this study booklet is the ongoing political debate among the governmental leaders within India regarding the desirability of developing their own nuclear weapons. Periodic

borders clashes with China and Pakistan, coupled with reduced foreign aid from the United States and other political developments, raised serious questions in India about the reliability of the American "nuclear umbrella" in case of a conflict. The cases for and against an independent nuclear force are summarized.

Chapter 6
WEAPONS TESTING AND RADIOACTIVE FALLOUT

Allardice, Corbin, and Edward R. Trapnell. *The Atomic Energy Commission*. New York and Washington: Praeger, 1974.
This book is one of a series on the functioning of various U.S. government agencies such as the Department of Agriculture and the Postal Service. The authors formerly were on the public information staff of the Atomic Energy Commission and are knowledgeable about its activities. They give an overview of the Manhattan Project and the formation of the AEC in 1947. They describe its role in regard to weapons production, the nuclear submarine program, federal research laboratories, and the civilian nuclear power program. The controversial Oppenheimer security hearing of 1954 is reviewed in a factual, nonjudgmental way. The political interaction of the AEC with the Joint Committee on Atomic Energy in Congress provides an interesting chapter.

Ball, Howard. *Justice Downwind: America's Atomic Testing Program in the 1950's*. New York: Oxford University Press, 1986.
From 1951 to 1958, the Atomic Energy Commission conducted more than one hundred atomic bomb test explosions at the Yucca Flats test site in southwestern Nevada. Some of the radioactive fallout carried downwind toward the region where New Mexico, Utah, and Nevada come together. The author is a professor of political science at the University of Utah who has made an extensive study of the lawsuit by citizens from the area, who are seeking compensation from the government for being exposed to excessive radiation doses. Detailed information is given about bomb tests, number of cancer deaths, and the ongoing litigation proceedings. An extensive appendix cites original sources used by the author.

Bradley, David. *No Place To Hide*. Boston: Little, Brown, 1948. Reprint, with new epilogue. Hanover, N.H.: University Press of New England, 1983.
The first atomic bomb explosion was the Trinity test in New Mexico, the second was at Hiroshima, and the third at Nagasaki. This books tells the story of the fourth and fifth explosions at Bikini in the summer of 1946, as observed by a medical officer in the U.S. Navy. He provides an eyewitness account in the form of a diary. The bombs at Bikini were exploded near a fleet of several dozen unmanned ships, to see how much damage they would sustain. The author describes how radiation levels were measured after the explosion in ships' hulls, water, fish, coral, and human urine samples. The plight of the 160 natives who could not return to their homes on the atoll is portrayed. Well written and informative.

Brues, Austin M., ed. *Low-Level Irradiation*. Washington, D.C.: American Association for the Advancement of Science, 1959.

A collection of ten essays on radioactive fallout, from a symposium organized by the AAAS and cosponsored by the Atomic Energy Commission. Scientific background information is presented on natural background radiation, meteorological factors in fallout distribution, and the biological effects of radiation on humans. One essay discusses public health concerns from medical X rays and industrial sources of radiation. Of particular interest in this collection is an article entitled "Responsibilities of the Press." It makes news when Dr. Albert Schweitzer warns against bomb tests, while another Nobel laureate, Dr. Willard Libby, says that fallout is no cause for concern. Journalists need to print both views in such a controversy, to clarify the technical issues without sensationalism.

Fradkin, Philip L. *Fallout: An American Nuclear Tragedy*. Tucson: University of Arizona Press, 1989.

The author is a professional writer who did considerable research on atomic bomb tests conducted at Yucca Flats, Nevada, in the 1950's. He provides a map of the test site and downwind communities such as St. George, Utah, which later was dubbed "Fallout City." One chapter, entitled "The Crime," is a strong indictment of the Atomic Energy Commission for giving false reassurances that fallout posed no danger. A chapter on "The Victims" provides individual case histories of radiation exposure and later cancer. The controversy among scientists about radiation effects, and the law suit against the government starting in 1979 are described. The trial judge awarded monetary damages to some of the plaintiffs, but an appeals court reversed the ruling. Sources of information are given in the appendix.

Fowler, John M., ed. *Fallout: A Study of Superbombs, Strontium 90 and Survival*. New York: Basic Books, 1960.

Contains twelve essays on fallout, with a foreword by Adlai Stevenson, then governor of Illinois and an advocate of halting nuclear test explosions. The authors provide knowledgeable explanations addressed to a nontechnical audience. One essay describes how radioactivity is carried from the South Pacific by the atmosphere. Another essay uses graphs to show the rising levels of radioactivity in soil, milk, and human bones. Another article explains radiation sickness, cancer, and genetic effects of radiation. Other articles deal with civil defense and the aftermath scenario of a nuclear war. The authors criticize Edward Teller and the Atomic Energy Commission for obscuring the fallout hazards from weapons testing.

Fuller, John D. *The Day We Bombed Utah: America's Most Lethal Secret*. New York: New American Library, 1984.

Describes how several thousand sheep died in Utah in the spring of 1953, not far from the site where atomic bomb tests were being conducted by the Atomic Energy Commission (AEC) at Yucca Flats, Nevada. The AEC denied any responsibility for the sheep deaths, claiming that the radioactive fallout was much too low to cause such harm; perhaps malnutrition or disease was to blame. Twenty-five years later, the Freedom of Information Act forced the AEC to release internal documents that showed a pattern of manipulated information to prevent interference with continued bomb testing. The author describes the problem of localized hot spots from fallout and gives Public Health Service data about excessive leukemia deaths among Utah residents. An angry book about government deception.

Hines, Neal O. *Proving Ground: An Account of the Radiobiological Studies in the Pacific, 1946-1961*. Seattle: University of Washington Press, 1962.
The Laboratory of Radiation Biology at the University of Washington conducted research under contract with the Atomic Energy Commission to monitor radioactivity in the environment following U.S. nuclear bomb tests in the South Pacific. Radioactivity was measured in ocean water, plankton, algae, fish, land animals and coral, sampling at different distances and times after the explosions. The various investigations are described in detail: Operation Crossroads at Bikini (1946); Operation Sandstone at Eniwetok (1948); Operation Greenhouse (1951); Operation Ivy, including the first hydrogen bomb (1952); Operation Castle, in which the Japanese fishing boat *Lucky Dragon* was seriously contaminated (1954); Operation Hardtack (1958). The progressively higher concentrations of radioactivity in large fish that feed on smaller ones is documented. Authoritative and informative, with photographs.

Kiste, Robert C. *The Bikinians: A Study in Forced Migration*. Menlo Park, Calif.: Cummings, 1974.
Bikini atoll is in the Marshall Islands, located about two thousand miles southwest of Hawaii. That isolated atoll was selected by the U.S. Navy for the first postwar atomic bomb tests in 1946, and its population of 170 men, women, and children had to move. The author of this monograph, an anthropologist, studied the disruption of the traditional Bikinian community structure after its forced resettlement. The natives were taken to an uninhabited atoll named Rongerik, but they nearly starved there. In 1948, they were moved to another island, but fishing was poor, while farming was too difficult an adjustment. The Bikinians became dependent on government relief shipments. The author cites references in *Life* magazine, *National Geographic*, and government publications to document the plight of these displaced people.

Kothari, D. S. *Nuclear Explosions and Their Effects*. 2d ed. Foreword by the prime minister of India, J. Nehru. Delhi, India: Publications Division, Ministry of Information and Broadcasting, 2nd edition, 1958.

A semitechnical discussion of the physical and biological effects caused by nuclear test explosions, addressed to nonscientist readers. The author describes blast damage, heat, and radioactivity from bomb explosions of different size. He presents tables of information to show the extent of radiation-induced leukemia, bone tumors, and genetic mutations. A chapter on global fallout analyzes the special problem of radioactive strontium in the world's milk supply. A detailed discussion is given about the Bikini test of March 1954, which produced dangerous levels of radioactivity for a Japanese fishing boat and also at Rongelap atoll a hundred miles away. The appendix presents additional data on radiation effects with a map of the contaminated area in the South Pacific.

Lang, Daniel. *From Hiroshima to the Moon: Chronicles of Life in the Atomic Age.* New York: Simon & Schuster, 1959.
Contains a collection of thirty-two articles that were published originally in *The New Yorker* magazine between 1945 and 1959. Some of the articles are based on personal interviews with scientists, such as the Oak Ridge physicist William G. Pollard, who became an ordained Episcopal priest. One essay tells the story of the Japanese fishing boat *Lucky Dragon*, which was contaminated by fallout, with a follow-up story about the radium watch dial painters who died of radiation sickness in the 1920's. The author witnessed a nuclear test explosion in Nevada in 1952 and describes how people reacted to such a sight. All the stories are reprinted as written, not updated, so they contribute to historical insights about the start of the atomic age.

Lapp, Ralph E. *Atoms and People.* New York: Harper & Brothers, 1956.
The author worked on the atom bomb project during World War II and later became a popular lecturer and writer on science for the general public. He gives an overview of nuclear physics, with good explanations of uranium fission, the first chain reaction, and the Manhattan Project. After the war ended, he was dismayed that the development of atomic energy was dominated by military weapons research. A long chapter is devoted to radioactive fallout from the 1954 Bikini test explosion. He is critical of the Atomic Energy Commission for withholding information and glossing over the hazards of continued bomb tests. He expresses strong support for President Eisenhower's "Atoms for Peace" proposal. Well written; for a nontechnical audience.

_____. *The Voyage of the Lucky Dragon.* New York: Harper & Brothers, 1957.
The *Lucky Dragon* was a Japanese fishing boat that was contaminated by radioactive fallout from a hydrogen bomb test explosion at Bikini atoll on March 1, 1954. Ralph Lapp is a physicist whose area of expertise is radioactivity. After reading all available news reports of the accident, he went to Japan to gather firsthand information about the twenty-three fishermen who had suffered from

"atomic bomb disease." He tells the dramatic story of the contaminated fish that were sold at the market before anyone realized it. The fear and hysteria of the Japanese people are described. One U.S. Congressman suggested that the fishermen were on a spying mission, which infuriated the Japanese press. This book raised worldwide concern about the danger of atomic explosions.

Lebedinsky, A. V. *What Russian Scientists Say About Fallout*. Translated from Russian. New York: Collier Books, 1962.
The introduction describes the situation in 1961, when both the United States and the Soviet Union were testing nuclear weapons of ever-increasing size. One enormous H-bomb explosion was equivalent to about 50 million tons (50 megatons) of TNT, which was eight times greater than the *total* explosives used in World War II. Many scientists on both sides of the Iron Curtain became opponents of testing because of worldwide radioactive fallout. This small paperback book gives English translations of outspoken Soviet dissidents, including the physicists Sakharov and Kurchatov. Active opposition to the nuclear arms race from within the Soviet Union was not well known in the West until these articles appeared.

Mawrence, Mel, with John Clark Kimball. *You Can Survive the Bomb*. Chicago: Quadrangle Books, 1961.
This book provides insight into the thinking about civil defense in the 1960's, when the threat of nuclear war was imminent. First the reader is told that total destruction is a myth. You can survive within three miles of a nuclear explosion if you have a fallout shelter. The cost of a family shelter is affordable, somewhere between the price of a new car and a summer suit. If a national alert comes, you are advised to dump wheelbarrows of dirt in your living room, to protect your family in the basement. Do not look at the flash, and keep calm. The style of writing is like a first aid manual, telling the individual what to do until outside help comes.

Melman, Seymour, ed. *No Place To Hide: Fact and Fiction About Fallout Shelters*. New York: Grove Press, 1962.
In 1961, the Department of Defense issued a booklet advocating the building of fallout shelters, claiming that 97 percent of the American population could survive a nuclear war in shelters. The essays in this paperback book oppose such a program from many points of view. Several articles anticipate severe problems for life inside a shelter during a nuclear attack: limited air supply, lack of water, mass diarrhea and nausea, defending one's shelter against outsiders. One article suggests that suburbs would need an armed militia to repel the refugees who are fleeing from a city. Other articles describe the likely postwar scenario: industrial breakdown, food resources destroyed by fallout, radiation-induced medical problems, martial law for survivors. The fallout shelter program generated intense opposition and was eventually abandoned.

O'Keefe, Bernard J. *Nuclear Hostages*. Boston: Houghton Mifflin, 1983.
The author is an electrical engineer who had major responsibilities for bomb detonation work at Los Alamos and in postwar testing at Bikini and Nevada. He provides a good historical overview of the scientific background for the atomic bomb. He describes his participation in the final checkout of the bomb assembly just before the B-29 took off for Nagasaki. He describes the frightening feeling of watching a 1953 artillery field test of a nuclear weapon in Nevada. In 1954, he was 25 miles from the Bravo test explosion, which produced so much fallout that his team had to be evacuated by helicopter. He sees improvements in Soviet-American relations and is hopeful that economic cooperation will eventually lead to political reconciliation. Well-written book, based on personal experiences.

Rapoport, Roger. *The Great American Bomb Machine*. New York: E. P. Dutton, 1971.
The author is an investigative reporter who presents an indictment against the nuclear weapons industry, singling out the Atomic Energy Commission for special criticism. He describes radioactive contamination problems in Nevada; at Los Alamos; at Rocky Flats, Colorado; and at the Pacific Test Site. Hydrogen bomb accidents over Spain in 1966 and at Thule, Greenland, in 1968 are recounted. The author blasts the public relations propaganda of the AEC, which gives false assurances about radiation hazards. He is disappointed that the general public seems to have more concern about lead-free gasoline or saving the redwood trees than the overwhelming danger of the continuing arms race.

Reynolds, Earle. *The Forbidden Voyage*. New York: David McKay, 1961.
In the summer of 1958, the author and his family decided to sail their small boat, the *Phoenix*, into a forbidden zone near Bikini atoll, where the Atomic Energy Commission was conducting nuclear test explosions. The Reynolds family embarked on this protest voyage after the crew of another sailboat, the *Golden Rule*, had been arrested and jailed in Hawaii for the same offense. The author, a radiation biologist by profession, expresses his moral and scientific objections to bomb tests. Much of the book deals with the circumstances of his arrest, trial, and appeal. His case received wide publicity and helped to alert the public to the fallout hazard, culminating in a moratorium on further testing announced by President Eisenhower on October 31, 1958.

Rosenberg, Howard L. *Atomic Soldiers: American Victims of Nuclear Experiments*. Boston: Beacon Press, 1980.
The author was an investigative reporter for newspaper columnist Jack Anderson. He tells about the American nuclear weapons testing program in Nevada in the 1950's. Not only were new bomb designs being tested, but also soldiers were to be trained there in atomic warfare under battlefield conditions. Corporal Russell Dann volunteered for this military exercise, attracted in part by the allure

of nearby Las Vegas. The author describes a typical indoctrination lecture about radioactivity for the troops, problems of inadequate radiation monitors, and contaminated clothing following a shot. Dann later suffered from severe medical problems, but the Veteran's Administration has been unwilling to acknowledge a connection between nuclear tests and disabilities. Testimony at a Congressional hearing in 1978 to consider possible compensation is presented.

Saffer, Thomas A., and Orville E. Kelly. *Countdown Zero*. Introduction by Stewart L. Udall. New York: G. P. Putnam's Sons, 1982.
Both authors were among the troops assigned to the nuclear testing program in the 1950's. Kelly, an Army veteran, witnessed twenty-two nuclear explosions at Eniwetok in the South Pacific. Saffer, a Marine, was at the Nevada test site, in trenches that sometimes were less than two miles from the blast center. Much of the book is a first-person narrative. The physical effects immediately after an explosion are described. Later disabilities (cancer, leukemia, neuromuscular problems) led to claims against the Veteran's Administration for compensation, but these were denied. Kelly was cofounder of the National Association of Atomic Veterans; he died of cancer in 1979. The last chapter is an angry indictment against government agencies that continue to deny a link between disabilities and radiation exposure.

Teller, Edward, with Allen Brown. *The Legacy of Hiroshima*. Garden City, N.Y.: Doubleday, 1962.
In this widely read book, Teller appeals to the American people to resist the drift toward appeasement in dealing with the Soviets. He expresses his conviction that Russian Communism is a greater danger than Nazi Germany; the Communists seek world domination, and the United States is losing the Cold War. The immediate issue in 1962 was the proposed test ban treaty. Teller thinks that the horror stories from Hiroshima have distorted people's judgment about fallout. He believes that the United States should be prepared to use small nuclear bombs in local conflicts. The political consequence of a test ban would be a further weakening of the free world because the Russians would continue testing in secret. He advocates building fallout shelters to overcome the doomsday mentality about nuclear war.

Titus, A. Constadina. *Bombs in the Backyard: Atomic Testing and American Politics*. Reno and Las Vegas: University of Nevada Press, 1986.
A well-written critique of nuclear weapons testing at the Nevada test site. The author gives an overview of the Manhattan Project. She then describes how the Atomic Energy Commission began bomb tests in the South Pacific; however, long-distance logistics were difficult, so President Truman approved the Nevada site in 1950. Local communities at first supported the testing because it was patriotic, it created jobs, and fallout hazards were downplayed by the AEC. More

recently, civilian and military personnel exposed to radiation from the tests have sought compensation through law suits, but with little success. The author suggests that Congress could pay for damages by special appropriation without admitting any legal responsibility, like the Agent Orange settlement for Vietnam veterans. Good bibliography; highly recommended.

Uhl, Michael, and Tod Ensign. *GI Guinea Pigs: How the Pentagon Exposed Our Troops to Dangers More Deadly Than War: Agent Orange and Atomic Radiation.* New York: Playboy Press, 1980.
The authors depict the plight of U.S. troops exposed to atomic radiation from bomb tests in the atmosphere, and also those exposed to Agent Orange in Vietnam. At the Nevada test site, there were eighty-three nuclear test explosions from 1950 to 1962, witnessed by more than 100,000 servicemen. The authors describe the experiences of soldiers who were assigned to trenches located only about two miles from the blast center. In some cases, soldiers were ordered to cross the nuclear explosion site within minutes after the blast, to see how they could function in a battlefield situation. The Atomic Energy Commission, the Pentagon, and the Veteran's Administration are charged with neglecting the long-term medical aftereffects on military personnel who now suffer from leukemia and other illnesses.

Chapter 7
THE H-BOMB AND THE NUCLEAR ARMS RACE

Ackland, Len, and Steven McGuire, eds. *Assessing the Nuclear Age: Selections from the Bulletin of Atomic Scientists*. Chicago: University of Chicago Press, 1986. The *Bulletin of Atomic Scientists* published a special fortieth anniversary issue in August, 1985, to provide a historical perspective about nuclear developments during the four decades since Hiroshima. The forty-one reprinted essays deal with a variety of topics, such as nonproliferation, the role of the weapons laboratories in the arms race, the Strategic Defense Initiative controversy, and the nuclear winter scenario. Some of the authors have written books that are annotated elsewhere in this bibliography: Victor Weisskopf, Richard Falk, Spencer R. Weart, Randall Forsberg, Robert Jay Lifton, Michael Mandelbaum, Bernard T. Feld, and others. A helpful bibliography is provided in the appendix. Informative articles by knowledgeable writers.

Aldridge, Robert C. *The Counterforce Syndrome: A Guide to U.S. Nuclear Weapons and Strategic Doctrine*. Washington, D.C.: Institute for Policy Studies, 1978. The author was employed for sixteen years as an engineer with Lockheed Corporation, working on the design of submarine-launched ballistic missiles. He resigned his position because he became aware that U.S. military strategy was shifting from a defensive posture of deterrence to an offensive first-strike capability against the Soviet Union. He presents a summary of the status of nuclear weapons technology, using nontechnical language suitable for a layperson. He explains clearly how the "counter-force" strategy, in which Trident missiles are aimed at Soviet Missile silos, is not consistent with deterrence. It only makes sense to target enemy launch sites if a first strike is planned, before they can fire their missiles. Informative, concise, and readable; highly recommended. Published in paperback.

_____. *First Strike! The Pentagon's Strategy for Nuclear War*. Boston: South End Press, 1983.
The author tells his personal story of growing frustration while working at Lockheed Corporation, doing engineering design of missiles for nuclear submarines. Gradually he became aware that the Pentagon war strategists were acquiring weapons for a preemptive first-strike capability against Soviet missile sites. The publicly proclaimed policy of deterrence would restrict the United States to fire its missiles only in retaliation; however, it makes no sense to target enemy missile silos unless the United States were planning to fire first, because otherwise the silos would already be empty. The author provides a comprehensive survey of modern weaponry, including the Minuteman, Trident, cruise missiles, bombers, and satellite technology. He argues that military expenditures have gone far beyond what is needed for defense while urgent civilian needs are unmet.

Allison, Graham T., Albert Carnesale, and Joseph S. Nye, Jr., eds. *Hawks, Doves, and Owls: An Agenda for Avoiding Nuclear War.* New York: W. W. Norton, 1985.
This book contains nine essays based on a 1984 seminar and ongoing discussions by the "Avoiding Nuclear War Project" at Harvard University's John F. Kennedy School of Government. Five possible paths to nuclear war are analyzed: an accidental or unauthorized missile launch; preemptive attack; escalation in Europe; escalation in the Middle East; a terrorist group or Third World dictator who acquires nuclear bombs. An extensive agenda of Dos and Don'ts for avoiding nuclear conflict is proposed. For example, do maintain a credible deterrent; do not adopt a launch-on-warming policy; do maintain civilian control over nuclear weapons; do not use nuclear weapons against third parties. Members of the academic community address these recommendations to governmental decision makers and military strategists. Stimulating, readable commentary.

Alperovitz, Gar. *Atomic Diplomacy: Hiroshima and Potsdam; The Use of the Atomic Bomb and the American Confrontation with Soviet Power.* New York: Simon & Schuster, 1965. Reprint. New York: Penguin Books, 1985.
An authoritative account of Soviet-American diplomacy in 1945, covering the first six months of Truman's presidency. The author has combined information from public documents and the private papers of various political leaders to provide a coherent interpretation of events. He presents evidence that Truman deliberately delayed the difficult negotiations with Stalin about postwar Eastern Europe until after the bomb had been proved. Also, he advances the thesis that the atom bomb was used on Japan to end the war quickly, in order to exclude the Soviets from any significant role in its occupation. The appendix includes an extensive bibliography and a review essay on the origins of the Cold War that has been widely used in college classes. A classic but controversial book on diplomatic history, highly recommended.

Ball, Desmond. *Politics and Force Levels: The Strategic Missile Program of the Kennedy Administration.* Berkeley: University of California Press, 1980.
A critical assessment of the U.S. intercontinental ballistic missile program in the 1960's. The author provides a detailed account of the "missile gap" controversy that was exploited by John F. Kennedy during his election campaign. By 1961, the missile gap had been shown to be an illusion, based on faulty intelligence about Soviet intentions. Nevertheless, Secretary of Defense Robert McNamara and the Kennedy administration initiated the largest peacetime military buildup in U.S. history. The author argues that policy decisions about the size of the missile force were determined more by domestic politics and bureaucratic infighting than by national security needs. The appendix lists pertinent books and articles, as well as the names of fifty-five top-level government officials and military leaders who were interviewed by the author.

Barash, David P. *The Arms Race and Nuclear War*. Belmont, Calif.: Wadsworth, 1987.

A well-written introduction to all aspects of the arms race, intended as textbook for a college course. Part 1 covers nuclear weapons technology, delivery systems, and the U.S. and Soviet military arsenals. Part 2 summarizes the effects of nuclear explosions, including fallout and nuclear winter. Part 3 discusses strategy issues, especially the concept of deterrence and its limitations. Part 4 gives an overview of the arms race, arms control negotiations and proliferation. Part 5 deals with domestic issues such as the economic cost of the arms race, the peace movement and some psychological implications of potential nuclear disaster. Each chapter contains well-chosen photographs, a list of key terms, and questions from both the hawk and dove viewpoints. Informative and stimulating; highly recommended.

Barnaby, Frank, and Ronald Huiskens. *Arms Uncontrolled*. Cambridge, Mass.: Harvard University Press, 1975.

Both authors are associated with the Stockholm International Peace Research Institute (SIPRI), which was set up in 1966 by the Swedish Parliament. This book provides authoritative information about the status of the nuclear arms race up to 1973. An interesting eight-page chronology gives a side-by-side comparison of U.S. and U.S.S.R. strategic arsenals since 1945. All nuclear test explosions are listed year by year. The number of bombers, land-based missiles, and submarine-launched missiles, the so-called "triad" of delivery systems, is enumerated. Existing arms control agreements are reviewed: Antarctic Treaty (1961), Atmospheric Test Ban (1963), Outer Space Treaty (1967), Non-Proliferation Treaty (1972), and others. The authors have collected and summarized the kind of information that conscientious citizens need to know about the arms race.

Beilenson, Laurence W. *Survival and Peace in the Nuclear Age*. Chicago: Regnery/-Gateway, 1980.

The author argues that nuclear war with the Soviet Union is more likely than not. He is opposed to the Strategic Arms Limitation Talks because the United States should "sharpen its swords, not sheathe them." Historical examples are used to show that treaties are unreliable, frequently broken by the more aggressive side. To prepare for a Soviet first strike, the United States should build civil defense shelters and an antiballistic missile system. After the disastrous experience of Vietnam, the United States should bring home its troops from foreign bases while helping NATO and Japan to develop nuclear weapons for their own defense. Finally, the author advocates using foreign aid to overthrow Communist governments, like America received help from France and Spain to win its independence from England.

Beres, Louis René. *Apocalypse: Nuclear Catastrophe in World Politics*. Chicago: University of Chicago Press, 1980.

The author has written many articles on the risks of continuing the nuclear arms race. He analyzes three possibilities that could lead to the use of nuclear weapons: conflict between the superpowers, proliferation of bombs in Third World countries, and acquisition of bombs by a terrorist group. He invents several scenarios that seem quite plausible. For example, the United States has more than seven thousand nuclear weapons stockpiled in Europe and elsewhere that are vulnerable to sabotage or theft by terrorists. He proposes a blueprint for action that includes a ban on further underground weapons testing, a no-first-use pledge, nuclear-free zones and an antiterrorist strategy. Many references to the current literature are given.

Bethe, Hans. *The Road from Los Alamos*. New York: American Institute of Physics, 1991.

Collected in this volume are essays written or coauthored by Bethe during his long and distinguished career as physicist and science adviser. Bethe, who was chairman of a testban study group and member of the President's Science Advisory Committee under Eisenhower, defends his opposition to building the hydrogen bomb and explains his views on arms control, a nuclear freeze, and nuclear power. His attitude about science and morality is presented in a section entitled "Advise and Dissent." "Five Physicists" contains personal reflections on colleagues and friends, including a notable obituary of J. Robert Oppenheimer. The final essay is on astrophysics, for which Bethe received the Nobel Prize in 1967. The preface contains the author's recent impressions about his essays viewed in retrospect.

Betts, Richard K. *Nuclear Blackmail and Nuclear Balance*. Washington, D.C.: Brookings Institution, 1987.

An analytical study of international political crises since 1945, in which the threat of using nuclear weapons was invoked to exert pressure on the opponents. Among the case studies cited by the author are the following: Berlin blockade, 1948; Korean War, 1950-1953; Suez crisis, 1956; Taiwan Straits (Quemoy and Matsu), 1958; second Berlin crisis, 1961; Soviet missiles in Cuba, 1962; Middle East War of 1973; Afghanistan invasion, 1980. The actions of presidents Eisenhower, Kennedy, Nixon, and Carter, along with their political advisers, are reviewed. Nuclear threats are characterized as "halfway between blackmail and bluff." The author warns that ambiguous threats are dangerous during the confusion of a crisis, because miscalculation of the opponent's intentions may trigger off an irreversible nuclear escalation. Footnotes and references are given.

Bidwell, Shelford, ed. *World War III: A Military Projection Founded on Today's Facts*. London: Hamlyn, 1978. Reprint. New York: Crown, 1983.

Contains a collection of fifteen essays by political analysts, journalists, and former military officers, all from Great Britain. Part 1 gives an up-to-date summary of weapons systems, including photographs of current missiles, submarines, and aircraft. One map pinpoints the location of the six Minuteman missile bases in the United States; another one shows the extent of arms exports to Third World countries. An interesting chapter on crisis management explains how the two superpowers have learned to avoid trespassing on each other's vital interests. In part 2, World War III is assumed to start in a confrontation between NATO and the Warsaw Pact. Over a period of three days, the fighting escalates rapidly from a localized conflict into an all-out nuclear exchange. An ominous projection of doomsday.

Blackett, Patrick M. S. *Fear, War, and the Bomb: Military and Political Consequences of Atomic Energy.* New York: McGraw-Hill, 1948.
Professor Blackett was a British physicist and Nobel laureate who played an active role as an adviser on atomic energy policy for his government. He describes the rapid deterioration of Soviet-American relations immediately after the defeat of Nazi Germany. He expresses the view that the atomic bombs used in Japan were intended primarily to obtain a favorable balance of power for the United States in the postwar world. He describes the Baruch Plan for control of atomic energy, which was unacceptable to the Soviets because it required inspections of military installations. On the other hand, the Gromyko plan was unacceptable to the United States because all atomic weapons plants would have to be dismantled. This well-written book provides interesting historical perspective and predicts with remarkable foresight how the Cold War arms race developed.

Boston Study Group. *Winding Down: The Price of Defense.* San Francisco: W. H. Freeman, 1979. Reprint. 1982.
An informative analysis of modern weapons and military strategy. The authors include Philip Morrison, physicist and past chairman of the Federation of American Scientists, and Randall Forsberg, leader in the Nuclear Freeze campaign. This book is intended to contribute to the public debate about national security, particularly to reconsider the large military buildup advocated by President Reagan. The authors argue that national security can be increased by *reducing* military spending by about 40 percent. They provide a well-documented comparison of U.S. and Soviet military power, and criticize the unnecessary investment in new weapons such as the MX missile and the B-1 bomber. They view the long-range cruise missile as a future attempt to obtain a nuclear advantage. Sources and notes are given in the appendix.

Boyer, Paul. *By the Bomb's Early Light: American Thought and Culture at the Dawn of the Atomic Age.* New York: Pantheon Books, 1985.

The author describes how the atomic bomb was viewed in American culture during the first five years after Hiroshima. He has made a thorough study of radio and newspaper commentaries, books, films, poetry, cartoons, country music; he summarizes the views of various religious leaders, scientists, and military spokesmen at that time. The reader is reminded about the widespread fear of nuclear destruction, the short-lived dreams for world government, the optimistic forecasts of life in the atomic age. One general theme that emerges from this broadly based study is the repeated cycle of activism and apathy toward nuclear weapons since 1945. Extensive references are provided in the appendix.

Brodie, Bernard, ed. *The Absolute Weapon: Atomic Power and World Order*. New York: Harcourt, Brace, 1946.
A collection of six essays on diplomacy in the atomic age by scholars at the Yale University Institute of International Studies. Written shortly after Hiroshima, these essays are chiefly of historical interest, to show what issues were uppermost at the time. The authors accurately predicted that the U.S. monopoly on atomic weapons would not last long. Also, already in 1946, they considered the possibility that rockets similar to the German V-2 could become carriers for atomic bombs. On the other hand, they did not foresee the great increase in explosive power and the radioactive fallout problem. They hoped that a Soviet-U.S. arms race could be avoided by international control of atomic energy through the newly formed United Nations.

Brodie, Bernard. *Strategy in the Missile Age*. Princeton, N.J.: Princeton University Press, 1959.
An excellent introduction to the role of nuclear weapons in military strategy, written with a minimum of technical jargon. The author discusses the failure of strategic bombing in Germany during World War II. He then gives a clear analysis of various strategic planning issues: missiles versus aircraft, preemptive attack, limited war, massive retaliation, credibility of threats, civil defense, missile bases in Europe, and so forth. His writing is objective but not impartial, that is, he considers various viewpoints but also gives his own conclusions. He argues that officers in the armed forces need a broad grasp of strategy in order to look beyond strictly military solutions. Clearly written; highly recommended.

Brown, Anthony Cave, ed. *Dropshot: The United States Plan for War with the Soviet Union in 1957*. New York: Dial Press, 1978.
"Dropshot" was an actual contingency plan for all-out war against the Soviet Union, prepared for the Joint Chiefs of Staff in 1949. It was made public in 1977 under the Freedom of Information Act. The editor has reprinted large portions of the document, with editorial comments to remind the modern reader about numerous political crises of the Cold War. Dropshot envisioned a war launched by Russian troops in Europe starting in 1959, a date selected for planning

purposes. The U.S. response would include three hundred atomic bombs carried by Strategic Air Command planes against targets in the Soviet Union. Intelligence estimates of allied and enemy military forces are given. A frightening document, reflecting a prevalent view of the Soviet menace in the postwar power struggle.

Brown, Neville. *Nuclear War: The Impending Strategic Deadlock.* New York: Praeger, 1964.
Presents a detailed assessment of the Soviet-U.S. military balance in the early 1960's. Specific information is provided about weapons such as the Titan land-based missiles, the B-52 bomber, the Hound-dog air-to-air missile, the French Mirage supersonic bomber, the KC-135 tanker for mid-air refueling and many others. One learns that the smallest nuclear bomb is the Davy Crockett mortar, developed for battlefield use, having a range of about one mile, a weight of only 150 pounds, and an explosive power of 500 tons of TNT. One also finds out that Minuteman solid-fuel rockets are always ready for launch within 32 seconds, but Polaris missiles on a nuclear submarine require one minute between successive firings. A coldly analytical writing style, but highly informative.

Burns, E. L. M. *Megamurder.* New York: Pantheon Books, Random House, 1967.
The author was a lieutenant-general in the Canadian armed forces. He condemns the nuclear arms race by the superpowers because it threatens unarmed civilians worldwide. He reminds his military colleagues that the professional soldier traditionally was honored for protecting the lives and property of noncombatants. In nuclear war, however, civilian populations will become the military targets. The author reviews how air warfare was used in World War II, when large cities such as Coventry, Dresden, Tokyo, and Hiroshima were destroyed. He reviews the political events that led up to the North Atlantic Treaty Organization (NATO) in 1949 and the placement of tactical nuclear weapons in Europe. From his broad knowledge of military history, he argues that more weapons can no longer buy added security.

Byers, R. B., ed. *Deterrence in the 1980's.* New York: St. Martin's Press, 1985.
Contains thirteen essays from a 1984 international conference on deterrence held at York University in Toronto, Canada. The stability of deterrence is questioned in view of the continuing arms race and the development of new weapons. Considerable criticism was expressed toward President Reagan's proposed Strategic Defense Initiative: It would cause an escalation of the arms race into space; it would weaken the NATO alliance by decoupling U.S. defense from what happens in Europe; it is an illusory technological fix, seeking to avoid difficult discussions with the Soviets on mutual security. Public concern about the vast number of weapons, the immorality of targeting enemy cities, and a distrust of strategic military analysts also prompts an overall rethinking of deterrence strategy. Thoughtful analysis.

Calder, Nigel. *Nuclear Nightmares: An Investigation into Possible Wars*. New York: Viking Press, 1980.

The author has written numerous books and articles on science for the general public. In 1979, the British Broadcasting Corporation asked him to investigate the status of the nuclear arms race. He describes four routes that could lead to nuclear war. One chapter, entitled "The German Volcano," describes the dangerous confrontation between NATO and the Warsaw Pact that could erupt during a crisis. "The Nuclear Epidemic" summarizes the problems of proliferation. "The Headless Dragon" symbolizes the loss of control and command by the military leadership when retaliation is automated by computers. "The Missile Duel" provides an overview of Trident submarines, the Soviet SS-18, and multiple warhead technology. Informative and well written; highly recommended.

Campbell, Christopher. *Nuclear Weapons Fact Book*. Novato, Calif.: Presidio Press, 1984.

A thorough compilation of the world's arsenal of nuclear weapons and delivery systems, with many half-page and full-page photographs. This book is not a critique of the arms race, but it gives informative, objective descriptions of existing weapons. Among these are the Minuteman, the Midgetman, the Pershing cruise missile, the Trident submarine, the B-52 and B-1 bombers, the Soviet Backfire bomber, the SS-19 and earlier Soviet missiles, and midair refueling technology, all shown with pictures. British, French, and Chinese weapons are summarized. A map showing all U.S. and Soviet missile launch sites is given. Other interesting diagrams show a Minuteman silo in cross-section and a proposed antisatellite space station. A glossary of acronyms and a chronology of the arms race up to 1983 are included. Highly informative.

Carlton, David, and Herbert M. Levine, eds. *The Cold War Debated*. New York: McGraw-Hill, 1988.

Nineteen controversial questions in the Cold War debate are presented, each one followed by two opposing points of view. The question, "Was détente of mutual benefit to the U.S. and the Soviet Union?" is answered "yes" by Henry Kissinger and "no" by labor leader George Meany, using reprints of their 1974 testimony to Congress. The cases for and against ballistic missile defense (the Strategic Defense Initiative) are debated in another chapter. Other contentious issues are whether United States influence in world affairs is declining, who is primarily responsible for the Cold War, and whether or not arms control agreements have improved the prospects for peace. Each chapter is followed by discussion questions and references for further reading, suitable for a college class on the nuclear arms race.

Carlton, David, and Carlo Schaerf, eds. *The Dynamics of the Arms Race*. New York: John Wiley & Sons, 1975.

Contains twenty-two articles presented at an international symposium on the arms race held in Italy at the University of Padua in 1974. Many of the authors are well-known scientists, analysts, and writers. Herbert York discusses the technology and deployment of multiple warheads for missiles. Kosta Tsipis describes the nearly invulnerable deterrent of submarine-launched nuclear missiles. Hans J. Morgenthau, distinguished political scientist, analyzes the implications of massive retaliation, counterforce, and first-strike strategies. Jules Moch, French disarmament negotiator, addresses problems of verification to prevent treaty violations. Alan Dowty, from Israel, discusses the role of international peace-keeping forces to prevent regional conflicts from escalating. Stimulating articles by knowledgeable contributors; highly recommended.

Carnesale, Albert, Paul Doty, Stanley Hoffmann, Samuel P. Huntington, Joseph S. Nye, Jr., and Scott D. Sagan. *Living with Nuclear Weapons*. Cambridge, Mass.: Harvard University Press, 1983.
An informative book of about 250 pages, designed for a college-level course on the nuclear arms race. Political changes in U.S.-Soviet relations and ongoing technological developments in weapons are discussed in clear, factual terms. Both the anticommunist rhetoric and the peace movement literature are criticized for presenting certain half-truths that hinder a genuine search for alternatives. An introduction by Derek Bok, president of Harvard University, reminds readers that an informed public opinion helped to bring about an end to slavery and produced other major social changes. The authors argue for setting realistic goals to reduce the danger of nuclear war in small steps; otherwise, fatalism and despair inhibit such efforts.

Chalfont, Alun. *Star Wars: Suicide or Survival?* Boston: Little, Brown, 1985.
A favorable endorsement of the Strategic Defense Initiative is provided in this book by a British author. He argues that deterrence based on mutually assured destruction is mutual suicide, so a defensive technology against enemy missiles should be developed. He gives an overview of the proposed SDI system, showing diagrams of surveillance satellites and space-based battle stations. He criticizes the nuclear freeze and disarmament movements for being naïve about Soviet military intentions. He discusses the favorable impact that SDI may have on arms control negotiations and the NATO alliance. The Outer Space Treaty of 1968 may need to be terminated if it is no longer in the U.S. interest. The appendix contains the text of President Reagan's SDI speech of 1983 and other documents.

Chayes, Antonia H., and Paul Doty, eds. *Defending Deterrence: Managing the ABM Treaty Regime into the 21st Century*. New York: Pergamon-Brassey's, 1989.
The Antiballistic Missile (ABM) Treaty of 1972 was an agreement to prohibit deployment of an ABM system because both superpowers felt that it would stimulate new offensive countermeasures, thereby accelerating the arms race. This

book contains twelve essays by writers knowledgeable on national security and arms control issues who analyze the implications of recent technical and political developments that will affect the treaty's future. One essay explores the Strategic Defense Initiative (SDI); deployment clearly would violate the ABM treaty, but research without actual testing would not. Scientific, military, political, and legal aspects are discussed by experts in those fields. Senator Sam Nunn provides an introduction. The book assumes that readers have some background knowledge about past nuclear weapons strategy.

Cimbala, Stephen J. *Nuclear War and Nuclear Strategy: Unfinished Business.* Westport, Conn.: Greenwood Press, 1987.
The author, a political scientist, provides a sophisticated analysis and critique of unresolved issues in nuclear strategy. Part 1 considers whether the deterrent threat of mutual vulnerability is relatively stable or unstable at this time. Part 2 asks how the United States would respond to the unlikely but still possible case of a Soviet "bolt from the blue" surprise attack. Part 3 analyzes the problems of maintaining command and control of nuclear forces after a war has started. Part 4 discusses the topic of extended deterrence, to include the NATO countries under the U.S. nuclear umbrella. Part 5 raises questions that are rarely asked about how a nuclear war, once started, could be terminated. Previous knowledge of nuclear strategy vocabulary and concepts is assumed.

Clarfield, Gerard H., and William M. Wiecek. *Nuclear America: Military and Civilian Nuclear Power in the United States, 1940-1980.* New York: Harper & Row, 1984.
A mixture of factual information and critical commentary about nuclear weapons and power plants. The scientific background, the Manhattan Project, and the Hiroshima and Nagasaki events are well described for the general readership. It is interesting that no high-level military officers were consulted by President Truman in the decision to use the bomb. The start of the Cold War, the hydrogen bomb, the fallout controversy, and the SALT I agreement are discussed in subsequent chapters, with brief quotations from key participants. The growth of the antinuclear movement and the controversial role of the Atomic Energy Commission in promoting both military and civilian nuclear activities are reviewed. The appendix contains a good selection of references with annotations.

Clark, Ian. *Limited Nuclear War: Political Theory and War Conventions.* Princeton, N.J.: Princeton University Press, 1982.
If war should break out between the two superpowers, a massive bombardment exchange of nuclear weapons would lead to pointless slaughter in both countries. The author argues that a strategy of limited nuclear war may prevail because both sides wish to prevent self-annihilation. The history of arms limitations and codes of conduct in warfare is reviewed. Some examples are the prohibition against

using poison gas, distinguishing between military and nonmilitary targets, and rules about treatment of captured enemy soldiers. Such restraints require cooperation between combatants. The author describes a code of "nuclear chivalry" that would include a pledge of no first use and some restriction on target selection. A scholarly overview and critique of the extensive literature on limited nuclear war.

Clark, Ronald W. *The Greatest Power on Earth: The International Race for Nuclear Supremacy.* New York: Harper & Row, 1980.
Presents an overview of the atomic bomb project and postwar developments, using sources of information that have only gradually become available to historians. The nuclear physics background and the specific contributions by scientists in Rome, Berlin, Chicago, and elsewhere are described in nontechnical terms. The postwar decision by England and France to develop their own nuclear weapons—the start of proliferation—is explained with appropriate documentation. Truman's controversial decision to build the H-bomb is presented in the context of the Berlin blockade and the first Soviet nuclear test explosion in 1949. Many interesting quotations by political leaders and scientists are woven into the narrative at critical points, with a complete listing of sources given in the appendix.

Coale, Ansley J. *The Problem of Reducing Vulnerability to Atomic Bombs.* Princeton, N.J.: Princeton University Press, 1947.
This small book is of historical interest, having been written in that brief span of four postwar years when the United States had a monopoly on the atomic bomb. A committee was established by the Social Science Research Council to consider various implications of this new weapon. Key issues at the time were possible evacuation of cities, construction of underground shelters, and negotiations for international control of atomic facilities. The destructive power of bombs is explained, as well as the methods of delivery by planes, submarines, or guided missiles. The vulnerability of maintaining a national administration if Washington, D.C., should be hit is anticipated. The doctrine of deterrence, based on the threat of retaliation, is foreseen as a basic defense against an enemy attack with nuclear weapons.

Cochran, Thomas B., William M. Arkin, and Milton M. Hoenig. *U.S. Nuclear Forces and Capabilities.* Vol. 1 in *Nuclear Weapons Databook.* Cambridge, Mass.: Ballinger, 1984.
An authoritative encyclopedia of the U.S. arsenal of nuclear weapons and delivery systems, with many photographs and tables of information. Three chapters are devoted to tactical nuclear weapons deployed by the Army, Navy, and Air Force, respectively. Strategic weapons are described separately, with detailed data about B-52, Minuteman, and Trident missile launch systems. One

chapter explains the newest cruise missile technology, with terrain recognition microprocessors and tiny jet engines for in-flight guidance control. A U.S. map shows all nuclear weapons installations; another one shows worldwide naval bases for nuclear-armed ships and submarines. The appendix gives a glossary of acronyms and special terms. An excellent reference book, factual and comprehensive.

Cochran, Thomas B., William M. Arkin, Robert S. Norris, and Jeffrey I. Sands. *Soviet Nuclear Weapons*. Vol. IV in *Nuclear Weapons Databook*. New York: Harper & Row, 1989.

An encyclopedic compilation describing the Soviet nuclear arsenal, including many photographs of Soviet missiles, planes, surface ships, submarines, and land-based launch facilities. The first three volumes in this series, published by the Natural Resources Defense Council, presented a similar compilation of U.S. nuclear weapons and delivery systems. In this book, the Soviet stockpile of about 33,000 warheads is broken down into subcategories of strategic and tactical weapons, with information about explosive power, range, accuracy, and the number deployed for each type. One chapter describes Soviet nuclear tests, including a seventeen-page listing of every underground explosion from 1961 to 1987. Maps are provided showing the location of uranium ore deposits, enrichment facilities, plutonium production reactors, and weapons laboratories. The most complete reference work available.

Codevilla, Angelo. *While Others Build: The Commonsense Approach to the Strategic Defense Initiative*. New York: Macmillan, 1988.

The author represents the conservative point of view, expressing his strong support for the Strategic Defense Initiative. He regards the Soviet Union as a dangerous opponent with a clear military superiority over the United States. Two decades of neglect allowed the Soviets to build a war-winning strategic missile system as well as to obtain a monopoly on antimissile defenses. He faults the Reagan administration for pursuing SDI half-heartedly, by funding only research without deployment. He proposes that a new military branch in addition to the Army, Navy, and Air Force is now needed, a "Strategic Defense Force" to push vigorously for an antimissile system with space-based weapons. He criticizes the ABM Treaty and SALT I for limiting U.S. options to counter the Soviet threat.

Cohen, Avner, and Steven Lee, eds. *Nuclear Weapons and the Future of Humanity: The Fundamental Questions*. Totowa, N.J.: Rowman & Allanheld, 1986.

A collection of twenty-five essays about the alarming escalation of the arms race in the early 1980's, written by philosophers and social scientists from the academic community. Among the well-known contributors are the following: John P. Holdren, national chairman of the Federation of American Scientists, writing on "The Dynamics of the Nuclear Arms Race"; Paul and Anne Ehrlich,

Stanford University, "Ecology of Nuclear War: Population, Resources, Environment"; Russell Hardin, University of Chicago, "Risking Armageddon"; Richard Falk, Princeton University, "Nuclear Weapons and the Renewal of Democracy"; Edmund Pellegrino, Georgetown University, "The Physician, Nuclear Warfare, and the Ethics of Medicine"; Louis R. Beres, Purdue University, "Preventing the Final Epidemic." The authors seek to uncover and explore ethical issues behind the nuclear weapons predicament. Thoughtful critique of current issues.

Cook, Fred J. *The Warfare State*. New York: Macmillan, 1962.
This book reminds us how grim the world situation was in 1962. *Life* magazine had just published an article on how to build a fallout shelter in one's basement, endorsed by a supporting letter from President Kennedy. The Berlin crisis, stories about Communist spies, the military draft, air raid drills in public schools, and hydrogen bomb explosions were the realities of the time. The author traces the growth of militarism and the idea of a permanent warfare state after World War II. President Eisenhower's farewell address, warning against the excessive influence of the military-industrial complex, forms the thesis of the book. A foreword by Bertrand Russell supports the message that fanatic anticommunism is being exploited for selfish political and economic gain.

Cottrell, Leonard S., and Sylvia Eberhart. *American Opinion on World Affairs in the Atomic Age*. Princeton, N.J.: Princeton University Press, 1948.
The authors are social scientists with a particular interest in public opinion surveys. In 1947 they questioned some six thousand people about their attitudes toward the atomic bomb and current negotiations for international control. The survey revealed that 98 percent of the respondents were aware of the A-bomb, but 33 percent did not know about the existence of the United Nations at that time. Most people had no opinion about what the United States should do to avoid nuclear war: "Let the government worry about it." Questions about Russia showed a widespread unfavorable viewpoint. The last half of the book contains interview questions and tabulated responses. An interesting glimpse of popular opinion shortly after Hiroshima.

Cox, Arthur Macy. *Russian Roulette: The Superpower Game*. New York: Times Books, 1982.
A pessimistic assessment about the deterioration of Soviet-American relations under the Reagan administration. The author describes the return to Cold War thinking of the 1950's, based on an exaggerated estimate of the Soviet military threat and U.S. vulnerability. President Reagan's appointments to the Arms Control and Disarmament Agency are identified as advocates of a large military buildup, not negotiators. The changing political scene in central Europe and the European nuclear disarmament movement are analyzed. Part of the blame for

increased tension between the superpowers is attributed to Soviet interventionism in Third World countries. A Soviet viewpoint is presented in a twenty-five-page commentary by George Arbatov, personal advisor to President Leonid Brezhnev. The author provides suggestions for several possible areas of negotiation.

Craig, Paul P., and John A. Jungerman. *Nuclear Arm Race: Technology and Society*. New York: McGraw-Hill, 1986.
An excellent textbook for a college-level course or an adult discussion group on the arms race. Part 1 describes the history of nuclear weapons and the development of missile systems with improved range and accuracy. Part 2 gives technical background on radioactivity, blast effects, fallout, hydrogen bomb design, and so forth. Part 3 deals with civil defense, proliferation, negotiations between the two superpowers, and the economics of the arms race. Each chapter has a list of discussion questions as well as graphs, tables, and timely cartoons. Highly recommended.

Cunningham, Ann Marie, and Mariana Fitzpatrick. *Future Fire: Weapons for the Apocalypse*. New York: Warner Books, 1983.
An informative summary of modern weapons technology, based on thorough research. Separate sections are devoted to the neutron bomb; the killer satellite; laser beam weapons; the nuclear triad of land-, sea-, and air-launched missiles; the Stealth bomber; the new MX missile; and multiple-warhead technology. Other chapters provide detailed information about nuclear weapons accidents in Spain, Greenland, and elsewhere; arms sales to developing nations; the cost of the massive military buildup promoted by President Reagan, and the increased dependence on computers to replace human judgment. The effects of the 20-kiloton explosion at Hiroshima are compared to an H-bomb explosion over an American city. A highly recommended reference, with clear explanations of technical details.

Dahl, Robert. *Controlling Nuclear Weapons: Democracy Versus Guardianship*. Syracuse, N.Y.: Syracuse University Press, 1985.
Contains five lectures given at Syracuse University in 1984. The author questions the desirability of delegating the power to determine nuclear weapons policies to a small group of experts in the government, with little opportunity for public debate. He discusses the historical background of the concept of "guardianship," where ideally the best-qualified, most competent people are chosen to make decisions for the welfare of all. He argues that the secret way in which the decision was made to use the atomic bomb in Japan is a poor model for the democratic process. He believes that citizens should have fuller access to information and need to exercise greater control over military and political issues. He proposes using a national referendum to provide genuine citizen participation.

Dotto, Lydia. *Planet Earth in Jeopardy: Environmental Consequences of Nuclear War*. New York: John Wiley & Sons, 1986.
A two-volume treatise published in 1985 on the environmental consequences of nuclear war was condensed into this shortened version for a general audience. Destruction of cities by blast, fire, and radiation are the direct bomb effects; however, indirect effects described in this study would be much more extensive. Sooty smoke clouds of continental size would reduce sunlight at the earth's surface, causing a temperature drop to winter levels possibly for several weeks. Other effects would include reduced rainfall and chemical pollution in the air. Agricultural productivity would drop greatly because of a shorter growing season and lack of supplies by farmers. Computer simulations show widespread starvation, causing more fatalities than the immediate bomb deaths. An informative summary of nuclear winter.

Douglass, Joseph D., and Amoretta M. Hoeber. *Conventional War and Escalation: The Soviet View*. New York: Crane, Russak, 1981.
This pamphlet from the National Strategy Information Center of Washington, D.C., is one of a series that tries to assess Soviet intentions in the Cold War. In the United States, initiating a nuclear war is considered impossible because it would lead to mutual annihilation. The authors warn that the Soviet leadership does not share this view. They quote from Soviet strategists who advocate using conventional weapons as just the first stage of a general offensive in which nuclear weapons would deal the decisive blow. The authors are greatly alarmed at the possibility of a nuclear surprise attack against NATO command and control centers in central Europe. Western strategists who believe that the Soviets would not resort to nuclear weapons are accused of wishful thinking.

_____. *Soviet Strategy for Nuclear War*. Stanford, Calif.: Hoover Institution Press, 1979.
The authors present a very threatening picture of Soviet military capability and intentions. The Soviet Union is described as an aggressive, expansionist power that is planning to fight and win a nuclear war against the United States. Communism and capitalism are viewed as irreconcilable enemies. Quoting from military textbooks and articles published in Russian, the authors claim that a nuclear first-strike surprise attack is the most likely scenario for Soviet world domination. After annihilating several U.S. cities, the Soviets would consolidate their victory by establishing a puppet government for the United States, with executions and mass deportations to control the population. This hawkish document was published when the Strategic Arms Limitation Treaty (SALT) negotiations were going on and was intended to rally public opposition to it.

Dyson, Freeman. *Weapons and Hope*. New York: Harper & Row, 1984.
The author is a physicist who emigrated from England to the United States after

World War II and is a longtime member of the prestigious Institute for Advanced Studies at Princeton, New Jersey. He has written and lectured extensively on war and peace issues. This volume contains twenty-four stimulating essays in which he tries to bridge the communication gap between the professional military establishment and peace activists. For example, the chapter on the antiballistic missile problem lists excellent arguments on both sides of the issue, without trying to shut off debate. Other chapters present a fresh perspective on Star Wars, pacifists, unilateral disarmament, and the arms race. His writing is filled with historical insights and literary quotations, rather than technical information. Thoughtful essays, with a hopeful attitude.

Ehrlich, Paul, Carl Sagan, Donald Kennedy, and Walter Orr Roberts. *The Cold and the Dark: The World After Nuclear War*. New York: W. W. Norton, 1984.
This book summarizes the 1983 Conference on Long-Term Worldwide Biological Consequences of Nuclear War, as reported by some of its most prominent participants. Carl Sagan, best known for the *Cosmos* TV series, describes atmospheric and climatic consequences of multiple nuclear detonations: clouds of dust and soot causing prolonged darkness and cold. Paul Ehrlich, whose writings on population explosion received wide publicity in the 1970's, summarizes the biological consequences on agriculture and marine life. One unique feature of this conference was the live satellite link to Moscow, where distinguished members of the Soviet Academy of Sciences contributed directly to the discussion. The appendix contains a reprint of the "TTAPS" article from the journal *Science* (named after its five authors, Turco, Toon, Ackerman, Pollack, and Sagan) which originally predicted drastic nuclear war aftereffects.

Enthoven, Alain C., and K. Wayne Smith. *How Much Is Enough? Shaping the Defense Program, 1961-1969*. New York: Harper & Row, 1971.
The author worked closely with Secretary of Defense McNamara as the assistant secretary for systems analysis. He describes the controversial role of civilian analysts who made independent assessments of military budget requests. In setting priorities among proposed weapons systems, they came into frequent conflict with the House Armed Services Committee and the Joint Chiefs of Staff. Three case studies of projects that were canceled over military and Congressional objections are described: the B-70 bomber, the Skybolt missile, and the F-111 fighter plane. One chapter discusses the change in NATO strategy, to reduce reliance on nuclear weapons while increasing conventional forces in Europe. Another chapter analyzes "how much is enough" for assured retaliation against a Soviet first strike. An interesting inside view of defense management.

Evans, Medford. *The Secret War for the A-Bomb*. Chicago: Henry Regnery, 1953.
A political diatribe against the menace of Communist world domination that reflects the superpatriotism of the early 1950's. The author identifies three groups

of people who are aiding the enemy. First are the atom spies such as Klaus Fuchs and Julius Rosenberg, as well as thieves who "may have stolen enough uranium for twenty atom bombs." Second are the Communist fellow travelers who have infiltrated U.S. atomic laboratories. The third and largest group are the college-educated intellectuals who promote the "One-World-Or-None nonsense," people such as Robert Hutchins, Leo Szilard, and David Lilienthal. They are criticized for being confused, blind, ignorant, foolish, and naïve. Adapting physics vocabulary to his cause, the author sees little difference between Communists and the "isotopically related" liberals.

Fallows, James. *National Defense*. New York: Random House, 1981.
The author, a journalist, provides a critique of faulty military thinking in the nuclear age. He argues that military planners have a "wonder-weapon" mentality, which means an overreliance on new technology without considering the realities of possible combat situations. In Vietnam, for example, the M-16 rifle performed very poorly under jungle conditions. In one chapter entitled "Theologians," he criticizes the war game analysts who obtain theoretical outcomes based on uncertain speculations about missile accuracy and Soviet intentions. He finds "ban the bomb" activists to be just as unrealistic as the hawks in Congress who endorse all new weapons indiscriminately. In his view, effective national defense has deteriorated because oversimplified slogans have replaced rational discussion about actual military requirements for maintaining security.

Feis, Herbert. *From Trust to Terror: The Onset of the Cold War, 1945-1950*. New York: W. W. Norton, 1970.
The author is a historian who provides not merely a description but an interpretation and evaluation of events that precipitated the Cold War. The alliance between the Soviet Union and the Western nations broke down almost immediately after Germany's surrender because of insoluble political disagreements over spheres of influence in central Europe. The author reviews key developments such as Churchill's "Iron Curtain" speech, Truman's policy of containment, the Marshall plan, the Communist coup in Czechoslovakia, the Berlin blockade, the formation of NATO, and the first Soviet nuclear explosion, all happening between 1946 and 1949. The failure to control atomic weapons development through the United Nations is interpreted as a consequence of mutual political mistrust in the East-West power struggle.

Fleming, D. F. *The Issues of Survival*. Garden City, N.Y.: Doubleday, 1972.
The author was a professor of political science who also became a radio commentator, newspaper columnist, and author of ten books. He provides a strongly negative assessment of the militarism and obsessive anti-Communism that dominated the internal life of the United States at that time. While the costly arms race continued, he points out urgent domestic problems that were being

neglected: schools, housing, mass transportation, poverty, and environmental pollution. In this short book, the author speaks his mind on the need for social changes, following up on his earlier two-volume analytical study, *The Cold War and Its Origins*.

Ford, Daniel F. *The Button: The Pentagon's Strategic Command and Control System*. New York: Simon & Schuster, 1985.
This book focuses attention on a weakness of the U.S. nuclear arsenal: the questionable reliability of the command, control, and communications network. The author visited Strategic Air Command (SAC) headquarters at Omaha, the Aerospace Defense Command at Cheyenne Mountain, Colorado, and other military facilities to gather his information. He exposes a number of embarrassing computer failures and past communication breakdowns. He envisions a frightening scenario during a major Soviet-U.S. political crisis if central control of weapons is lost and submarine or field commanders have to make missile launch decisions. Retaliation against an actual Soviet missile attack is quite insecure; therefore, the author asserts, the Pentagon in fact has planned to launch a first strike in an impending confrontation. Many quotations are cited.

Fryklund, Richard. *100 Million Lives: Maximum Survival in a Nuclear War*. New York: Macmillan, 1962.
The author begins with a critique of military strategy in the 1950's. Under President Eisenhower, the United States had threatened "massive retaliation" against the Soviet homeland if the Communists attacked anywhere in the world. As the Soviet's nuclear arsenal increased, however, this policy had to be abandoned because it would lead to mutual devastation. In searching for a more flexible deterrent, Pentagon analysts doing computerized war simulation exercises discovered a new concept, the "No-City" theory. Each side would attack the opponent's military targets only, while cities would be spared. In such a limited nuclear war, perhaps a hundred million lives could be saved. The author argues persuasively that the Soviets have the same incentive to avoid annihilation of cities as we do. A good example of 1960's thinking.

Gallois, Pierre. *The Balance of Terror: Strategy for the Nuclear Age*. Translated from French by Richard Howard. Boston: Houghton Mifflin, 1961.
The author was a general in the French Air Force. He presents persuasive arguments that mutual deterrence based on a balance of nuclear weapons is the best strategy to maintain world peace. A surprise attack by either superpower could not bring quick victory because both sides would have enough weapons left to retaliate. He argues against nuclear disarmament because when a conflict develops, a threatened country could quickly reestablish its nuclear stockpile. The author reminds readers of recent conflicts in Korea, the Near East, and Hungary, none of which escalated to the point that nuclear weapons were used. He justifies

the French nuclear program because a strong national defense helps collective security. Clearly written; highly recommended to understand the basis for a strategy of deterrence.

Garfinkel, Adam M. *The Politics of the Nuclear Freeze*. Philadelphia: Foreign Policy Research Institute, 1984.

The nuclear freeze movement was a proposal to stop the "testing, production, and deployment of nuclear weapons and of missiles" that received widespread support from 1981 to 1984. The author analyzes the freeze as viewed across the political spectrum from the far left to the far right. From his perspective, the extreme left includes the World Council of Churches, Common Cause, and various peace groups. On the far right are Jerry Falwell, the John Birch Society, and others. He places the Reagan administration at the political center as the "conservative mainstream." He strongly criticizes Randall Forsberg, founder of the Freeze movement, and quotes approvingly from Richard Perle, Reagan's Assistant Secretary of Defense. A scholarly rejection of the Nuclear Freeze.

Garthoff, Raymond L. *Perspectives on the Strategic Balance*. Washington, D.C.: Brookings Institution, 1983.

In this small pamphlet, the author describes many difficulties that arise in trying to compare the relative strength of U.S.S.R. and U.S. strategic nuclear weapons. Should one count the number of missiles or number of warheads on each side? Are land-based and submarine-launched missiles equivalent? How should differences in explosive power and aiming accuracy be taken into account? In a 1981 television address, President Reagan displayed a graph showing a six-to-one Soviet "margin of superiority" in strategic weapons. A careful analysis later revealed that the president had included bombers on the Soviet side, but omitted cruise missiles on the U.S. side. The author criticizes such distorted data because it falsely influences public perception and cuts off serious dialogue about arms control. Knowledgeable and informative.

Gay, William, and Michael Pearson. *The Nuclear Arms Race: A Digest with Bibliographies*. Chicago: American Library Association, 1987.

An excellent overview of the nuclear arms race, with an extensive, annotated bibliography of pertinent literature. This book should be particularly useful for scholars who need guidance to locate relevant source material. The following topics are included: the Manhattan Project, hydrogen bomb development, nuclear weapons testing, the debate over deterrence, the problem of proliferation, the social and economic costs of military spending, the Strategic Defense Initiative, attempts at arms control, and the influence of the peace movement. The appendix gives a list of useful scholarly journals, research organizations, and government publications that deal with various aspects of nuclear weapons. Highly recommended.

Gilpin, Robert. *American Scientists and Nuclear Weapons Policy*. Princeton, N.J.: Princeton University Press, 1962.

The author presents an analysis of the difficult role of scientists as technical advisors on controversial political issues. He cites four case studies. First was Truman's decision to use the atomic bomb against Japan, which was opposed by the Franck Report but supported by the official Scientist's Advisory Committee. Second was the argument about developing a hydrogen bomb in 1949. Third was the debate over the production of small tactical nuclear weapons. Fourth was the dispute over fallout and a nuclear test ban, in which Edward Teller and Linus Pauling were the main protagonists. The author shows that political and scientific issues are inevitably intertwined. Therefore, he argues, the process of soliciting advice from opposing technical experts is a good way to produce an acceptable political compromise.

Green, Harold P., and Alan Rosenthal. *Government of the Atom: The Integration of Powers*. New York: Prentice-Hall, 1963.

The focus of this study is the Joint Committee on Atomic Energy (JCAE), through which Congress maintains its oversight of the Atomic Energy Commission. The authors describe the political process of conflict and compromise between the executive and legislative branches of government through which decisions on policy are reached. Some key issues analyzed in this treatise are the following: the crash program to develop a hydrogen bomb; whether to share nuclear weapons information with Great Britain and other allies; construction of plutonium production reactors; the civilian nuclear power plant controversy; vigorous arguments about the nuclear test ban treaty; cancellation of the aircraft nuclear propulsion project. The JCAE is characterized as a committee that initiates policy rather than merely responding to problems.

Green, Philip. *Deadly Logic: The Theory of Nuclear Deterrence*. Columbus: Ohio State University Press, 1966.

The author, a social scientist, challenges assumptions and raises questions about the strategy of deterrence. One chapter gives a detailed, negative assessment of Herman Kahn's book *On Thermonuclear War* (Princeton University Press, 1960.) In particular, Kahn's aura of scientific objectivity is rejected by identifying hidden value judgments and speculative reasoning. Another chapter criticizes the game theory approach to deterrence used by Thomas Schelling in *The Strategy of Conflict* (Harvard University Press, 1960.) Game theory does not replicate actual conditions of international conflict, in which misperceptions of enemy intentions become important. Maintaining a large stockpile of retaliatory weapons is a subjective decision based on a Cold War bias. An alternative policy, such as negotiated disarmament, is defended as equally valid but arising from other assumptions. Sophisticated and thoughtful analysis.

Greene, Owen, Ian Percival, and Irene Ridge. *Nuclear Winter: The Evidence and the Risks*. Cambridge, England: Polity Press, 1985.
This book is addressed to nonscientist readers who want to understand the basis for the nuclear winter scenario that would follow a large-scale nuclear war. Predictions of worldwide climate changes resulting from firestorms, dust, and smoke clouds are described, based on past observations of large volcanic eruptions. Extended darkness and cold temperatures would bring about the collapse of advanced agriculture, with a return to subsistence farming. Famine and devastating epidemics would follow, with sanitation and medical services unable to cope with the problems. The authors characterize present superpower arsenals as a "doomsday machine" that could be set off by a regional crisis or by an accident. Nuclear winter heightens the urgency of reducing the stockpile of weapons that threaten human survival. Brief and well written.

Griffiths, Franklyn, and John C. Polanyi, eds. *The Dangers of Nuclear War*. Toronto: University of Toronto Press, 1979.
What is the likelihood of nuclear war by the year 2000? A group of invited experts from eleven countries gathered for a conference thirty-three years after Hiroshima to grapple with questions about political negotiations and nuclear weapons. Some of the notable contributors to this book are W. George McBundy, former special assistant to the president for national security (1961-1966); S. Freier, head of the Israeli Atomic Energy Commission (1971-1976); and Lord Zuckerman, scientific adviser to the government of Great Britain. Some of the timely topics under discussion are nuclear proliferation, escalation of local conflicts, and international arms sales to Third World dictators. Prime Minister Pierre Trudeau of Canada contributes a foreword to this authoritative collection of foresighted essays.

Grinspoon, Lester, ed. *The Long Darkness: Psychological and Moral Perspectives on Nuclear Winter*. New Haven, Conn.: Yale University Press, 1986.
Contains nine essays by distinguished contributors who express their urgent concern about the clear and present danger of nuclear extermination. Carl Sagan, professor at Cornell University, author, and television personality, describes how nuclear wars of varying size would affect climate and agriculture worldwide. Stephen Jay Gould, biologist and popular writer, shows that there is no basic genetic reason why antagonism should dominate over cooperation between human races. Robert Jay Lifton, psychiatrist and author, discusses psychological responses of repression, anger, fear, or resignation to the possibility that the world may come to an end. The nuclear winter scenario provides a vivid picture for the imagination to deal with the real threat of nuclear annihilation.

Grodzins, Morton, and Eugene Rabinowitch, eds. *The Atomic Age: Scientists in National and World Affairs*. New York: Basic Books, 1963.

Contains reprints of sixty-five articles published in the *Bulletin of the Atomic Scientists* between 1945 and 1961. Dr. Rabinowitch was the founder and editor of the *Bulletin* and contributed frequent editorials on issues involving technology and society. Among the eminent scientist-authors in this collection of essays are Leo Szilard, Albert Einstein, Edward Teller, Ralph E. Lapp, Max Born, and several Soviet scholars. A wide range of problems are discussed: fallout shelters, Soviet espionage, hydrogen bomb tests, world government, the Oppenheimer security hearing, international scientific cooperation, proliferation of nuclear weapons, computer technology, and nuclear power plants. Each article has a brief introduction by the editors. An excellent historical overview from the leading journal in its field.

Hafemeister, David, ed. *Physics and Nuclear Arms Today*. New York: American Institute of Physics, 1991.
This volume is the fourth in a series of reprinted articles taken from the periodical *Physics Today*, which is published by the American Institute of Physics for professional physicists. The reprints collected here are divided into eight sections that deal with effects, testing, and limits on offensive nuclear weapons, as well as defensive alternatives, proliferation, history, commentaries, and references. The list of authors includes many prominent physicists including Edward Teller and Andrei Sakharov, who respectively led the teams of scientists who developed hydrogen bombs for the United States and the Soviet Union. This reference is a source of published debates on controversial issues, with most of the articles being appropriate for non-technical readers.

Halliday, Fred. *The Making of the Second Cold War*. London: Verso Editions, 1983.
The author divides postwar U.S.-Soviet relations into four distinct time periods: the first Cold War, ending in 1953 with the Korean armistice; oscillatory antagonism from 1953 to 1969; cautious cooperation in the 1970's, called détente; and Cold War II, starting in 1979. A Cold War is characterized by military buildup, belligerent propaganda against the enemy, internal persecution of dissenters, and increasing Third World conflicts. The rise of a militant right-wing political movement in the 1980 election campaign is analyzed. The rhetoric of the Reagan administration, advocating the restoration of military superiority and war-winning capability, is critically assessed. The author is a British writer who provides interesting insights into historical events and international politics. A good balance of factual information and stimulating interpretation.

Halperin, Morton H. *Limited War in the Nuclear Age*. New York: John Wiley & Sons, 1966.
This volume is part of a series of scholarly studies on basic world problems published by Harvard University's Center for International Affairs. The author

reviews postwar confrontations in which the United States and the Soviets were on opposite sides, but escalation was avoided. Examples cited include Korea, Indochina, the Suez Canal, Cuba, and Berlin. In Korea, the United States had committed its combat forces, but President Eisenhower ended the fighting without victory in 1953. Several reasons are suggested why the United States refrained from employing tactical nuclear weapons there. The two superpowers have a mutual interest to avoid crossing the threshold of first nuclear use. The author argues that even though local conflicts are inevitable, restraints exist to prevent escalation into all-out strategic war.

Hardin, Russell, John J. Mearsheimer, Gerald Dworkin, and Robert E. Goodwin, eds. *Nuclear Deterrence: Strategy and Ethics*. Chicago: University of Chicago Press, 1985.
The twenty-one articles in this collection were first presented at a conference on "Ethics of Nuclear Deterrence" in 1984 and then published in a special issue of the journal *Ethics* in 1985. The conference was designed to bring together two rather different academic groups, philosophers and social scientists, with a mutual concern about military strategy. Some of the authors argue that deterrence is working well, that it has made the leaders on both sides quite cautious and has successfully prevented conventional wars in Europe and elsewhere. Critics of deterrence believe that threatening civilian targets is basically immoral, that advances in military technology make for instability, and that nuclear weapons undermine democratic governance because war planning decisions are made in secret. Thoughtful presentations of diverse viewpoints.

Harwell, Mark A. *Nuclear Winter: The Human and Environmental Consequences of Nuclear War*. New York: Springer-Verlag, 1984.
On October 31, 1983, an international conference entitled "The World After Nuclear War" was held in Washington, D.C. More than five hundred participants from twenty countries met to analyze the validity of the nuclear winter scenario. The author presents a 165-page synopsis of the results, including quantitative data in the form of tables and graphs. Among the major problems following an assumed 5,000-megaton nuclear war would be disastrous climate changes, fallout, atmospheric pollution, and the collapse of agriculture and health care. Even a preemptive first strike, in which country A devastates country B with no return strike, would shut down food production in country A as a result of a nuclear winter. Political and military issues were deliberately omitted from the conference in order not to distract from the scientific message.

Herken, Gregg. *Counsels of War*. New York: Alfred A. Knopf, 1985.
The author gives a thoroughly documented, historical overview of nuclear strategy issues since 1945. He interviewed well-known scientists, civilian defense analysts, and government policymakers, including three former secretaries of

defense. He provides fascinating personal anecdotes as well as succinct summaries of the viewpoints held by leading personalities in the ongoing debate over strategy. Some key issues discussed in the book are the concept of deterrence, the "missile gap" controversy, the nuclear test ban, tactical nuclear weapons, multiple warhead technology, the single integrated operational plan (SIOP) and the Strategic Defense Initiative for space warfare. The views of people such as Robert McNamara, Robert Oppenheimer, Herman Kahn, Edward Teller, Henry Kissinger, and others are clearly depicted. Provides helpful perspective for the general reader.

_____. *The Winning Weapon: The Atomic Bomb in the Cold War, 1945-1950*. New York: Alfred A. Knopf, 1980.
A scholarly analysis of the start of the Cold War, viewed from a historical perspective thirty years later. Key events are described: the failure of the Baruch Plan for international control of atomic weapons through the United Nations; the Berlin crisis of 1948; the first Soviet nuclear explosion; President Truman's hydrogen bomb decision; the hysteria over Soviet espionage; the start of the Korean War in 1950. The author asserts that American policy was dominated by an illusion about the power of the atomic bomb: the "winning weapon" of World War II supposedly would give the United States a decisive political advantage to dictate the terms of international settlements. When this myth was shattered, the stage was set for an intensified, continuing arms race. Careful documentation, provocative writing.

Hewlett, Richard G., and Francis Duncan. *Atomic Shield, 1947-1952*. Vol 2 in *A History of the United States Atomic Energy Commission*. University Park: Pennsylvania State University Press, 1969.
An extensive history of the first five years of the Atomic Energy Commission is provided here, continuing the high quality of historical scholarship found in volume 1. Many controversial issues faced by the Commission are described with fascinating details: the battle over civilian versus military custody of the nuclear weapons stockpile; labor unrest at Oak Ridge Laboratory; Congressional bickering over new appointments to the Commission; proposed reactor development for Navy submarines; justification for nuclear weapons testing; the debate over hydrogen bomb development. The impact of pertinent historical events is described: Truman's surprising election victory in 1948; the first Soviet nuclear explosion in 1949; the outbreak of the Korean War in 1950. Authoritative and readable, with thorough documentation given in the appendix.

_____. *Nuclear Navy: 1946-1962*. Chicago: University of Chicago Press, 1974.
Both authors are historians employed by the U.S. Atomic Energy Commission. For this project, they were given unrestricted access to the records of the Navy

Department, the Atomic Energy Commission, and the Division of Naval
Reactors, as well as the files and correspondence in Admiral Rickover's office.
They conducted interviews with naval officers, scientists, shipyard workers, men
in the fleet, and industrial managers. The building of the first atomic submarine,
the *Nautilus*, is described in detail. Admiral Rickover was the key personality
in overcoming initial opposition within the Navy bureaucracy, in managing the
industrial contractors, and in training the submarine crews. The original concept
of nuclear power for propulsion rapidly evolved into a new role for the Navy,
using the submarine as a mobile launching platform for missiles. Authoritative
and readable.

Iklé, Fred Charles. *The Social Impact of Bomb Destruction*. Norman: University
of Oklahoma Press, 1958.
The author is a social scientist who attempts to describe the overall impact of a
nuclear war. He argues that doomsday warnings about the end of civilization
discourage any rational planning; a more realistic assessment of possible recovery
can be obtained by studying historical examples of major disasters. Among his
illustrations are the London plague of 1665, the siege of Moscow of 1942, and
the bombing of cities in World War II. He provides numerical data showing
temporary sharp decreases in population, housing, and consumer goods, followed
by a remarkably fast recovery. One graphs shows that Nagasaki's population had
returned to its prewar level already by 1953; however, emergency aid from
nearby cities was essential for rapid restoration. A relatively optimistic analysis
of survival probability.

Jastrow, Robert. *How To Make Nuclear Weapons Obsolete*. Boston: Little, Brown,
1983.
This book contains a mixture of two things: a semitechnical explanation of the
proposed Strategic Defense Initiative (SDI) to shoot down Soviet missiles, and
a political justification to deploy such an SDI system. The author argues that U.S.
strategic forces, especially Minuteman missiles and B-52 bombers, have become
vulnerable to a Soviet first strike. He explains how lasers, electron beams, X
rays, or other high-tech devices could be placed into satellites that would be
capable of intercepting 80 percent of enemy missiles in flight. He asserts that the
Soviets already have made substantial progress on their Star Wars technology in
spite of the antiballistic missile treaty of 1972, and the United States needs to
catch up.

Kahn, Herman. *On Escalation: Metaphors and Scenarios*. New York, Washington,
London: Praeger, 1965.
This is the author's third book on military strategy, following after *On Thermonuclear War* (1960) and *Thinking About the Unthinkable* (1962). He does not
advocate any specific course of action, but tries to reason through various options

to clarify the range of possible consequences. As a framework for discussing the subject of escalation, he uses the metaphor of a ladder, with forty-four rungs from low to high. Starting at the bottom of the ladder, among the rungs he discusses are the following: political crisis; show of force; breaking off diplomatic relations; nuclear ultimatum; embargo or blockade; crossing the nuclear threshold; attack on a military target; civilian devastation attack. He also discusses the process of de-escalation after a crisis, using examples from recent history. A provocative analysis.

_____. *On Thermonuclear War*. 1st ed., Princeton, N.J.: Princeton University Press, 1960. Oxford, England: Oxford University Press, 1960; 2d ed., New York: Free Press, 1969.
This book of more than six hundred pages was based on a series of lectures dealing with military strategy options in the nuclear age. It was addressed primarily to professionals in the defense establishment but was also widely read and discussed in the media. The author seeks to replace guesswork and vague reasoning with sophisticated, analytical techniques and quantitative calculations. He provides data on radioactivity in the environment after a nuclear war and the possibility for economic recovery. He differentiates between several "tragic but distinguishable" postwar scenarios, assuming from 2 to 160 million deaths. His unemotional, scientific style of analysis provoked a hostile reaction from many readers; however, he stimulated more concrete thinking about various levels of deterrence, how best to avoid a crisis that everyone feared.

_____. *Thinking About the Unthinkable*. New York: Avon Books, 1962.
In the past, there was a taboo against discussing in public certain topics such as prostitution or mental illness. The author of this influential book argues that the time has come to face the fact that a nuclear war is possible. How can military deterrence be made more stable? What are some ways in which a nuclear war might start? Is civil defense, including fallout shelters, practical? In order to promote more concrete thinking about nuclear strategy, he presents good arguments for fourteen alternatives, from unilateral disarmament to a preemptive first strike. Like a doctor expected to use cool logic in advising about a life-threatening illness, Kahn defends the need for objective, analytical reasoning in planning for the future. Well written; for a nontechnical audience.

_____. *Thinking About the Unthinkable in the 1980's*. New York: Simon & Schuster, 1984.
Herman Kahn (1922-1983) became famous in the 1960's as an analyst who used possible nuclear war scenarios to generate realistic thinking about the consequences of various defense options. Writing in the early 1980's, he rejects the nuclear freeze, unilateral disarmament (called "preemptive surrender"), and the doomsday image of a nuclear holocaust. He gives arguments favoring civil defense,

antiballistic missiles, and postwar recovery planning, in case deterrence should fail. He states that there was no arms race during the last two decades because United States defense efforts were very lax. He views the possibility of a massive nuclear exchange as very improbable; instead he envisions a protracted political crisis leading to limited nuclear exchange with "proportional retaliation" to avoid mutual annihilation. Provides intellectual justification for the Reagan administration's military buildup.

Katz, Arthur M. *Life After Nuclear War: The Economic and Social Impacts of Nuclear Attacks on the United States*. Cambridge, Mass.: Ballinger, 1982.
In 1979, the author wrote a report for a Congressional committee chaired by Senator William Proxmire, to investigate the economic and social effects of nuclear war. This book presents the same information to a broader audience. It gives quantitative results of computer studies using several levels of nuclear bombardment. In one scenario, a 1-megaton attack on each of the seventy-one largest metropolitan centers in the United States is analyzed. Beyond the immediate physical destruction, other consequences to be considered include unavailability of clean water, sanitation, and medical care followed by economic chaos, lack of law and order, and disruption of energy supplies. This study was completed before the cumulative effects of nuclear winter were published, which would make social recovery even more unlikely.

Kegley, Charles W., and Eugene R. Wittkopf, eds. *The Nuclear Reader: Strategy, Weapons, War*. New York: St. Martin's Press, 1985.
A collection of twenty-four essays expressing a broad range of viewpoints on nuclear weapons strategy, with introductory comments by the editors. Some articles of special interest are the following: "Star Wars: A Critique," by the Union of Concerned Scientists; "On Russians and Their Views of Nuclear Strategy," by Freeman Dyson; "Nuclear War and Climatic Catastrophe," by Carl Sagan; "The Irrelevance of a Nuclear Freeze," by Harold Lewis (a critic); "Toward Ballistic Missile Defense," by Keith B. Payne and Colin S. Gray (supporters of the Strategic Defense Initiative.) One article on "Strategic Build-Down" describes a proposed procedure for gradually reducing the nuclear arsenals of the two superpowers. Well-chosen essays to stimulate reader interest. A glossary of specialized vocabulary is provided.

Kennan, George F. *The Nuclear Delusion: Soviet-American Relations in the Atomic Age*. New York: Random House, 1982.
The author was in the U.S. Foreign Service for nearly thirty years, specializing in Soviet affairs. In 1953 he became a member of the Institute for Advanced Studies at Princeton. This book contains selections from his writings published between 1950 and 1982. He criticizes the exaggerated, menacing image of the Soviet military threat as depicted by the media. He suggests that anti-Soviet

hysteria revived in the 1970's because American frustration over Vietnam and domestic economic problems needed an external enemy as an outlet. With remarkable foresight, he predicts that the countries of Eastern Europe and even the non-Russian republics in the Soviet Union will reassert their independence. He argues that better understanding between the two superpowers is essential to halt the disastrous arms race. Thoughtful insights from a knowledgeable observer.

Kissinger, Henry A. *Nuclear Weapons and Foreign Policy.* New York: Harper & Brothers, 1957.

A wide-ranging, scholarly treatise on America's role in world affairs, based on discussions by a distinguished committee of thirty-five scientists and military and political leaders assembled by the Council on Foreign Relations. The major issue was how to deal with the Soviet threat. The author argues that clear communication of one's intentions toward an enemy is vital; keeping him guessing is a dangerous strategy in the nuclear age. Based on the lesson of the Korean conflict, he believes that limited use of nuclear weapons would be an effective strategy against an aggressor. He discusses the importance of diplomatic flexibility to strengthen the Western alliance and to counter Soviet propaganda. Dr. Kissinger later became National Security Adviser and Secretary of State under President Nixon.

Lapp, Ralph E. *Arms Beyond Doubt: The Tyranny of Weapons Technology.* New York: Cowles, 1970.

The title of this book comes from President Kennedy's inaugural address in 1961: "Only when our arms are beyond doubt can we be certain that they will never be employed." The author criticizes such militaristic rhetoric because, as Secretary of Defense McNamara later admitted, "We built more missiles than we needed." A dangerous escalation of the arms race in the 1960's was the placement of multiple warheads on Minuteman III and Poseidon submarine-launched missiles. The story of the antiballistic missile (ABM) debate in Congress is told, ending with a dramatic 50-to-50 tie vote in the Senate. The author presents current evidence to support President Eisenhower's warning against the undue political influence of the military-industrial complex and the scientific-technical elite.

_____. *The Weapons Culture.* New York: W. W. Norton, 1968.

The author begins with a factual description of military spending for weapons development. At that time, more than half the federal budget and 10 percent of the civilian labor force were allocated to the defense industry. He reviews the rhetoric of the 1960 presidential campaign, when Kennedy raised the issue of a missile gap and promised the voters "arms sufficient beyond doubt." He gives an authoritative overview of the thirteen-day Cuban Missile Crisis, the Chinese atomic bomb development, and the fallout shelter controversy. The author is highly critical of a proposed Nike-X antiballistic missile (ABM) system, which would benefit the aerospace and electronics contractors but would provide little protection. A thoughtful speech by Secretary of Defense McNamara opposing ABM is reprinted in the appendix.

Larus, Joel. *Nuclear Weapons Safety and the Common Defense.* Columbus: Ohio State University Press, 1967.
The author presents a thoroughly documented study of nuclear weapons accidents since 1950 (called "Broken Arrows" by the Air Force.) A very serious one occurred in 1961 at Goldsboro, North Carolina, when a 24-megaton hydrogen bomb fell in a field without exploding. Another accident happened over Palomares, Spain, where one of the four hydrogen bombs landed in the ocean. The author provides sources of information for each incident, using *The New York Times, Bulletin of Atomic Scientists,* and other reputable publications. He gives a descriptive overview of bomb design, techniques of detonation, and safety mechanisms. A particular worry at this time was the problem of proliferation. As the nuclear arsenal continued to grow, the probability of an unintentional explosion or missile launch would increase. Informative and alarming.

Laurence, William L. *The Hell Bomb.* New York: Alfred A. Knopf, 1950.
This book, written by a journalist, is notable for its virulent antagonism toward communism. First he explains how an atom bomb would be used to trigger the fusion of hydrogen nuclei, to produce an explosion that would be a thousand times more powerful than the one at Hiroshima. Then he warns his readers that if the United States does not have the H-bomb but the Soviets do, they can issue an ultimatum to "surrender or be destroyed!" The Korean War, which started in 1950, "unmasked the Kremlin's intention to enslave mankind." He argues for haste in the American H-bomb program, to aid in the battle of freedom versus tyranny.

Lehman, John F., and Seymour Weiss. *Beyond the SALT II Failure.* New York: Praeger, 1981.
John Lehman, an outspoken advocate for a large U.S. military buildup, became Secretary of the Navy under President Reagan. This book contains eleven essays by the authors that depict growing Soviet military superiority over the United States in the 1970's. The Strategic Arms Limitation Talks (SALT I, signed in 1972) allowed a massive Soviet arms advantage to develop. The authors argue that cruise missiles should be deployed in Europe, and the B-1 bomber, the MX missile (both canceled by President Carter) and additional Trident submarines are urgently needed to counter the Soviet threat. The foreword compares arms control negotiations with the Soviets to the infamous Munich pact of 1938 which gave in to Hitler's demands. The appendix contains the text of the controversial SALT II proposal.

Lens, Sidney. *The Bomb*. New York: E. P. Dutton, Lodestar Books, 1982.
Historical overview of the nuclear arms race between the United States and the
Soviet Union, written at a level suitable for high school students. A brief review
is given on military confrontations in Korea, Cuba, Berlin, Vietnam, Israel, and
elsewhere, where the use of nuclear weapons was threatened in order to accomplish political goals. The increasingly sophisticated weapons delivery systems are
described, from B-52 bombers to ballistic missiles, from nuclear submarines to
satellites in space. The concept of action and reaction is used to explain why the
weapons buildup continues: Both sides in the Cold War are reacting out of fear
that the opponents may get one step ahead.

_____. *The Day Before Doomsday: An Anatomy of the Nuclear Arms Race.*
Garden City, N.Y.: Doubleday, 1977.
A critical assessment of the continuing arms race, written at the time of President
Carter. The author traces the development of the U.S. fixation on "victory over
Communism," promoted by the self-serving interests of the military-industrial
complex. The shifting political vocabulary of counterforce, deterrence, and
détente, under six presidents since Truman, all have led to more weapons, not
less. Does the United States really need more than twenty thousand nuclear
bombs? Winston Churchill's graphic comment is quoted: "You reach a point
where more bombs only make the rubble bounce." The last chapter finds hope
for the future in a vision of global partnership, to overcome the obsolete goal of
national security based on weapons.

_____. *The Maginot Line Syndrome: America's Hopeless Foreign Policy.*
Cambridge, Mass.: Ballinger, 1982.
The Maginot Line was built by France in the 1930's at enormous cost, but it
lasted less than six weeks against the Nazi blitzkrieg. It has become a symbol
for military futility. The author argues that atomic weapons are similarly futile
in attaining the political goal of containing the spread of communism. He cites
a pertinent quotation from Albert Einstein: "The atomic bomb is to America what
the Maginot Line was to France before 1939. It gives us imaginary security, and
in this respect it is a great danger." He advocates a supranational global partnership to deal with international environmental problems and the rising expectations
of the developing countries.

Lewis, Flora. *One of Our H-bombs Is Missing . . .* New York: McGraw-Hill, 1967.
The author is a journalist who has written numerous articles for the Associated
Press, the *Washington Post,* and various news magazines. She describes the 1966
accident over Palomares, Spain, where a B-52 bomber carrying four hydrogen
bombs collided in midair with its refueling tanker. Forty thousand gallons of jet
fuel burst into flames, killing most of the crew. The dramatic story of searching
for the bombs is described with many fascinating details. Three bombs landed

on the ground, causing local radioactive contamination. Nearly five thousand barrels of contaminated soil were removed to North Carolina. The fourth bomb was found in the ocean after an eighty-day search with submarines. Seven pages of photographs and an informative map of the ocean bottom near Palomares are provided. Well-written, factual reporting.

Lieberman, Joseph I. *The Scorpion and the Tarantula: The Struggle To Control Atomic Weapons, 1945-1949*. Boston: Houghton Mifflin, 1970.
The author has made a thorough study of political efforts in the 1940's to prevent a nuclear arms race. As early as 1944, Niels Bohr met privately with Roosevelt and Churchill to push for international control of atomic energy. Pertinent events of 1945 are reviewed: opposition to bomb use by scientists within the Manhattan Project, the Potsdam Conference, and world reaction to Hiroshima. In 1946, a Soviet espionage ring was uncovered in Canada; Congress opposed sharing atomic information with other countries; and the Bikini nuclear test explosions took place. After 1947, negotiations about nuclear weapons in the United Nations became simply an exchange of propaganda. The author shows how diplomacy failed to stop the arms race because old thinking about national security had prevailed.

London, Julius, and Gilbert F. White, eds. *The Environmental Effects of Nuclear War*. Boulder, Colo.: Westview Press, 1984.
This volume is a record of the 1983 symposium on "The Effects of Thermonuclear War," sponsored by the American Association for the Advancement of Science (AAAS). It is a collection of reports by various authors on environmental and ecological consequences of nuclear war, radiation effects on humans, short-term consequences on civilian population, unresolved scientific problems in evaluating the effects, and suggestions for action by scientists. A bibliography is provided. Eight appendices contain declarations from various scientific communities stating their concerns about nuclear war. Notable among these are the Russell-Einstein Manifesto of 1955 and the Declaration on Prevention of Nuclear War. This book is a good source of graphs and tables dealing with nuclear war issues and radiation effects.

Mandelbaum, Michael. *The Nuclear Future*. Ithaca, N.Y.: Cornell University Press, 1983.
A well-written, brief introduction to the nuclear arms race for the general reader. The author provides clear explanations of the essential vocabulary needed to understand the nuclear debate: strategic versus tactical weapons, first-strike and second-strike strategy, partial test ban, cruise missiles, nonproliferation treaty, mutually assured destruction, and so on. He describes how the anti-Soviet belligerence of the Reagan administration generated widespread support for a nuclear freeze movement in the United States and in Europe. His personal

assessment is that neither the nightmare of nuclear war nor the dream of nuclear disarmament are probable. He foresees a continuation of the present nuclear stalemate between the superpowers because "the Soviet bloc is not about to dissolve!" Interesting historical perspective.

_____. *The Nuclear Revolution: International Politics Before and After Hiroshima*. Cambridge, England: Cambridge University Press, 1981.
In what ways have nuclear weapons affected international politics? The traditional ways of thinking and negotiating have seen little change. The author analyzes why the attempts to avoid an arms race failed after Hiroshima: political relations were still based on sovereign, independent countries seeking their own national security. He finds interesting historical parallels for the current world situation. For example, an active "military-industrial complex" already existed before World War I in both Great Britain and Germany, which worked to promote the need for a large fleet of warships at the time. The present NATO alliance, with its strengths and strains, is compared to the ancient Greek system of city-states. The appendix contains fifty pages of notes and references to selected source material.

Markusen, Ann, and Joel Yudken. *Dismantling the Cold War Economy*. New York: Basic Books, 1992.
The first half of this book documents the enormous military expenditures during nearly fifty years of the Cold War. The rise of the aerospace, communications and electronics industries was funded by lucrative Pentagon procurement contracts. In the middle 1980's, almost 70 percent of American scientists worked in military-related jobs. The U.S. became technologically the strongest power in the world, as demonstrated in the Gulf War against Iraq. Meanwhile, consumer products such as automobiles and home electronics lost out to foreign competition. The great difficulties of converting from military to civilian production are described through several case studies. The authors call for a new national economic strategy that will give priority to the environment, human health and community development. Informative and stimulating analysis.

Mastny, Vojtech, ed. *Disarmament and Nuclear Tests, 1964-69*. New York: Facts on File, 1970.
This book reviews newsworthy developments in disarmament negotiations and nuclear testing, organized chronologically year by year. It presents factual information on controversial topics without bias or criticism. Senator Goldwater's objections in the 1964 presidential campaign to the Nuclear Test Ban Treaty are summarized. In 1966, one learns, the United States conducted 38 underground nuclear tests, the Soviet Union had nine, France had five (all in the atmosphere), and China had three, including its first H-bomb. In 1967, a ban on nuclear weapons in Central and South America was negotiated. In 1968, placing multiple

warheads on each missile (called MIRV) escalated the arms race. Also, a B-52 bomber carrying four hydrogen bombs crashed in Greenland; the bombs were not recovered. An informative summary of current events of the time.

McBride, James Hubert. *The Test Ban Treaty: Military, Technological, and Political Implications*. Chicago: Henry Regnery, 1967.
The Nuclear Test Ban Treaty, prohibiting nuclear test explosions in the atmosphere, was signed in 1963 by U.S. and Soviet negotiators and has been ratified by more than one hundred nations since then. The author of this book is thoroughly opposed to the treaty. He presents twenty-three reasons why it is harmful to U.S. interests. Testimony against the treaty by the Joint Chiefs of Staff, by conservative political leaders, and by scientists doing weapons research is prominently quoted. Fallout from nuclear tests is described as a false alarm that has produced exaggerated fear, promoted by Communist propaganda. From the one-sided arguments in this book, the reader can appreciate why arms limitation treaties are very difficult to get approved.

McNamara, Robert S. *The Essence of Security: Reflections in Office*. New York: Harper & Row, 1968.
The author was the Secretary of Defense from 1961 to 1968. He describes the difficult task of managing a huge enterprise that consumes 10 percent of the gross national product, or about half of the federal budget. He discusses numerous international trouble spots that developed during his tenure in office: Berlin, Cuba, Taiwan, the Near East, and others. The dangerous policy of massive retaliation with nuclear missiles gradually was replaced by flexible response with conventional weapons. He argues that national security does not depend on military might alone, but also requires economic growth, political stability, and progress in racial integration. Increased foreign aid to developing nations may accomplish more than weapons in the competition with communism. Strangely, the war in Vietnam is hardly mentioned.

_____. *Blundering into Disaster: Surviving the First Century of the Nuclear Age*. New York: Pantheon Books, 1986.
The author was president of Ford Motor Company, then Secretary of Defense for seven years under presidents Kennedy and Johnson, and president of the World Bank from 1968 to 1981. The author refutes a series of nuclear myths: The Soviets have nuclear superiority; the Soviets cheat, so agreements are worthless; the United States can be technologically superior; nuclear weapons can serve political ends. These ideas are all viewed as dangerous misperceptions that fuel the arms race. One chapter describes the author's long-term vision for reducing the risk of nuclear war during the period from 1990 to 2040. A minimum deterrent of less than five hundred nuclear weapons is proposed for each side, which would be a 98 percent reduction from present stockpiles. Knowledgeable commentary and advice; highly recommended.

Moss, Norman. *Men Who Play God: The Story of the H-Bomb and How the World Came to Live with It*. New York: Harper & Row, 1968.

The first U.S. hydrogen bomb test explosion took place in November 1952, and the Soviet Union followed in August 1953, much sooner than anyone had anticipated. The author traces the military developments from atom bomb to hydrogen bomb, from bombers to intercontinental missiles, from tactical weapons to multiple warheads. The parallel development of political strategy is described, from the policy of massive retaliation under Eisenhower to deténte under Kennedy. To personalize the debate over strategy, three biographical sketches are given: Edward Teller, the physicist; Herman Kahn, the analyst from the RAND corporation; and Mrs. Pat O'Connel, a British activist, to represent the peace movement. A critical assessment of the inflationary weapons spiral.

Moulton, Harland B. *From Superiority to Parity: The United States and the Strategic Arms Race, 1961-1971*. Westport, Conn.: Greenwood Press, 1973.

A history of the Cold War from 1945 to 1971, with special attention to the 1960's. The U.S. position with regard to strategic nuclear weapons is separated into four time periods: nuclear monopoly, 1945-1953; massive retaliation, 1954-1960; flexible response, 1961-1968; and nuclear sufficiency, 1969-1971. The Vietnam War required a substantial commitment for increased production of conventional weapons and munitions. Eventually, the overwhelming U.S. nuclear superiority that had been built up under presidents Truman, Eisenhower, and Kennedy gave way to approximate parity with the Soviet Union after 1968. The author presents key arguments on both sides of some major controversies, such as the Nuclear Test Ban Treaty, the bombers versus missiles debate and civil defense preparations. Well documented, informative, and readable.

Murray, Thomas E. *Nuclear Policy for War and Peace*. Cleveland: World Publishing, 1960.

The author was one of the five appointed members of the Atomic Energy Commission from 1950 to 1957, and later became a consultant to the Congressional Joint Committee on Atomic Energy. Based on his extensive experience, he makes some strongly worded criticisms of U.S. weapons policy. He states that massive retaliation is wrong because it relies too much on superweapons, so that the military cannot respond appropriately to limited war. He reviews the Christian tradition of civilized warfare and urges that bombs larger than 1 megaton should be dismantled. On the other hand, he is firmly opposed to the moratorium on nuclear test explosions because of the continuing Soviet threat. This book provides interesting insights into the policy controversies of the time.

Nacht, Michael. *The Age of Vulnerability: Threats to the Nuclear Stalemate*. Washington, D.C.: Brookings Institution, 1985.

The author, a professor of international relations, provides an analysis of unresolved dilemmas in the U.S.-Soviet arms race. He begins with an instructive chapter on the Soviet national character, dominated by weakness in its civilian economy and political unrest in neighboring countries. The United States is characterized as having a dual personality—wanting to win the arms race while promoting world peace—thus creating inconsistent policies. The author summarizes the development of various new weapons systems, while arms control negotiations made no progress between 1972 and 1985. He discusses several factors that would unbalance the nuclear stalemate, such as a military technological breakthrough or the acquisition of nuclear weapons in the Near East. Knowledgeable and clearly written.

National Research Council. *The Effects on the Atmosphere of a Major Nuclear Exchange*. Washington, D.C.: National Academy Press, 1985.
In 1983, the National Research Council appointed a committee of recognized technical experts with diverse backgrounds to evaluate the status of knowledge about possible atmospheric changes caused by a nuclear war. This report presents their conclusions about dust and smoke clouds, surface temperature changes, and chemical pollutants resulting from fires. Social and biological consequences are not considered in this study. Each chapter contains graphs and tables of data, supported by an extensive listing of articles published in professional journals. The report emphasizes the large uncertainties in estimating burning time, soot particle size, and many other factors. Nevertheless, present evidence supports the prediction of severe atmospheric perturbations. Suitable for a reader with some technical background.

Newhouse, John. *War and Peace in the Nuclear Age*. New York: Alfred A. Knopf, 1989.
A comprehensive history of the Cold War from the 1940's to 1988, paralleling a series of thirteen PBS television programs with the same title as the book. One chapter, entitled "The End of Illusion," describes the shocked U.S. reaction to the first Soviet nuclear explosion in 1949. "Mad Momentum" recalls the high anxiety caused by a reported missile gap, based on faulty intelligence, that accelerated the arms race. "Black Saturday" presents fascinating inside information about President Kennedy and his advisers during the Cuban Missile Crisis. "The Inconstant Presidency" details the vacillations of the Carter administration. "Opportunity Lost" gives a critical assessment of President Reagan and the new Soviet leadership. Knowledgeable interpretation of events and personalities, with cartoons, photographs, and other documentation; highly recommended.

Nichols, K. D. *The Road to Trinity*. New York: William Morrow, 1987.
From 1942 to 1946, General Nichols was the military deputy working directly under General Groves in the Manhattan Project. He describes his personal role in the overall administration of the project: construction of major facilities at Oak

Ridge, Hanford, and Los Alamos; negotiations with industrial suppliers; town planning for scientists and their families; setting deadlines and handling crises as they developed. He expresses his uncompromising views on controversial issues: to use the atom bomb against Japan, to develop the hydrogen bomb, to take away Oppenheimer's security clearance. He urged the use of atomic bombs during the Korean War in 1952, to show United States resolve in deterring Communist aggression. Writing in the middle 1980's, he expresses strong support for the Strategic Defense Initiative.

Nolan, Janne E. *Guardians of the Arsenal: The Politics of Nuclear Strategy*. New York: Basic Books, 1989.
President Reagan gave a television speech in 1983 proposing a new Strategic Defense Initiative (dubbed "Star Wars" by the media). SDI presumably would provide an umbrella of surveillance satellites and computer-controlled high-tech laser guns to defend the United States from Soviet missiles. The author's analysis shows that SDI represented only 2 percent of the defense budget, but it effectively diverted public attention away from the huge military buildup at the time. A parallel situation occurred in 1970 when the antiballistic missile debate hid a dramatic increase in offensive weapons resulting from multiple warhead technology. The author cites other examples to show that military decisions by the Strategic Air Command and the Pentagon are virtually autonomous from civilian oversight by Congress. Many interesting details based on thorough research.

Nogee, Joseph L. *Soviet Policy Towards International Control of Atomic Energy*. Notre Dame: University of Indiana Press, 1961.
The author presents an analysis of Soviet-American negotiations from 1945 to 1953 regarding international control of atomic weapons through the United Nations. The Baruch Plan, offered by the United States in 1946, is described in some detail. It proposed international control and licensing of all atomic activities, including mining, with on-site inspections to deter violations. The Soviets were strongly opposed to a continued American monopoly of the atomic bomb and rejected the inspections as an infringement of national sovereignty. The U.N. debates of 1948 through 1952 are depicted as a shrewd propaganda effort by the Soviets to gain favorable world opinion while stalling for time to build their own atomic weapons.

Nye, Joseph S., Jr., Graham T. Allison, and Albert Carnesale, eds. *Fateful Visions: Avoiding Nuclear Catastrophe*. Cambridge, Mass.: Ballinger, 1988.
This book is a continuation of a preceding volume entitled *Hawks, Doves, and Owls* (W. W. Norton, 1985) by the same authors, based on ongoing discussions at Harvard University's Avoiding Nuclear War Project. Some long-range alternatives to the present policy of deterrence are described. A vast reduction

of nuclear weapons to near zero is discussed, with careful analysis of the problems it raises. Another vision, called defense dominance, is advocated by supporters of the Strategic Defense Initiative. "Lengthening the fuse" suggests removing nuclear weapons from front lines, such as Europe. Moving away from large national armies toward an increased civilian militia is another option. Analysis of superpower relations progressing from confrontation to cooperation and U.S. responses to Soviet decline as a world power anticipates some major issue of the 1990's.

Panofsky, W. K. H. *Arms Control and SALT II*. Seattle: University of Washington Press, 1979.
This pamphlet contains two public lectures given in 1979 defending the benefits of the Strategic Arms Limitation Talks (SALT II) then in progress. The author was a Stanford University physicist, speaking as a representative of the technical community to warn the general public about the urgent need for continuing arms control negotiations with the Soviet Union. He provides a general assessment of the content of SALT II, including the controversy over the Soviet Backfire bomber and U.S. forward-based cruise missiles in Europe. The author argues that the strategy of deterrence is hazardous and that the cost of world armament, currently about $500 billion annually, is a great burden. After the Soviet invasion of Afghanistan, SALT II was withdrawn from Senate consideration and was never ratified.

Paul, Ellen Frankel, Fred D. Miller, Jr., Jeffrey Paul, and John Ahrens, eds. *Nuclear Rights/Nuclear Wrongs*. Oxford, England: Basil Blackwell, 1986.
Contains eleven essays on ethical questions about nuclear deterrence, written by scholars whose academic backgrounds are either in philosophy or political science. One article on deterrent threats argues that both countervalue targeting (enemy cities) and counterforce targeting (military installations) should be replaced by a strategy of minimum deterrence, which clearly is not capable of a first strike. Another article endorses President Reagan's Strategic Defense Initiative (SDI). One author advocates dismantling nuclear weapons while relying only on conventional arms as a deterrent. Some of the articles contain intricate arguments with subtle distinctions, for which a reader must be willing to learn the specialized vocabulary of philosophical debate.

Plate, Thomas Gordon. *Understanding Doomsday: A Guide to the Arms Race for Hawks, Doves, and People*. New York: Simon & Schuster, 1971.
At the time of this book, two new additions to the arms race were being planned: the antiballistic missile (ABM) system to intercept enemy missiles, and multiple warheads for each missile. Since neither side can win a nuclear war, what drives the arms race to ever higher levels of military spending? The author's analysis shows how candidates for public office are under great political pressure to

support new weapons because otherwise they can be accused of weakness. Also, economic pressure to maintain jobs supplied by defense contracts is an important campaign issue. Senator George McGovern has written a foreword, and the appendix gives a list of the fifty biggest Department of Defense contractors.

Pogodzinsky, Michael. *Second Sunrise: Nuclear War, The Untold Story*. Thorndike, Me.: Thorndike Press, 1983.
The author's stated goal is to find a middle ground between the nuclear weapons advocates, who scare people with the "Communist menace," and peace activists, who likewise frighten people with "end of civilization" scenarios. He gives an excellent overview of the major developments in the arms race since 1945, divided into convenient five-year segments. Additions to Soviet and U.S. weapons systems, such as Trident submarines, Stealth planes, and the SS-18 missile, are evaluated. A case study of the most likely targets for Soviet missiles in New England is given. Civil defense at the personal and national level and problems of long-term survival are described. Each chapter lists sources of information with the author's assessment of their reliability.

Powaski, Ronald E. *March to Armageddon: The United States and the Nuclear Arms Race, 1939 to the Present*. New York: Oxford University Press, 1987.
A well-written overview of the nuclear arms race since its beginning. Brief quotations from leading personalities are cited to bring historical events alive for the modern reader. The Manhattan Project, the Trinity test explosion, and President Truman's decision to use the bomb against Japan are reviewed. The start of the Cold War, the hydrogen bomb controversy, and the Eisenhower-Dulles policy of massive retaliation are described. Key events are discussed in their historical setting: the "missile gap" scare of 1960, radioactive fallout and the atmospheric test ban treaty, SALT I negotiations, antiballistic missiles, Trident submarines, the Strategic Defense Initiative, and the Nuclear Freeze movement. The author's guiding theme is that arms control has been a failure while the nuclear buildup continued under seven presidents.

Pressler, Larry. *Star Wars: The Strategic Defense Initiative Debates in Congress*. Foreword by James Schlesinger. New York: Praeger, 1986.
Senator Larry Pressler (Republican from South Dakota) was Chairman of the Foreign Relations Subcommittee on Arms Control at the time of President Reagan's 1983 speech that proposed the Strategic Defense Initiative (SDI). The viewpoints of both the supporters and opponents of SDI, as expressed in Congressional hearings, are fairly presented in this book. A shield in space to protect the United States against enemy missiles has great popular appeal; however, opponents argue that SDI would continue the escalation of the nuclear arms race from its present land, sea, and bomber forces into space. After considerable debate, Congress voted funds for research only, while forbidding testing and deployment. Readers are left to draw their own conclusions from the arguments presented.

Prins, Gwyn, ed. *The Nuclear Crisis Reader*. New York: Random House, Vintage Books, 1984.

An outstanding collection of sixteen essays with fresh thoughts about needed reforms in military strategy. Among the distinguished contributors are the former commander of U.S. military operations in Europe and the Middle East, Rear Admiral Eugene Carroll; George Kennan, frequent writer on international relations and former ambassador to the U.S.S.R.; the former commander-in-chief of all U.S. forces in the Pacific, Admiral Noel Gayler; and Robert Neild, first director of the Stockholm International Peace Research Institute (SIPRI). Military and diplomatic leaders at the highest levels of responsibility are asserting that the practical usefulness of nuclear weapons is an illusion, that national security in the nuclear age truly depends on reducing, not increasing, the number of weapons. Highly recommended.

Quester, George H. *Nuclear Diplomacy: The First Twenty-Five Years*. New York: Dunellen, 1970.

Presents a chronological overview of the nuclear arms race from 1945 to 1969. The author identifies significant military developments: the B-52 long-range bomber with midair refueling; the hydrogen bomb; the Polaris missile launched from a submarine; intercontinental ballistic missiles; high-altitude reconnaissance from airplanes and later from satellites. He provides a scholarly analysis of diplomatic turning points such as the Berlin blockade and the Cuban Missile Crisis. He describes the domestic political struggle by the Navy against the Strategic Air Command for its exclusive control of nuclear weapons. He traces the test ban treaty of 1963 back to Adlai Stevenson's presidential campaign of 1956. Knowledgeable and interesting commentary from a historical perspective.

Riordan, Michael. *The Day After Midnight: The Effects of Nuclear War*. Palo Alto, Calif.: Cheshire Books, 1982.

This is an edited version of *The Effects of Nuclear War*, previously published by the Office of Technology Assessment in 1979. Editing was done to make the original report more accessible to the general reader and "to bring forth the more human elements of the original report." A fictional attack on Charlottesville, Virginia, which was an appendix in the original report, has been revised and constitutes the first chapter of this book. Much of the organization and data from the original has been unaltered, but some sections dealing with detailed attack scenarios and civil defense have been simplified or omitted altogether. Like the original, this is a sobering portrayal of how a nuclear war might be fought.

Roberts, Chalmers M. *The Nuclear Years: The Arms Race and Arms Control*. New York: Praeger, 1970.

A short history of the arms race and efforts to control it, from 1946 to 1970. The author saw the ruins of Hiroshima a few weeks after the bombing ("rubble,

rubble is everywhere") and later became a reporter for the *Washington Post*. He reviews Soviet-American negotiations and confrontations, with quotations and cartoons that capture the key issues of the time. In 1970, a new technological development made it possible to put multiple warheads on each rocket. Diplomatic efforts to prevent deployment of such a weapons system are described. The appendix contains reprints of several documents, including the Baruch Plan of 1946 and the Non-proliferation Treaty of 1968.

Russett, Bruce. *Prisoners of Insecurity: Nuclear Deterrence, the Arms Race, and Arms Control*. San Francisco: W. H. Freeman, 1983.
A well-written, brief introduction to key issues in the nuclear arms race, addressed to "conscientious citizens" who do not want to leave strategy decisions to technical experts. The author is an academic social scientist with extensive experience as a governmental advisor. One chapter discusses why the arms race continues: action-reaction between the superpowers, technological innovations, domestic politics, profits for the defense industry, and competition for Third World resources. Clear explanations are given for important concepts such as proliferation, extended deterrence, command and control problems, limited war and escalation, first-strike versus second-strike capability, and counterforce targeting. Eighteen arms control agreements from 1959 to 1979 are summarized. Some unilateral steps toward weapons limitations, not requiring a negotiated treaty, are suggested.

Russett, Bruce, and Fred Chernoff, eds. *Arms Control and the Arms Race: Readings from Scientific American*. New York: W. H. Freeman, 1985.
Contains sixteen articles on the arms race reprinted from the monthly magazine *Scientific American*, with introductory commentary by the editors. Among the articles, "The Debate over the Hydrogen Bomb" gives a retrospective view by Herbert York. "Intermediate Range Nuclear Weapons" discusses the difficult category of weapons in between tactical and strategic range. "Enhanced Radiation Weapons" describes the so-called neutron bomb. "Verification of a Comprehensive Nuclear Test Ban" explains advances in seismology to improve detection of underground nuclear explosions without requiring on-site inspection. Other articles provide critical assessments of proliferation, antisubmarine warfare, space-based ballistic missiles, and preemptive nuclear attack. Authoritative and readable.

Sagan, Carl, and Richard Turco. *A Path Where No Man Thought*. New York: Random House, 1990.
An authoritative presentation about nuclear winter written by two of its most influential proponents, intended for a general audience with no special scientific expertise. The authors address pertinent topics such as climate change, radioactive fallout, six scenarios of nuclear warfare, impact on noncombatant

nations, critique of the present strategy of deterrence, and a proposal for minimum sufficient deterrence. Interspersed in the text are charts and short essays on special topics such as major human catastrophes of the past, the climatic effect of volcanic eruptions, and the Soviet fallout shelter system. The appendix contains more than one hundred pages of notes and references, giving worldwide reactions (both confirmations and objections) to the nuclear winter concept since its origination in 1982. Highly recommended; well written.

Scheer, Robert, with Narda Zacchino and Constance Matthiessen. *With Enough Shovels: Reagan, Bush, and Nuclear War*. New York: Random House, 1982.
This book contains transcripts of tape-recorded interviews conducted by the author between 1979 and 1982 with Paul Warnke, Eugene Rostow, Robert McNamara, Cyrus Vance, Ronald Reagan, George Bush, Herbert York, and Hans Bethe. Two contrasting views of the nuclear arms race are explored. On one side is the Reagan military buildup, based on the fear of potential Soviet world domination. On the other side is the nuclear freeze movement and the conviction that a nuclear war would be mutual suicide. The book title is a quotation from Reagan's Deputy Undersecretary of Defense, Thomas K. Jones, telling how a nuclear war could be survived: If there are " . . . enough shovels to go around," people could dig individual fallout shelters. Skillful interviews and commentary; highly recommended.

Schelling, Thomas C. *The Strategy of Conflict*. Cambridge, Mass.: Harvard University Press, 1963.
The author was an economist at Harvard University and with the RAND Corporation. This influential book deals with the general topic of conflicts between adversaries. Maneuvering in a political crisis, negotiating with terrorists or hostage takers, collective bargaining between labor and management, or competitive games with winners and losers all have some similar features. A decisive showdown may be so costly for both sides in a conflict that negotiations for limited objectives would be preferable. The author is particularly concerned with bargaining situations in which the antagonists are mutually interdependent. A general theory of gamesmanship is developed to provide insight for the U.S.-Soviet nuclear standoff. Deliberate deception, misperception of enemy intentions, and reciprocal fears of surprise attack are analyzed. Provocative ideas, skillfully presented.

Schloming, Gordon C. *American Foreign Policy and the Nuclear Dilemma*. Englewood Cliffs, N.J.: Prentice-Hall, 1987.
This paperback book would be an excellent text for a college course on the nuclear arms race. The author presents a knowledgeable overview of arms control negotiations, Star Wars strategy, and other contemporary issues. Each chapter has open-ended questions for discussion, an extensive list of references for

assigned student papers, and a unique counterpoint section to assert opposing points of view. The reader is encouraged to question various assumptions of the Cold War. Can deterrence be maintained indefinitely? What does "national security" mean beyond its military aspect? What role have American political campaigns played in public perception of the Soviet threat? This book provides a bridge between the academic ivory tower and the practical world of politics. Highly recommended.

Scoville, Herbert. *MX: Prescription for Disaster*. Cambridge, Mass.: MIT Press, 1981.
The author has been an observer and critic of the nuclear arms race for some thirty years. His credentials include working for the Atomic Energy Commission, the Department of Defense, and the Arms Control and Disarmament Agency. He provides a strongly negative assessment of the proposed MX missile system. The MX was designed to replace Minuteman missiles, because the Minuteman silos were becoming vulnerable to Soviet weapons of increased accuracy. The MX would be mobile, not in silos, to keep the Soviets guessing about their location. The author describes the immense construction project of roads and rails that would have to be built in Utah and Nevada. He argues that nuclear submarines already provide an invulnerable deterrent, so a $100 billion MX system is unnecessary and would create a threatening escalation of the arms race.

_____. *Toward a Strategic Arms Limitation Agreement*. New York: Carnegie Endowment for International Peace, 1970.
This fifty-page pamphlet was written at the time when the United States and the Soviet Union had started Strategic Arms Limitation Talks (known by the acronym SALT). The author reviews the existing triad of strategic weapons, consisting of long-range bombers, nuclear submarines and intercontinental ballistic missiles in hardened silos. He shows that the two superpowers were not equal in each category, but, nevertheless, an overall parity existed. The debate in 1970 focused on two impending new developments: antiballistic missiles (ABM), and multiple warheads for each missile. The author argues that a general freeze agreement on strategic arms and a halt to new weapons systems were in the best interests of both sides. SALT I, signed in 1972, did stop ABM, but multiple warhead technology was deployed.

Scribner, Richard A., Theodore J. Ralston, and William D. Metz. *The Verification Challenge: Problems and Promise of Strategic Nuclear Arms Control Verification*. Basel, Switzerland: Birkhauser, 1985.
The American Association for the Advancement of Science, in cooperation with Stanford University, provided support and guidance for this informative publication. Negotiations with the Soviets have produced a number of arms control agreements, such as the 150-kiloton limit on underground nuclear tests, the

Strategic Arms Limitation Treaty (SALT I), and others. The authors have prepared a thorough summary of the modern technology that is used to assure compliance with the terms of an agreement. They describe various high-tech surveillance methods such as satellite photography, seismic detectors, radar, and communication monitors that are available to detect possible cheating. The appendix contains the text of several treaties, an extensive glossary of missile vocabulary, and a bibliography of source material. Informative and readable.

Segal, Gerald, Edwina Moreton, Lawrence Freedman, and John Baylis. *Nuclear War and Nuclear Peace*. New York: St. Martin's Press, 1983.
The authors present a knowledgeable analysis of the nuclear arms race as viewed from Great Britain. They emphasize that deterrence based on mutually assured destruction is working. The nuclear freeze movement in the United States and the Campaign for Nuclear Disarmament in England are criticized for giving unrealistic answers to a complex problem. They argue that reduction of nuclear weapons, rather than their elimination, is a more reasonable goal. Since conflicts in international relations will continue, a minimum level of deterrence will always be needed. Writing in 1983, they described the East-West division of Europe as "stabilized" and predicted that the Soviet Union would be a fixture in Europe for the rest of this century. They did not anticipate the rapid disintegration of Communism in eastern Europe in the late 1980's.

Sherwin, Martin J. *A World Destroyed: The Atomic Bomb and the Grand Alliance*. New York: Random House, 1973. Reprint. New York: Vintage Books, 1977.
A short book based on extensive historical scholarship, describing the deterioration of the wartime Soviet-U.S. alliance and the start of the Cold War. The author has consulted original sources of information at the Library of Congress, the National Archives, the Atomic Energy Commission, the Truman Library, and elsewhere. He gives direct quotations from the diaries and published writings of various political leaders. He conducted interviews with ten of the leading Manhattan Project scientists. He analyzes the Potsdam Conference of 1945, where Truman received word of the first successful bomb test explosion. The immediate continuation from World War II into the Cold War is attributed to the policy of using the threat of atomic weapons to win foreign policy concessions from the Soviets.

Smith, Gerard. *Doubletalk: The Story of the First Strategic Arms Limitation Talks*. Garden City, N.Y.: Doubleday, 1980.
The first Strategic Arms Limitation Talks (SALT I) were a series of scheduled meetings between Soviet and U.S. negotiators, held periodically during the years 1969 to 1972 in Helsinki and Vienna. Gerard Smith, appointed Chief U.S. Delegate to SALT I by President Nixon, gives a detailed inside account of the negotiations. The greatest success of SALT I was the agreement to halt the

deployment of an antiballistic missile (ABM) system. The greatest failure was the lack of progress in placing any limitations on the arms race in strategic weapons—hence the "doubletalk" in the book title. No control over multiple-warhead technology or on submarine-launched missiles was accomplished. The author expresses frequent frustration with Henry Kissinger for using personal diplomatic contacts that bypassed the SALT negotiators. Informative and readable.

Strauss, Lewis L. *Men and Decisions*. Garden City, N.Y.: Doubleday, 1962.
Lewis Strauss (1896-1974) became a member of the first Atomic Energy Commission in 1947 and was appointed its chairman in 1953. In this autobiography, Strauss describes his modest family background in Virginia and his first public service under Herbert Hoover. He became a successful financier and an officer in the Naval Reserve. He first heard about the possibility of an atomic bomb from Leo Szilard in 1937. Several chapters deal at length with controversial decisions: the use of the atomic bomb against Japan; whether to develop the hydrogen bomb or not; the Oppenheimer case; and, finally, the nuclear test ban. Strauss promoted the idea of peaceful uses for atomic energy. One historic photograph shows him with Dag Hammerskjold, opening the Geneva Conference in 1958.

Sylves, Richard T. *The Nuclear Oracles: A Political History of the General Advisory Committee of the Atomic Energy Commission, 1947-1977*. Ames: Iowa State University Press, 1987.
The General Advisory Committee (GAC) was a panel of nine distinguished scientists appointed by the president to provide advice from the science communi-ty to the Atomic Energy Commission. The author presents the major issues faced by the GAC during a span of thirty years, based on declassified records from more than 140 meetings. He provides brief biographies of the fifty-five individuals who served on the GAC and describes how the wartime facilities at Los Alamos, Oak Ridge, and elsewhere evolved into national laboratories. Of special interest is a chapter dealing with the hydrogen bomb controversy in the fall of 1949. Informative and authoritative, with an extensive bibliography.

Szulc, Tad. *The Bombs of Palomares*. New York: Viking Press, 1967.
On January 17, 1966, a B-52 bomber carrying four hydrogen bombs had a midair collision during a refueling operation over Spain. Tad Szulc, bureau chief for The New York Times in Madrid, tells the dramatic story of the accident and the ensuing search to recover the bombs. Three of the bombs were found within twenty-four hours by helicopter and ground search near the town of Palomares. The fourth bomb apparently had landed offshore in the Mediterranean Sea. After eighty days of strenuous effort, it was found at a depth of about 2,500 feet by the two-man submersible ship *Alvin*. The author describes how military secrecy

and concern about international publicity complicated his work to get the full story.

Talbott, Strobe. *Deadly Gambits: The Reagan Administration and the Stalemate in Nuclear Arms Control.* New York: Alfred A. Knopf, 1984.
The author is a senior staff member and writer for *Time* magazine. In 1970 he was the translator and editor of Nikita Khrushchev's memoirs. In this book, he gives a revealing portrait of the political conflicts within the Reagan administration that lead to a breakdown of arms control negotiations in 1983. Bureaucratic battles between the National Security Council, the State Department, and the Pentagon are described in detail. The cast of political figures includes Eugene Rostow, Arms Control and Disarmament Agency; Alexander Haig, Secretary of State; Richard Perle, Department of Defense; Paul Nitze, U.S. negotiator at Geneva. President Reagan's participation at cabinet meetings on national security matters shows remarkably little comprehension of issues. A fascinating and disturbing inside view of how arms negotiations were thwarted by domestic politics.

Tirman, John, ed. *The Fallacy of Star Wars.* New York: Random House, 1984.
A negative assessment of the Strategic Defense Initiative (SDI), prepared by the Union of Concerned Scientists, a well-respected public interest group. The book is in three parts: the evolution of space weapons, the technology of ballistic missile defense, and antisatellite warfare. Serious objections to SDI are voiced: it would extend the arms race into space; feasibility depends on breakthroughs in laser technology that show little promise of success; deployment of a complete system would be extremely expensive, and surveillance satellites would be vulnerable; Soviet countermeasures could defeat the defense; computer capability can be overwhelmed by a large number of simultaneous targets. SDI is criticized as a technological illusion that would be a setback for genuine arms negotiations between the superpowers.

Tsipis, Kosta, Anne C. Cahn, and Bernard T. Feld, eds. *The Future of the Sea-Based Deterrent.* Cambridge, Mass.: MIT Press, 1973.
A collection of ten essays based on a symposium held in 1972 to investigate whether improved underwater detection methods may make U.S. nuclear submarines vulnerable to a Soviet first strike. Mutual deterrence is based on the idea of assured retaliation. Therefore, any weakness in the capability to retaliate endangers the stability of the East/West nuclear stalemate. One essay describes the technology of underwater acoustics. Another essay compares existing Polaris submarines to the proposed Trident with its larger size, less noise, and 6,000-mile missile range. Political and technical issues that threaten to escalate the arms race further are analyzed. The symposium participants conclude that a decisive, preemptive strike against the opponent's fleet of nuclear submarines is not a realistic possibility.

Wade, Nicholas. *A World Beyond Healing: The Prologue and Aftermath of Nuclear War*. New York: W. W. Norton, 1987.

The author presents a knowledgeable overview of the nuclear stalemate, emphasizing how fragile the policy of deterrence has become. He summarizes the large arsenal of nuclear warheads and considers specific ways in which a war might start, such as a false alert or an escalating political crisis. He reviews the devastation at Hiroshima and the importance of outside help for survivors. The nuclear winter scenario, based on computer simulation of a 10,000-megaton nuclear war, considers the effect of massive fire storms added to local blast, fire, and fallout damage. Extrapolating historical data from huge volcanic eruptions in Indonesia in 1883 and 1816, the model predicts changes in worldwide weather patterns leading to a severe food production crisis. Clear explanations without emotional exaggeration; highly recommended.

Weston, Burns H., ed. *Toward Nuclear Disarmament and Global Security: A Search for Alternatives*. Boulder, Colo.: Westview Press, 1984.

A collection of forty-five essays, mostly from books and magazine articles published after 1980, suitable for a college class or adult discussion group. Some of the notable authors include George F. Kennan, Robert S. McNamara, Randall Forsberg, Robert J. Lifton, and Jonathan Schell. Other sections are public statements by groups such as the Catholic bishops, a committee of lawyers, and a United Nations team of international representatives. The material is arranged into twelve chapters, each one followed by discussion questions and a bibliography. The wide variety of expressed viewpoints encourage the reader to reexamine his or her perception of the Soviet threat, the meaning of deterrence, and the social costs of the continuing arms race.

Wigner, Eugene P., ed. *Survival and the Bomb: Methods of Civil Defense*. Bloomington: Indiana University Press, 1969.

The editor of this book was a 1963 Nobel laureate in physics who had major responsibility for design of the plutonium production reactors at Hanford during the Manhattan Project. He became an outspoken advocate for building an antiballistic missile system and fallout shelters to protect against the Soviet threat. Various authors have contributed pertinent essays to this collection: design of fallout shelters, both in homes and in subway tunnels; civil defense efforts outside the United States; psychological response to living underground and the siege of Budapest during World War II; ecological and economic recovery after nuclear war. The message of this book is that active preparations for survival should be pursued vigorously. Well-written essays, but objections to civil defense are not included here.

Willrich, Mason, and Theodore B. Taylor. *Nuclear Theft: Risks and Safeguards*. Cambridge, Mass.: Ballinger, 1974.

The authors are a professor of law and a physicist who have a long-standing interest in issues involving technology and society, and have participated in international arms control negotiations. This study, financed by the Ford Foundation, explores the potential connection between civilian nuclear power and nuclear weapons proliferation. Two major concerns are the possible theft of nuclear material by a terrorist group or secret diversion of reactor fuel by a Third World government. Present safeguards include limiting personnel access to nuclear facilities, guarding fuel shipments, and requiring strict accounting with on-site inspections. The authors analyze the technical requirements to construct a bomb once some fuel has been obtained. The large difference in fuel enrichment required for reactors and bombs respectively is also discussed.

Wohlstetter, Albert, Thomas A. Brown, Gregory Jones, David C. McGarvey, Henry Rowen, Vince Taylor, and Roberta Wohlstetter. *Swords from Plowshares: The Military Potential of Civilian Nuclear Energy.* Foreword by Fred Charles Iklé. Chicago: University of Chicago Press, 1979.

When applied to nuclear technology, the "swords" are bombs and the "plowshares" are nuclear power plants to produce electricity. This book is based on a project sponsored by the U.S. Arms Control and Disarmament Agency (ACDA) in 1975, to clarify the connection between peaceful and military uses of uranium fission. The authors explain how power reactors generate plutonium as a by-product, which could be extracted and used for weapons. The economics of reprocessing and the problems of policing this technology worldwide are discussed. One chapter, entitled "Life in a Nuclear Crowd," dramatizes the consequences of weapons proliferation. A sixty-page appendix summarizes world nuclear facilities. The foreword provides an excellent overview. Authoritative and readable.

York, Herbert. *Race to Oblivion: A Participant's View of the Arms Race.* New York: Simon & Schuster, 1970.

Herbert York has seen the arms race from the inside, as head of the Livermore weapons laboratory from 1952 to 1957, as Director of Defense Research and Engineering under President Eisenhower, and as frequent consultant for government agencies. He has become convinced of the futility of the arms race. He reviews the buildup of new weapons systems and missiles, whose funding frequently is justified by false rumors and exaggerations of the Soviet military threat. Rivalry between the Army, Navy, and Air Force, as well as partisan politics, continues to drive the arms race. The author reminds readers that Eisenhower spoke out not only against the military-industrial complex, but also warned against the "scientific-technical elite" who try to sell their latest technological gadgets for self-serving reasons.

Zuckerman, Solly. *Nuclear Illusion and Reality*. New York: Viking Press, 1982.
Reprint. New York: Vintage Books, 1983.

The author was chief scientific adviser to the Ministry of Defense and the British Government from 1960 to 1971. In this short book, he argues that the policy of building a larger arsenal of nuclear weapons in order to produce greater military security is an illusion. He describes a scenario of destruction that would result if just a single 1-megaton bomb were to explode over Detroit. He promotes, in contrast to the policy of massive retaliation, the idea of minimum deterrence. In a strongly worded conclusion, he blames the continuing arms race primarily on the military-industrial complex and the government weapons laboratories.

Chapter 8
THE PEACE MOVEMENT

Adams, Ruth, and Susan Cullen, eds. *The Final Epidemic: Physicians and Scientists on Nuclear War*. Chicago: Educational Foundation for Nuclear Science, 1981.
Twenty-two distinguished contributors, including Helen Caldicott, George B. Kistiakowsky, and John Kenneth Galbraith, originally presented these talks to symposia that were organized by the group Physicians for Social Responsibility. Some issues addressed in the essays are the anticipated medical problems after a nuclear attack, the effects of radiation at various dose levels, and the heavy financial burden of a nuclear arms race. A postattack scenario portrays the chaos when medical resources are overwhelmed: hospitals destroyed, electricity and water unavailable, medical supplies and personnel inadequate, deteriorating sanitation as a result of decomposing corpses. The need for citizen participation in a peace movement is urgently advocated to prevent a final epidemic.

Aizenstat, A. J. *Survival for All: The Alternative to Nuclear War with a Practical Plan for Total Denuclearization*. New York: Billner and Rouse, 1985.
The author reviews the colossal destructiveness of nuclear weapons that now make them unsuitable for military purposes. The concept of deterrence is used by military strategists to justify a continuing arms race, but the Achilles heel of deterrence is uncertainty about effective command and control in a crisis. Arms control negotiations with the Soviets are criticized as mere "running in place." The author argues against the fatalistic view that nothing can be done to stop the nuclear menace. He proposes a denuclearization plan that would eliminate present nuclear stockpiles and prevent future manufacture. A nuclear control board jointly managed by the superpowers would have powers of inspection and verification. Denuclearization involves risks, but the risk of letting the arms race continue is even greater. Well-informed and hopeful.

Arnow, Saul, Frank R. Ervin, and Victor W. Sidel, eds. *The Fallen Sky: Medical Consequences of Thermonuclear War*. New York: Hill & Wang, 1963.
The three editors who prepared this short paperback book are medical doctors who are members of a group called Physicians for Social Responsibility. In the early 1960's, the federal government was promoting a program of civil defense, including fallout shelters. Articles in this booklet describe the large number of medical casualties that would result from a hypothesized 1,446-megaton nuclear attack on the United States. Skin burns, blindness, infectious disease, and lack of medical supplies would overwhelm the surviving health facilities. One essay discusses the psychological effects of fallout shelters. An article by Gerard Piel, "The Illusion of Civil Defense," is reprinted from *Scientific American*. The conclusion of the editors is that prevention of a nuclear catastrophe is the only effective therapy.

Barash, David P., and Judith Eve Lipton. *The Caveman and the Bomb: Human Nature, Evolution, and Nuclear War*. New York: McGraw-Hill, 1985.
The authors are a social biologist and psychiatrist, applying their professional tools of analysis to the predicament of nuclear weapons. Part 1 presents their thesis that outmoded patterns of behavior, the so-called Neanderthal mentality, still dominate modern thinking. The roots of militant nationalism are traced back to tribal instincts, that developed because group survival depended on defeating an enemy. A propaganda of fear, with exaggerated images of outside threats, leads to constant preparation for war. Part 2 describes the antithesis, the idea that shared relatedness with other people can be discovered by individuals and nations. Thoughts, feelings, and beliefs are explored, with well-chosen quotations from many sources. Part 3 expresses a hopeful synthesis that old ways of thinking can be overcome to create the conditions for human survival. Many interesting insights.

_____. *Stop Nuclear War! A Handbook*. New York: Grove Press, 1982.
The authors are a psychologist and a medical doctor who have worked in the peace movement through the organization Physicians for Social Responsibility. They give a brief history of nuclear weapons and the political doctrine of deterrence. They describe the economic and psychological cost of the continuing weapons buildup. They urge people to become personally involved in the peace movement, to consider committing 10 percent of their time, money, and effort to reverse the arms race. The appendix gives names and addresses of peace organizations, listed according to professions: musicians, lawyers, physicians, scientists, educators, nurses, and so forth.

Bennett, John C., ed. *Nuclear Weapons and the Conflict of Conscience*. New York: Charles Scribner's Sons, 1962.
A small collection of essays that raised ethical questions about the escalating arms race in the 1960's. The authors are two political scientists, three Christian theologians, one physicist, and one psychologist (Eric Fromm, author of several popular books). All the authors share the opinion that military strategy issues overly dominated the thinking at the time. One essay criticizes the concept of calculating "acceptable damage" from a nuclear war because the quality of life of survivors is not being considered. Another essay presents the case for unilateral disarmament. Many people may think that disarmament is naïve, but the author argues that the policy of building a huge arsenal and thinking it will never be used is also naïve. Thoughtful and stimulating readings.

Brembeck, Howard S. *Making Nuclear War Impossible*. Goshen, Ind.: Alternative World Foundation, 1984.
The author is an inventor and businessman with a company that manufactures agricultural equipment. In this brief book, he presents his alternative to the

nuclear arms race. He proposes a trade embargo against any nations that supply offensive weapons to other nations. The embargo would apply to all manufactured goods and technology, but would not limit trade in raw materials such as oil or food products. The threat of an economic world boycott, he believes, would bring an end to the arms race. Unfortunately, the author makes no mention that the United States is a major supplier of weapons on the world market. It is not clear how sanctions would be applied while the United States is one of the culprits in the armament industry.

Bigelow, Albert. *The Voyage of the* Golden Rule: *An Experiment With Truth.* Garden City, N.Y.: Doubleday, 1959.
Four men in a thirty-foot sailing ship set out from San Francisco in March of 1958, to protest the continuing nuclear test explosions in the South Pacific. Their goal was to sail to the Marshall Islands, to the same restricted test site where Japanese fishermen on the *Lucky Dragon* had been contaminated with radioactive fallout in 1954. The author, the ship's captain, traces the roots of nonviolent protest back to Martin Luther King, Jr., Gandhi, and William Penn of the Religious Society of Friends. He tells the story of the crew's arrest, trial, and jail sentence in Honolulu. Their act of civil disobedience aroused public opinion, as shown by editorials in major U.S. newspapers and many personal letters of support.

Caldicott, Helen. *Missile Envy: The Arms Race and Nuclear War.* New York: Bantam Books, 1984. Rev. ed., 1986.
The author was a pediatrician who gave up her medical career to become a spokesperson against nuclear weapons. The arms race is described as a life-threatening illness. The "Terminal Event" is nuclear war, with worldwide consequences of radioactive fallout and nuclear winter. The "Physical Examination" summarizes the present arsenal of land, sea, and air-launched missiles. "Germs of Conflict" deals with U.S. and Soviet intervention in Third World countries such as Nicaragua, Iran, and others. "Psychopathology" presents the concept of missile envy as a symbol of male dominance. The "Prognosis" concludes that the outlook for survival is poor when weapons are proliferating. Finally, the suggested "Therapy" is the preventive medicine of nuclear disarmament.

_____. *Nuclear Madness: What You Can Do!* New York: Bantam Books, 1978.
Caldicott tells about her successful experience during the early 1970's to halt French bomb tests in the South Pacific by mobilizing large protest rallies in Australia. Her urgent message to Americans is that survival depends on "abolishing nuclear weapons permanently and halting the nuclear power industry." Nuclear weapons and nuclear reactors are portrayed as equal evils. The book is

an emotional plea for people to enlist in a crusade against all aspects of radiation. Dramatic exaggeration is used to generate fear and opposition to the menace.

Cornell University Peace Studies Program. *Crisis Stability and Nuclear War*. Ithaca, N.Y.: Cornell University, 1987.

This one-hundred-page pamphlet contains a series of recommendations for reducing the risk of nuclear war, representing a consensus from seventeen distinguished members of the Cornell Peace Studies program. Among the contributors are Kurt Gottfried, project director; Hans Bethe, physicist; Richard L. Garwin, consultant on national security affairs; Henry W. Kendall, chairman of the Union of Concerned Scientists; and Hillman Dickinson, former Director of Command, Control and Communications Systems for the Joint Chiefs of Staff. The major focus of this study was not the size of the nuclear arsenal, but rather the danger that the chain of command could break down in a political crisis. If military command centers lose communication, the risk of escalation becomes acute. Practical suggestions for preserving stability during a crisis are provided.

Cousins, Norman. *In Place of Folly*. New York: Harper & Brothers, 1961.

Norman Cousins was a well-known author, lecturer and long-time editor of the magazine *Saturday Review*. He expresses his deep concern for the survival of humankind when threatened by nuclear, biological, and chemical weapons. He characterizes the military and political leadership not as evil, but as people who are caught up in a system in which national security requires them to build up military superiority. The result is "competitive insecurity" for both sides in the arms race. He points to violence in sports and entertainment as a problem that should be recognized. His version for a better future includes a greatly expanded role for the United Nations and a personal commitment by all to join in the search for world security.

Cox, Donald W. *The Perils of Peace: Conversion to What?* Philadelphia and New York: Chilton Books, 1965.

One of the obstacles to halting the arms race is the economic impact that a cutback in defense spending would have on communities that depend on military contracts for their livelihood. The author describes what happened in 1964 when Secretary of Defense McNamara proposed that the Brooklyn Navy Yard should be closed. The governor, mayor, members of Congress, and labor union leaders all pledged their vigorous opposition to the closing. The author suggests that we need a "Pentagon for Peace" to rechannel defense expenditures toward civilian needs in health care, education, and so forth. A speech by Senator George McGovern on economic conversion and an appeal by Dr. Benjamin Spock are reprinted.

Cox, John. *Overkill: Weapons of the Nuclear Age*. New York: Thomas Y. Crowell, 1977.

The author is an engineer in England and former chairman of the Campaign for Nuclear Disarmament. He describes the proliferation of nuclear weapons in two directions: horizontally, as more countries become nuclear powers; and vertically, as the United States and the Soviet Union develop weapons that are bigger, have longer range and greater accuracy, and carry multiple warheads. He quotes excerpts from *Hiroshima Diary, Voyage of the* Lucky Dragon, and the 1955 *Manifesto for Nuclear Disarmament*. He criticizes the fatalistic attitude that many people have toward the arms race, thinking that, like an earthquake, there is nothing that can be done about it. An informative, short book with a good selection of photographs and a glossary.

Day, Samuel H., ed. *Nuclear Heartland: A Guide to the 1000 Missile Silos of the United States*. Photos by John Hooten. Madison, Wis.: Progressive Foundation, 1988.

The United States has more than one thousand underground silos containing Minuteman missiles aimed at targets in the Soviet Union. The missiles are concentrated at six regional sites: two in North Dakota; one in South Dakota near the Black Hills; one in Montana; one near Cheyenne, Wyoming; and one near Kansas City, Missouri. The peace organization Nukewatch undertook a two-year project in 1985 to map the location of each underground silo, as an attempt to arouse public awareness and perhaps protests against nuclear weapons. Each individual silo is shown as a red dot on a map, with road directions to nearby towns. Peaceful rallies at missile site fence lines, acts of deliberate trespassing, and conversations with Air Force security guards are described. Many photographs.

Dellums, Ronald V., with R. H. (Max) Miller, H. Lee Halterman, and Patrick O'Heffernam, eds. *Defense Sense: The Search for a Rational Military Policy*. Cambridge, Mass.: Ballinger, 1983.

Ronald Dellums, a member of Congress from California, sponsored six days of hearings in 1982 before the Armed Services Committee to examine the Reagan administration's military budget. Dellums was strongly opposed to the proposed expansion in weapons production at the expense of domestic welfare. This book contains twenty-five essays by articulate, distinguished witnesses who testified at the hearings, with follow-up questions by members of the committee. Among the selections are the following: Paul Warnke, "The Need for Arms Control"; former Senator J. William Fulbright, "National Security and the Reagan Arms Buildup"; Seymour Melman, "Military Spending and Domestic Bankruptcy"; Episcopal Bishop John T. Walker, "The Immorality of the Arms Race." The concluding essay by Dellums gives his vision of a constructive alternative to the continuing arms race. Highly recommended.

Drinan, Robert F. *Beyond the Nuclear Freeze*. New York: Seabury Press, 1983.
The author is a Catholic priest and professor of law who served five terms in the
U.S. House of Representatives. He analyzes the deep-rooted Cold War mentality
that has frustrated arms control negotiations with the Soviets over the past forty
years. The Reagan administration's military buildup and anti-Soviet rhetoric have
intensified fears about nuclear war. The nuclear freeze rally in New York in June
of 1982 drew 700,000 people, the largest demonstration in U.S. history. The
author describes growing opposition to the arms race by concerned groups of
physicians, lawyers, and the religious community. He urges continued public
pressure to bring about political changes as a necessary precondition for fruitful
negotiations on arms control.

Filcher, Dietrich. *Preventing War in the Nuclear Age*. Totowa, N.J.: Rowman &
Allanheld, 1984.
The author reminds readers of the extremely dangerous situation in which they
live, where nuclear war could start by accident, by escalation of local conflicts,
or by preemptive strike. He believes there are some widespread misconceptions
about peace and security that block the negotiation process. One chapter lists
various steps that the United States, or any nation, could take unilaterally to
reduce the danger of war, by shifting from offensive to nonthreatening, defensive
weapons. Another chapter discusses new ideas in the study of conflict resolution,
based on the recent book *Getting to Yes: Negotiating Agreement Without Giving
In*, by R. Fisher and W. Ury. A hopeful contribution to peace literature.

Ford, Daniel, Henry Kendall, and Steven Nadis. *Beyond the Freeze: The Road to
Nuclear Sanity*. Boston: Beacon Press, 1982.
This informative paperback book reviews the status of the nuclear arms race
during President Reagan's first term in office. Reagan had initiated the largest
peacetime U.S. military buildup in history, including the new MX missile system,
the B-1 bomber, the six-hundred-ship Navy, and laser weapons in space. The
three authors are members of the Union of Concerned Scientists (UCS), a
Massachusetts group known for its careful analysis of issues involving technology
and society. They describe the background of the nuclear freeze movement, with
its simple plan to halt the building and testing of nuclear bombs and missile
systems. Each chapter is introduced with a short quotation from a notable
personality, such as Albert Einstein, Richard Nixon, or Admiral Rickover.

Gerson, Joseph, ed. *The Deadly Connection: Nuclear War and U.S. Intervention*.
Philadelphia: American Friends Service Committee, New Society Publishers,
1986.
A collection of articles and speeches by twenty-three authors condemning the
continuing nuclear arms race. Randall Forsberg, nuclear freeze organizer, tells
how she gradually came to realize that the purpose of the excessive U.S. nuclear

arsenal was for political intimidation of Third World countries. Daniel Ellsberg, of Pentagon Papers fame, reviews twelve occasions when the United States threatened nuclear intervention to accomplish foreign policy objectives. Other writers discuss the nuclear-political connection in the Middle East, Korea, Central America, and the Philippines. The editor, Joseph Gerson, calls on the peace movement to unify its efforts by opposing both the arms buildup and foreign interventionism.

Hutchins, Robert M. *The Atomic Bomb and Education*. London: National Peace Council, 1947.
The author was the chancellor of the University of Chicago and a well-known spokesman for the importance of liberal education. This pamphlet is the text of a radio broadcast that he gave on the BBC. He describes his vision of world government as the only hope for avoiding atomic destruction. With remarkable foresight, he anticipated the important role of universities to offer adult continuing education to prepare people for the drastic changes in society that are needed. He expresses rather naïve optimism about a coming era of leisure and material abundance, based on peaceful atomic energy. He asserts the necessity of religious faith to build a durable world community in the atomic age.

Katz, Milton S. *Ban The Bomb: A History of SANE, the Committee for a Sane Nuclear Policy, 1957-1985*. New York; Westport, Conn.: Greenwood Press, 1986.
The author presents a chronological study of SANE's contributions to the peace movement in the United States. SANE published newspaper advertisements, staged public rallies, promoted petitions, and raised money for political campaigns. They deliberately rejected civil disobedience and more radical activism in order to retain broad public support. The early leadership roles of Norman Cousins and Linus Pauling are described. Several of SANE's full-page advertisements are reproduced. In 1962, Dr. Benjamin Spock, author of *Baby and Child Care*, was shown with the caption "Dr. Spock is Worried" to publicize radioactive fallout from nuclear testing. A 1971 advertisement, entitled "America Has a Tapeworm," showed how military expenses were devouring resources at the rate of $200 million dollars per day. Well written and informative.

Kenny, Anthony J. *The Logic of Deterrence*. Chicago: University of Chicago Press, 1985.
The author is on the faculty of Oxford University, Great Britain, and has published numerous books and articles on issues in philosophy and ethics. He presents a scholarly analysis of the idea of a just war and argues that nuclear weapons that are targeted to annihilate civilian population centers can not be justified. He criticizes the concept of deterrence because it is based on mutual fear, so the arms race never stops. He supports continuation of East-West

negotiations to limit nuclear weapons. At the same time, he proposes some unilateral steps that would help the cause of peace, such as phasing out land-based Minuteman missiles, while retaining nuclear submarines as a credible minimum deterrent. Persuasive arguments addressed to thoughtful readers.

Keys, Donald, ed. *God and the H-Bomb*. New York: Bellmeadows Press, distributed by Random House, 1961.
Contains a collection of twenty-eight short essays by Protestant, Catholic, and Jewish leaders that address urgent moral questions about the nuclear arms race. Among the authors are Bishop James A. Pike (Episcopal), Paul Tillich (Harvard University), the Conference of American Rabbis, the World Council of Churches, Pope Pius XII, and several editors of influential religious journals. The introduction to the book emphasizes that these essays do not support Communist tyranny or unilateral disarmament. They do, however, reject the present policy of deterrence based on force. They advocate a policy of reconciliation, which would include serious negotiations on weapons reductions and economic aid to developing nations. In the tradition of the biblical prophets, they try to provide religious guidance for the survival of the human race.

Keyes, Ken. *The Hundredth Monkey*. Coos Bay, Oreg.: Vision Books, 1982.
The title of this book refers to a tribe of Japanese monkeys who learned to wash the dirt off their potatoes before eating them. Biologists observed that the number of monkeys who washed their food increased quite slowly up to a critical value, at which point the habit suddenly spread to all the rest of the tribe. In the same way, the author hopes that the antinuclear crusade will gradually win more converts until a sudden, dramatic change in many people's consciousness will bring an end to the nuclear nightmare. Each page of this book contains only a few sentences printed in large type, to emphasize the urgency of the call to action. The author gives well-chosen quotations by Dr. Helen Caldicott, Carl Sagan, and others.

Lapp, Ralph E. *Kill and Overkill: The Strategy of Annihilation*. New York: Basic Books, 1962.
The author is a nuclear physicist with a talent for explaining in simple terms how the arms race has come about. He describes the disappointment of scientists who pushed for a civilian Atomic Energy Commission only to see it become a munitions producer. He summarizes the effects of nuclear weapons, considering blast, fire, and fallout. He describes the development of Polaris and Minuteman missiles. He tells about imaginary scenarios of attack and defense played out on computers by Pentagon strategists. He points to the terrible danger in the concept of "peace through mutual terror." Finally, he advocates an immediate halt to further weapons production and proposes an Office of Industrial Reorientation to plan for conversion from military to civilian projects.

Larson, Jeanne, and Madge Micheels-Cyrus. *Seeds of Peace: A Catalogue of Quotations*. Philadelphia: New Society Publishers, 1987.
Contains more than 1,600 quotations on war, peace, and nonviolence, with an index of authors. A useful resource for writing speeches, newsletters, or sermons. Some examples: "You cannot simultaneously prevent and prepare for war" (Albert Einstein). "We have a choice today: nonviolent coexistence or violent coannihilation" (Martin Luther King, Jr.). "Mankind must put an end to war or war will put an end to mankind" (John F. Kennedy). "The term 'arms race' is misleading. It implies that the side with the most weapons will be the winner" (Teachers for Social Responsibility). "No one is right if no one is left" (bumper sticker).

Learning, Jennifer, and Langley Keyes, eds. *The Counterfeit Ark: Crisis Relocation for Nuclear War*. Cambridge, Mass.: Ballinger, 1984.
Physicians for Social Responsibility published this critical assessment of the Federal Emergency Management Agency (FEMA) and its Crisis Relocation Planning project. FEMA promotes plans for population evacuation of cities and construction of shelters, so that perhaps 80 percent of Americans could survive a nuclear war. Each chapter in the book begins with an extended quotation from a Civil Defense document, followed by a systematic rebuttal of its assumptions and conclusions. For example, the greatest natural disaster in this century was 5000 casualties from the Galveston flood, which is hardly comparable to 45 million from a nuclear war. Other chapters deal with problems of fallout, medical shortages, agriculture, debris clearance, maintaining law and order, and psychological trauma. Civil defense is called a dangerous illusion that distracts public attention away from efforts to prevent nuclear war.

Lifton, Robert Jay, and Richard Falk. *Indefensible Weapons: The Political and Psychological Case Against Nuclearism*. New York: Basic Books, 1982.
The term "nuclearism" is defined as psychological, political, and military dependence on nuclear weapons to provide national security. The first half of the book, written by the psychologist Robert Jay Lifton, points out several fallacies of nuclearism: the illusion that a limited nuclear war would not spread, the deception of civil defense preparations, and the false hope of recovery after a nuclear war. The second half, written by the political scientist Richard Falk, discusses the continuing arms race, justified by anti-Soviet rhetoric and the fear of falling behind in new weapons development. Both authors advocate an end to passive acquiescence toward nuclearism. They find hope in the growing protest activities of professional organizations and citizen groups.

Lilienthal, David E. *Change, Hope, and the Bomb*. Princeton, N.J.: Princeton University Press, 1963.
The author became a well-known public figure as head of the Tennessee Valley

Authority in the 1930's and as the first Chairman of the Atomic Energy Commission. Writing during the Cold War era of the Cuban Missile Crisis and the race to build bigger hydrogen bombs, he brings a message of faith in the future that is worth rereading today. He believes that an overwhelming preoccupation with the bomb has diverted attention from other problems of society. He finds great hope in the European Common Market, where mutual economic benefits make a future outbreak of war between Germany and France most unlikely. In the same way, he believes that disarmament negotiations will only succeed after greater mutual trust is established by international cooperative projects. Highly recommended.

Loeb, Paul Roget. *Nuclear Culture: Living and Working in the World's Largest Atomic Complex*. Philadelphia: New Society Publishers, 1986.
Hanford, Washington, was selected in 1943 as the site for building several nuclear reactors to produce plutonium for weapons. The author describes what has become of the town and its people, based on personal visits and interviews in the 1980's. As an antinuclear activist, he is outraged by the placid attitude of employees who are "doing their job" without giving thought to the resulting bombs that can bring about the end of civilization. Comparison is made to the Nazi concentration camps, and to townspeople who lived nearby closing their eyes to what was happening. The author makes a strong indictment of the nuclear weapons culture and then extends his arguments to the potential hazards of nuclear power plants.

Masters, Dexter, and Katherine Way, eds. *One World or None*. McGraw-Hill, 1946.
This historic document is a collection of sixteen short essays about the grave implications of the atomic bomb, written mostly by distinguished scientists who were leaders in the Manhattan Project. Hans Bethe calculates that Russia probably can duplicate the U.S. bomb development in about five years. J. R. Oppenheimer says that the Hiroshima bomb was an "infant" in size compared to anticipated future weapons. Leo Szilard writes on the question, "Can We Avert an Arms Race?" Albert Einstein envisions a world in which national armies have to be disbanded to make way for a supranational military force under the United Nations. Other contributors include Arthur H. Compton, Niels Bohr, Eugene P. Wigner, and Walter Lippmann. The urgent message to avoid nuclear warfare is authoritatively presented.

Merton, Thomas. *Original Child Bomb: Points for Meditation to be Scratched on the Walls of a Cave*. Drawings by Emil Antonucci. New York: New Directions, 1962.
The author is a Trappist monk who is known for *The Seven-Storey Mountain* and other writings. How can the story of the first atomic bomb be told with a minimum number of words? One can imagine the survivors of a nuclear war

living in a cave, trying to preserve a record of how it all got started. Merton uses an understated style of writing to weave together the essential threads. Brief mention is made of the roles played by Truman, Churchill, Japanese military leaders, the B-29 crew ("as excited as little boys on Christmas Eve"), Emperor Hirohito, the scientists, the Soviet leadership. "Original Child" is a translation of one name that the Japanese gave to the Hiroshima bomb. An effective message for peace.

Morland, Howard. *The Secret That Exploded*. New York: Random House, 1981.
The author was a Vietnam veteran who became a journalist and antiwar activist in the 1970's. He gained national attention for his article "The H-Bomb Secret," which was published in *The Progressive* magazine in November, 1979. The government tried to prevent publication of the article based on national security, while the magazine claimed freedom of the press guaranteed by the First Amendment. The author describes how he gathered information on the design of the H-bomb. He consulted previously published material, interviewed numerous scientists, and made site visits to Los Alamos and elsewhere. A complete reprint of the *Progressive* article is given in the appendix, including the sections that originally had been deleted by censors in the Department of Energy.

Muste, Abraham J. *Not by Might. Christianity: The Way to Human Decency* and *Of Holy Disobedience*. 1947 and 1952. Reprint. New York: Garland, 1971.
A. J. Muste (1885-1967) was an uncompromising spokesman for the pacifist movement. With eloquence and emotional intensity, he calls on people to join the great crusade for peace. One chapter is addressed specifically to atomic scientists to renounce further work on weapons. In forceful words, Hiroshima is described as an atrocity that set an all-time record for instantaneous mass slaughter. Another chapter expresses his support for draft resistors and conscientious objectors. In order to overcome repressive authoritarianism, he advocates nonviolent resistance in the tradition of Gandhi, Thoreau, and Jesus. He exposes the moral fallacy of German war criminals who tried to evade responsibility for their actions because they were following orders. He appeals to the individual conscience to provide persistent witness against the nuclear arms race.

Myrdal, Alva. *The Game of Disarmament: How the United States and Russia Run the Arms Race*. 1976. Rev. ed. New York: Random House, Pantheon Books, 1982.
The author is a recognized authority on the arms race and has represented the Swedish government at various disarmament conferences. She expresses her discouragement about the deteriorating world situation in 1982, with President Reagan's anti-Soviet rhetoric and the continuing waste of funds and brainpower on military buildup. She presents up-to-date information about chemical weapons and the danger of nuclear proliferation. One chapter describes the psychological

impact of militarism on people's attitude toward violence in everyday life. She sees hope in the rising tide of public protests, for a nuclear-free zone in Europe and a nuclear freeze in the United States. She also calls on engineers and workers to refuse employment in the weapons industry, as a personal commitment to halt the arms race.

Nathan, Otto, and Heinz Norden, eds. *Einstein on Peace*. New York: Schocken Books, 1960.

The general public is familiar with Einstein as the famous physicist who invented relativity, but his lifelong effort as an opponent of militarism is not so widely known. The editors of this volume have selected extensive quotations from Einstein's public speeches and private letters, interspersed with helpful background information. The chapters are arranged chronologically, beginning with World War I and ending in the middle 1950's. Einstein's letter to President Roosevelt in 1939, urging government support for atomic research on uranium, is discussed in detail. It is fascinating to read firsthand some of Einstein's correspondence with renowned contemporaries such as Sigmund Freud, Thomas Mann, and Bertrand Russell. The need for international cooperation to end the threat of war was a dominant theme in this later writings. He was a persistent spokesman for peace.

National Conference of Catholic Bishops. *The Challenge of Peace: God's Promise and Our Response. A Pastoral Letter on War and Peace*. Washington, D.C.: U.S. Catholic Conference, 1983.

This document of about one hundred pages was adopted by the American bishops of the Catholic Church, meeting in Chicago in May, 1983. It is a strong denunciation of the arms race. Among the specific recommendations are deep cuts in the arsenals of both superpowers and a halt to underground nuclear testing. The arms race is characterized as an act of aggression against the poor, because billions are spent on weapons while the homeless suffer. Special words of concern are addressed to public officials, to people in defense industries, to soldiers, and to scientists. People are called to be peacemakers, to listen for God's word. The policy of military deterrence is rejected as a basis for lasting peace. Challenging and hopeful, a widely publicized statement.

Newman, James R. *The Rule of Folly*. New York: Simon & Schuster, 1962.

The author was a mathematician who became widely known as editor of *The World of Mathematics*. This small book is a collection of articles and letters to the editor written by Newman expressing his intense opposition to the nuclear arms race. He ridicules the idea of fallout shelters, which were being advocated at the time. He criticizes the excessive stockpile of nuclear weapons, which can be justified only if war is accepted as an ultimate resort. His review of Herman Kahn's book *On Thermonuclear War* is reprinted, in which he declares its mathematical calculations of survival probabilities to be lunacy. He calls upon people to have the courage to protest against the military and political leaders who have brought the world to the brink of nuclear war.

Pauling, Linus. *No More War!* New York: Dodd, Mead, 1958, 1962.
Linus Pauling (1901-   ) was a recipient of the Nobel Prize for Chemistry in 1954 and won a second Nobel Prize for Peace in 1962. At the time of this book, both the United States and the Soviet Union were testing hydrogen bombs of incredible explosive power. Pauling expresses strong criticism of the Atomic Energy Commission for misleading the public about the dangers of radioactive fallout. He describes the scientific basis for calculating worldwide increases in cancer and birth defects resulting from fallout. In 1958, Pauling presented a petition to the United Nations signed by more than nine thousand scientists calling for an end to nuclear weapons testing. He urges the establishment of a World Peace Research Organization. Pauling was an outspoken and effective advocate for the peace movement.

Paulson, Dennis, ed. *Voices of Survival in the Nuclear Age.* Introduction by Carl Sagan. Santa Barbara, Calif.: Capra Press, 1986.
The editor of this paperback book is a writer, world traveler, and director of a conference center in California. He has collected short statements by 120 well-known public figures giving their views about the threat of nuclear war. Representative comments were obtained from political leaders, physicians, journalists, musicians, scientists, religious leaders, psychologists, actors, and peace activists. Among the authors are Hugh Downs, Indira Gandhi, Joan Baez, Edward Teller, Karl Menninger, George Bush, Mario Cuomo, William F. Buckley, Jr., Andrei Sakharov, and Pope John Paul II. Many of the writers are greatly alarmed by the continuing Soviet-U.S. arms race and advocate active individual involvement in a popular movement for peace. The general theme is, Don't leave it to the experts! Well-chosen quotations.

Rosenthal, Debra. *At the Heart of the Bomb: The Dangerous Allure of Weapons Work.* Reading, Mass.: Addison-Wesley, 1990.
The locale for this book is New Mexico, where the author conducted numerous personal interviews at the two main U.S. nuclear weapons facilities. Los Alamos is responsible for weapons design, while Sandia Laboratory builds the bombs and also monitors the total military stockpile of some thirty thousand weapons worldwide. Among the people who were interviewed are technicians, recent Ph.D.'s, old-timers at the labs, antinuclear activists, and townspeople. The author records various rationalization for doing bomb work: the Soviet threat, employment opportunities, becoming engrossed in the technical challenge of each project, availability of funds for nonmilitary applications. The author criticizes the attitude of many interviewees who reject any personal responsibility for the

arms race because they claim they were only doing their assigned job. Informative and well written.

Schell, Jonathan. *The Abolition*. New York: Alfred A. Knopf, 1984.
This is a follow-up to the author's widely quoted earlier book, *The Fate of the Earth* (1982). A new public awareness about the dangers for a nuclear holocaust arose from several factors: breakdown of the Strategic Arms Limitation Talks (SALT II), President Reagan's proposal for weapons in space (SDI), the likely nuclear winter scenario following a nuclear war, and the dramatic TV film *The Day After*. The author finds hope in the widespread support for a nuclear freeze. He criticizes the military deterrence theory for having lulled people into a false sense of security. He envisions the complete abolition of nuclear weapons as a goal that is attainable by a series of gradual steps. Thoughtful and provocative writing.

_____. *The Fate of the Earth*. New York: Alfred A. Knopf, 1982.
In this widely read book, the author begins with a depressing analysis of the effects of nuclear war. In addition to the immediate casualties, survivors would be decimated by lack of food, water, sanitation, and medical care. Epidemics and ecological disasters that threaten the survival of humankind are so incomprehensible that many people have put up mental barriers against thinking about it. The author contrasts human thinking about one's own death, which is inevitable and requires acceptance, with nuclear extinction, which can be avoided and requires rejection. He criticizes the political strategy of deterrence based on mutually assured destruction because it is fundamentally unstable. The basic message of the book is that a nuclear holocaust is avoidable if public apathy can be overcome.

Schweitzer, Albert. *On Nuclear War and Peace*. Edited by Homer A. Jack. Elgin, Ill.: Brethren Press, 1988.
Albert Schweitzer (1875-1965) had three careers: professional musician, theologian, and medical missionary in East Africa. For his humanitarian work, he received the Nobel Peace Prize in 1952. The editor's introduction tells how Schweitzer resisted all efforts to join the campaign against nuclear weapons until he was in his eighties. He did not feel qualified to speak out on political issues until a personal visit by Norman Cousins persuaded him that his moral stature could help to arouse public opinion against the arms race. Schweitzer's "Declaration of Conscience" (published in 1957) and three radio addresses on "Peace or Atomic War" (1958) are reprinted. Also, his correspondence with Bertrand Russell, Linus Pauling, Pablo Casals, President Kennedy, and others provides insight and inspiration for the reader.

Sterba, James P., ed. *The Ethics of War and Nuclear Deterrence.* Belmont, Calif.: Wadsworth, 1985.
The author is a philosopher at the University of Notre Dame with an interest in ethical issues raised by the nuclear arms race. Nineteen articles with a variety of viewpoints are reprinted, most of them written in the early 1980's. A major theme of this book is a philosophical critique of the concept of nuclear deterrence. Among the authors are Jonathan Schell, George F. Kennan, Caspar W. Weinberger, the U.S. Catholic bishops, and Herbert F. York. The Nuclear Freeze Resolution of 1982 by Senators Ted Kennedy and Mark Hatfield is reprinted, followed by an opposing statement from the Department of Defense entitled "Security through Military Buildup." A useful selection of readings for a college course.

Thompson, Edward P. *Beyond the Cold War: A New Approach to the Arms Race and Nuclear Annihilation.* New York: Pantheon Books, 1982.
The author was a leading spokesman for the Campaign for Nuclear Disarmament (CND) in Great Britain, which paralleled the nuclear freeze movement in the United States. This book contains speeches and articles published by Thompson in the early 1980's. The CND vigorously opposed both the deployment of the cruise missile by NATO and the Soviets' SS-20. The United States and Soviet Union represented two monolithic adversaries, each distorting the opponent's intentions to justify its own weapons buildup. The author envisions a nuclear-free zone across central Europe, brought about by a new international bonding between peace movements on both sides. The loosening Soviet rule in Eastern Europe and the internal problems of the American economy were viewed as signs that the Cold War was coming to an end. Foresighted and outspoken.

Thompson, James. *Psychological Aspects of Nuclear War.* New York: John Wiley & Sons, 1985.
This pamphlet contains a statement that was adopted by the British Psychological Society at its annual conference in 1984, to delineate how the field of psychology can contribute to the nuclear weapons debate. One section discusses psychological reactions to major disasters such as a dam failure, the Hiroshima bomb, and the Black Death plague of 1350. Another section is concerned with human fallibility under stress, creating a heightened possibility of accidents. Examples cited include nuclear submarine collisions, missile silo explosions, aircraft accidents, and false radar alerts. Drug and alcohol abuse among military personnel and the danger of an unplanned nuclear missile launch are noted. Finally, psychological research on conflict resolution provides suggestions for more effective political negotiations toward arms limitations agreements. Informative; highly recommended.

Van Ornum, William, and Mary Wicker Van Ornum. *Talking to Children About Nuclear War*. New York: Continuum, 1984.
The authors are a clinical psychologist and a journalist who specialize in educational materials for young people. They are concerned about the communication gap between adults and children on the subject of nuclear war. They present examples of letters and stories written by children that show that the threat of nuclear annihilation is very much on their minds; however, there seems to be a taboo that prevents open discussion of such worries, similar to the inability that many people have to talk about death with a person who has a terminal illness. Specific suggestions are given for adults who genuinely want to share their feelings of fear and hope with young people.

Woodworth, Elizabeth M. *What Can I Do? Citizen Strategies for Nuclear Disarmament*. Victoria, Canada: Cream Books, 1987.
The author reviews the destructive power of nuclear weapons and the continuing arms race. She points out that arms control treaties and summit meetings by political leaders have not accomplished any reductions in weapons, but instead have led to mutually agreed higher levels of armament. The focus of this book is on what individual people can do to promote peace. The most important step, Woodworth emphasizes, is to overcome the fatalistic attitude that nothing can be done. She provides a list of fifty activities to awaken public opinion, such as teach-ins, letters to the editor, and nonviolent protest marches. The appendix lists more than a hundred peace organizations that individuals can join for mutual support and encouragement.

World Health Organization, United Nations. *Effects of Nuclear War on Health and Health Services*. 1st ed. Geneva: World Health Organization, 1984.
The World Health Organization (WHO) appointed an international committee of six members and nine technical advisers to study the effects of nuclear war on health services. Their quite depressing conclusions are presented in this pamphlet: localized blast, fire, and radiation, followed by superfires, smoke, climate changes, famine, and disruption of social, communication and economic systems worldwide. A study of London, England, envisages 7,500 hospital beds to cope with a million immediate casualties. Another article focuses on the acute psychological problems of postdisaster behavior. Nuclear war is described as such an overwhelming disaster that all attempts to deal with its medical problems are viewed as futile and illusory. Diagrams, graphs, and references to professional journal publications are given in the appendix.

_____. *Effects of Nuclear War on Health and Health Services*. 2d. ed. Geneva: World Health Organization, 1987.
The International Committee of Experts in Medical Sciences and Public Health had recommended that the World Health Organization periodically should inform

the World Health Assembly of studies concerning the effects of nuclear war on health and health services. This is the second such report, which differs from the first by including information about climatic effects from blast and fire, as well as how the threat of nuclear war is perceived by people. As in the first edition, the majority of the information is contained in the appendices, emphasizing the psychological and social aspects of nuclear war in this volume. Extensive references are given. Again, the Committee of Experts concludes that prevention is the only way to deal with the potentially disastrous health effects of nuclear warfare.

Willens, Harold. *The Trimtab Factor: How Business Executives Can Help Solve the Nuclear Weapons Crisis.* New York: William Morrow, 1984.
The "trimtab" is a small rudder that is attached to the main rudder of a big ship. One person applying a small amount of leverage to the trimtab can turn the main rudder and eventually the whole ship. The author is a successful business executive who uses this analogy to urge the business community to utilize its leverage to change the course of the runaway nuclear arms race. Nuclear war is described as "omnicide," the killing of everything. Willens shows that building more weapons is doing great damage to the economy. He was state chairman in 1982 for the California Nuclear Freeze Initiative, which received nearly four million votes. Well written, with good quotations and a short bibliography.

Zuckerman, Edward. *The Day After World War III.* New York: Viking Press, 1979.
A thoroughly documented study of contingency plans actually developed by government agencies, industrial companies, and the military, in case of a nuclear war with the Soviets. Many examples are cited that make the reader wonder about the bizarre mentality of the planners. The Post Office has plans to distribute emergency change-of-address cards to survivors. The Federal Emergency Management Agency (FEMA) has published rules for sleeping arrangements separated by sex in fallout shelters. Bus companies will be permitted to expand their normal routes. The boards of directors of large corporations are authorized to make decisions with a reduced quorum. The Air Force is to retain sufficient nuclear weapons to deal with potential future aggressors. The magnitude of a nuclear holocaust is reduced to such minor shifts in normal procedures.

Chapter 9
VIDEOCASSETTES, DOCUMENTARIES, AND MOVIES

After the Fall of New York. Dir.: Martin Dolman. Cast: Michael Sopkiw, Valentine Momnier, Anna Kanakis, George Eastman. 1983 Nuova Dania Cinematografica (Vestron Video). Color. 95 min. R.
This clearly dubbed Italian offering takes place twenty years after a nuclear holocaust. The American alliance has been driven underground in Alaska. Their opponents, the Euracs—a monarchy founded on a European, African, and Asian alliance—have taken over New York City. Since all the females are now infertile, the only hope for humanity is a single woman who has been kept in suspended animation since the war in the ruins of New York City. She is ultimately recovered and sent to another planet in the Alpha Centauri system. Many of this movie's themes are done better in other movies such as *On the Beach* or the Mad Max trilogy; however, a sense of hopelessness among the survivors is apparent, caused by the destructiveness of nuclear war that leads to the abandonment of Earth.

Akira Kurosawa's Dreams. Dir.: Akira Kurosawa. Cast: Akira Terao, Martin Scorsese, Mitsuko Baisho, Toshie Negishi, Mieko Harada, Mitsunori Isaki, Toshihiko Nakano, Yoshitaka Zushi. 1990 Akira Kurosawa U.S.A. (Warner Bros.) Color. 120 min. Japanese with English subtitles. PG.
This collection of film shorts from famed director Akira Kurosawa contains three vignettes of interest here. *The Tunnel* (18 minutes) provides a strong antiwar statement by exploring the feelings of a surviving commanding officer as he confronts his dead troops. *Mount Fuji in Red* (7 minutes) explores the horrors of radiation as six nuclear power plants around Mr. Fuji explode and scatter radioactive gases over the countryside. *The Weeping Demon* (17 minutes) depicts a wasteland created by nuclear explosions, inhabited by mutated plants and people (the demons). Although lacking in complete scientific accuracy (these are, after all, "dreams"), the images Kurosawa presents are striking and haunting.

Amazing Grace and Chuck. Dir.: Mike Newell. Cast: Jamie Lee Curtis, Alex English, Gregory Peck, William L. Petersen, Joshua Zuehlke. 1987 Tri-Star Pictures and Rastar. Color. 115 min. PG.
Chuck, a 12-year-old and star pitcher on a Montana little league team, decides to give up baseball after being shown a missile silo. His protest catches on with the athletes and the children of the world until ultimately all nuclear weapons are dismantled. Although well intentioned, the plot is predictable and lacks thorough discussion of relevant issues.

American Masters: "Einstein—The World as I See It." Dir.: Richard Kroenling. Narrator: William Hurt. Documentary. 1991 VPI—Videfilm Producers Interna-

tional (Educational Broadcasting Corp.-WNET) Color. 60 min. Not rated.
Similar in nature to *Nova:* "Einstein," this production relies more on interviews
with Einstein's colleagues and friends than the earlier film; however, some
original interviews with Einstein are included along with some of his writings,
many of which have been collected in a book of the same name. A segment
(about 15 minutes or so) deals with Einstein's involvement with the letters to
President Roosevelt that launched the Manhattan Project. Einstein's reaction to
the use of atomic weapons, as well as to the notoriety that followed, is detailed.
A brief indication of his relationship with Oppenheimer and his reaction to
Oppenheimer's hearing is included. Recommended for its insights into Einstein's
personality, this film does provide a useful resource for someone wishing to study
the political atmosphere just before and after the atomic bomb as well as the
creators of the atomic age.

Atomic Cafe. Dir.: Kevin Rafferty, Jayne Loader, Pierce Rafferty. 1982 The
Archive Project, Inc. Black and white. 88 min. Not rated.
This is not so much a film as a collection of films about the atomic bomb and
nuclear preparedness. Taken from newsreels, propaganda films, training films,
and civil defense films, it juxtaposes the thinking of the 1950's and 1960's with
the actual effects of the Hiroshima and Nagasaki bombings. An excellent source
of film segments illustrating nuclear blasts and their effects, and of "duck and
cover" films, in which the viewers are instructed in procedures to follow in order
to survive an initial atomic blast. This film effectively documents how the United
States first tried to deal with the threat of nuclear weapons. This film is part of
the MacArthur Library and has been given to many libraries throughout the
United States along with supplementary materials for classroom use.

Boy and His Dog, A. Dir.: L. Q. Jones. Cast: Don Johnson, Suzanne Benton, Jason
Robards, Jr. 1974 Third L.Q.J. Inc.(1985 MEDIA Home Entertainment, Inc.)
Color. 87 min. R.
This screen adaptation of a Harlan Ellison novel depicts two contrasting societies
left after a five-day nuclear war. On the surface, near present-day Phoenix,
Arizona, a violent and uncivilized world exists where people must scavenge for
food preserved before the nuclear holocaust. This is the world of the boy
(Johnson) and his dog who depend on each other for survival until one day the
Boy is lured underground by a girl he has saved from a pack of scavengers.
Underground he discovers a society where the "council" controls all aspects of
the citizens' lives and that he was brought there to revitalize the genetic material
of the colony. The boy escapes this sterile underground world with the help of
the girl who lured him there, but sacrifices her to save his dog. Both societies
are bleak statements against nuclear warfare and an interesting contrast to H. G.
Wells's Eloi and Morlocks in *The Time Machine.*

By Dawn's Early Light. Dir.: Jack Sholder. Cast: Powers Boothe, Rebecca De-
Mornay, James Earl Jones, Martin Landau, Darren McGavin, Rip Torn, Peter
MacNichol. 1990 Home Box Office, Inc. Color. 104 min. Not rated (made for
television).
This is a depiction of a limited nuclear engagement between the United States
and the Soviet Union. Powers Booth and Rebecca DeMornay play a B-52 pilot
and copilot who turn back from total war and give the Russians and Americans
a chance to de-escalate the war. Martin Landau is an injured president trying
desperately to stop the destruction before everything is destroyed. Meanwhile,
Darin McGavin is the Secretary of the Interior who mistakenly succeeded to the
presidency and is trying to "win" the war for the United States. In many
respects, this movie is an update of *Fail Safe* and has several notable points. It
suggests how easily the United States and the Soviet Union could be duped into
beginning a nuclear war, and how difficult it would be to limit that war once it
began. Various reasons for escalating and for de-escalating the conflict are
brought out. Also, this film conveys a sense of the chaos that even a limited
nuclear engagement would produce. Integrated into the story are some of the
systems and procedures the United States has instigated to control such a conflict.
Worth viewing.

Daniel. Dir.: Sidney Lumet. Cast: Timothy Hutton, Mandy Patinkin, Lindsay
Crouse, Edward Asner, Amanda Plummer. 1983 Paramount. Color. 129 min.
R.
Based on E. L. Doctorow's book *The Book of Daniel*, this is essentially a
retelling of the Rosenberg case as seen through the eyes of the son Daniel
(Hutton). Beginning in the era of Vietnam War protests, Daniel's troubled past
and the story of his parents' arrest, trial, and execution for espionage is told
through a series of flashbacks. His sister, Susan, is so disturbed by the events
of her past that she is eventually confined to a mental hospital. This dramatization
of the Rosenberg case asserts the innocence of the "Issacson" parents and
emphasizes the tragedy of their punishment by revealing its effects on their family
and friends.

Day After Trinity, The. Dir.: Jon Else. Documentary. 1980 Jon Else and KTEH,
San Jose. Color and black and white. 88 min. Not rated.
This documentary of the life of J. Robert Oppenheimer not only chronicles his
life but the Manhattan Project and the post-World War II era as well. Fascinating
interviews with brother Frank (also a physicist) and other scientists who knew
and worked with J. Robert Oppenheimer years before World War II as well as
at Los Alamos on the "gadget" are mixed with contemporary film. The
interviews reveal the thoughts and moods of those most affected during the
development of the first atomic bombs, as well as anecdotes of life during the
project. Paranoia during the McCarthy era led to hearings and the eventual

withdrawal of Robert Oppenheimer's security clearance. His subsequent disillusionment is discussed, as are the hearings. Film clips of Oppenheimer himself reveal his thoughts on the political developments affecting nuclear weapons after World War II. This film's title is taken from one such clipping, in which Oppenheimer comments on Robert Kennedy's efforts to begin negotiations with the Russians by saying, "It's twenty years too late. It should have been done the day after Trinity." Very highly recommended, this film is part of the MacArthur Library and has been given to many libraries throughout the United States along with supplementary materials for classroom use.

Day the Earth Stood Still, The. Dir.: Robert Wise. Cast: Michael Rennie, Patricia Neal, Hugh Marlowe, Sam Jaffe, Billy Gray. 1951 Twentieth Century-Fox Film Corp. Black and White. 92 min. Not Rated.
In this classic science-fiction thriller, Klaatu (Rennie) comes to warn Earth that aggressive use of atomic power will not be tolerated by other planets. Only a scientist (Jaffe), a young widow (Neal) and her son are willing to give the visitor a chance while the politicians and soldiers discourage and hunt him down. In the end the message is clear—nations must learn to live with each other or be destroyed.

. . DEADLINE . . Dir.: Arch Nicholson. Cast: Barry Newman, Trisha Noble, Bill Kerr, Bruce Spence, Alwyn Kurts, John Ewart. 1981 Hanna-Barbera Pty. Ltd. Color. 94 min. Not Rated.
Extortionists have constructed two nuclear devices form stolen plutonium in this Australian film. The first is detonated in the desert while the second is armed and placed in Sydney for ransom. The government wants to hush it up but reporters figure out what's going on and ultimately save Sydney. The discussion among government officials concerning evacuation of Sydney raises some interesting points as does the conflict between the journalists and government.

Dr. Strangelove: Or, How I Learned To Stop Worrying and Love the Bomb. Dir.: Stanley Kubrick. Cast: Peter Sellers, George C. Scott, Sterling Hayden, Slim Pickens, Keenan Wynn, Peter Bull, James Earl Jones. 1964 RCA/Columbia. Black and white. 93 min. Not rated.
Much has been written on this masterly black comedy about a fanatical U.S. general who manages to singlehandedly launch a nuclear attack on the Soviet Union. Scenes switch between the general's Strategic Air Command (SAC) base, the B-52 bomber that eventually drops the first bomb of the war, and the U.S. president's war room, where options and scenarios are debated. Kubrick, who helped rewrite Peter George's novel *Two Hours to Doom* into a script, drives this movie with the irony of a defensive nuclear arsenal and the paranoia of the time. Some scenes are unforgettable such as Slim Pickens riding a hydrogen bomb to its target, the president's conversation with the Soviet premier, and Dr. Strange-

love's advice for survival of the social elite. This movie is a fascinating statement about the absurdity of nuclear war and the ease with which such a war might be initiated.

Elephant Parts. Dir.: William Dear. Cast: Michael Nesmith, Jonathan Nesmith, Bill Martin, Lark Alcott, Robert Akerman, Katherine McDaniel. 1981 Michael Nesmith (The Pacific Arts Corp., Inc.) Color. 60 min. Not rated.
This is former-Monkee Michael Nesmith's first "video record," containing a number of songs and skits. One skit is of particular interest here. It is a fake advertisement for Neighborhood Nuclear Superiority (NNS)—a company that sells nuclear weapons that can attach to a garden hose. While making fun of international nuclear threats by bringing them down to a neighborhood arena, Nesmith has also summarized the paranoia and fear that lead to nuclear buildup. It is also sobering to think that strategic weapons (now dismantled) could have been used by a field commander in a way not unlike these fictional NNS devices. This skit lasts for about one and a half minutes and starts about 19 minutes into the film.

Enola Gay: The Men, the Mission, the Atomic Bomb. Dir.: David Lowell Rich. Cast: Billy Crystal, Kim Darby, Patrick Duffy, Gary Frank, Gregory Harrison. 1980 Viacom. Color. 150 min. Not rated (made for television).
Enola Gay was the name given by Colonel Paul Tibbets to the B-29 bomber that dropped the first atomic bomb on Hiroshima. This movie provides interesting insights into the development of the mission, Tibbets' command of the mission and its effect on his personal life, crew selection and training, modifications to the B-29 bomber, the decision to drop the bomb, and Japanese feelings at the time. The final scenes are of a destroyed Hiroshima and of brief updates of the persons depicted in the film. This is a convenient source of several details about the mission that are likely to be true as many of the original crew members, including Tibbets, were technical advisers for this movie.

Fail-Safe. Dir.: Sidney Lumet. Cast: Henry Fonda, Walter Matthau, Fritz Weaver, Dan O'Herlihy, Sorrell Booke, Larry Hagman, Frank Overton, Dom DeLuise. 1964 Columbia Pictures Industries, Inc. Black and white. 111 min. Not rated.
A computer malfunction sends U.S. bombers toward Moscow as if a nuclear war with the Soviet Union had begun. Attempts to call the bombers back fail, and the president (Fonda) is faced with trying to convince the Soviets that it was all a mistake. In order to avert an all-out nuclear war, the president orders New York City to be destroyed when Moscow is bombed. *Fail-Safe* is a chilling look at what might be and a comment on the danger of the nuclear arms race. It should be compared with *Dr. Strangelove* and *By Dawn's Early Light*, and is based on a novel by Eugene Burdick and Harvey Wheeler.

Fat Man and Little Boy. Dir.: Roland Joffe. Cast: Paul Newman, Dwight Schultz, Bonnie Bedelia, John Cusack, Laura Dern, John McGinley. 1989 Paramount Pictures. Color. 127 min. PG-13.

This dramatization of the Manhattan Project focuses on the Los Alamos laboratory and three principal characters. Paul Newman plays General Leslie Groves, the military director of the project, while Dwight Schultz plays J. Robert Oppenheimer, the scientific leader of the project. The plot also revolves around the fictional character Mike Merriman, played by John Cusack. Merriman is a composite character who seems to be everywhere and through whose perspective much of the drama is revealed. As development of the atomic bomb progresses, questions of the morality of building and using such a weapon are addressed. The horror of radiation sickness is brought out near the end of the movie when Merriman receives a lethal dose of radiation while conducting tests. Contrasting opinions between the scientists and the military are emphasized. Although historically accurate in many respects, some inaccuracies are apparent when compared to a documentary such as *The Day After Trinity*. A viewer is advised to remember the disclaimer at the end of the credits, which states: " . . . the names of certain characters portrayed have been changed and certain incidents portrayed have been dramatized." Nevertheless, this motion picture does pique interest and could provide a beginning for further study or discussion on the morality of using such weapons.

Final Chapter?, The. Dir.: W. Longul (TVO); Yutaka Aida, Goro Koide (NHK). Documentary. Narrator: Christopher Plummer. 1985 The Ontario Educational Communications Authority. Color and black and white. Not rated.

This documentary explores many aspects of the results of nuclear war, including radiation effects on plants and animals, nuclear winter, stratospheric ozone depletion, conflagration, and fallout. This is a source of numerous interviews, and films of bomb tests and could easily stimulate discussions on the horrors of nuclear war.

Fourth Protocol, The. Dir.: John Mackenzie. Cast: Michael Cain, Pierce Brosnan, Joanna Cassidy, Ned Beatty. 1987 Lorimar. Color. 100 min. R.

This film, based on the book by Frederick Forsyth, deals with nuclear terrorism, espionage, and politics. Pierce Brosnan plays a cold, violent Russian agent charged by direct orders of the head of the KGB to assemble and detonate a nuclear device near a U.S. base in England. The bomb is smuggled into England piece by piece and then assembled in Brosnan's attic. The purpose is to simulate a nuclear accident that would destroy NATO and break the last remaining secret protocol of the 1968 SALT treaty. Michael Cain plays the British agent who detects the plot and ultimately prevents detonation of the bomb. Although oversimplified, this film illustrates basic elements of bomb design, the threat of subversion, and the relative ease by which such threats could be implemented.

Hiroshima Maiden. Dir.: Joan Darling. Cast: Susan Blakely, Tamlyn Tomita, Steven Dorff, Richard Masur. 1988 Wonder Works. Color. 58 min. Not rated (made for television).

In 1955, twenty-four Japanese women who were injured during the Hiroshima bombing came to the United States for medical treatment. This is a dramatization of one of those visits. The film is told from the point of view of the adolescent son of one of the host families. His initial attitude toward his family's guest is one of animosity since he thinks she is a spy. This opinion is shared by most of the neighborhood, especially by one of the neighbors who was a veteran of the Pacific theater in World War II but never saw Hiroshima or the victims there. As the story progresses, the son's opinions change as he grows to accept and understand his Japanese guest's fears and victimization. Ultimately, he becomes one of her defenders in the community. This film's ability to deal with the themes of fear and prejudice in a way that is suitable for all ages make it very worth-while. It also provides insights into the cultural atmosphere in the United States a decade after World War II and into the feelings of the victims of war and atomic destruction.

Hiroshima, Mon Amour. Dir.: Alain Resnais. Cast: Emmanuele Riva, Eiji Okada, Stella Dassas, Pierre Barband. 1959 Argo Films S.A. Black and white. 91 min. French with subtitles. Not rated.

Drawing parallels between the war in Europe and the destruction by atomic blast and rebuilding of Hiroshima, this film centers around a French actress and a Japanese architect and their relationship fourteen years after World War II. The first part is concerned with Hiroshima's destruction and recovery. Scenes of the Hiroshima Atomic Museum and of the rebuilt city are integrated into the story line. The last (and longer) part deals with the actress' history in war-torn France. Just as he helped rebuild Hiroshima, the architect helps the actress rebuild her life. The use of symbolism and the need for subtitles may limit the audience for this movie; however, it is thought-provoking and does depict the conditions in Europe near the end and just after World War II.

Hunt for Red October, The. Dir.: John McTiernan. Cast: Sean Connery, Alec Baldwin, Scott Glenn, James Earl Jones. 1989 Paramount. 135 min. PG.

The threat of nuclear war is imminent when a Russian submarine commander and his officers attempt to defect to the United States. Connery plays the masterful Russian submarine commander who hopes to avert an all-out nuclear war by bringing the latest Soviet submarine to the West—a missile-carrying submarine constructed for the sole purpose of launching a Soviet first strike against the United States. Exciting entertainment with a subtle antiwar message, this drama provides an unusual look at submarine warfare and provides insight into the place and importance of submarines as delivery systems for nuclear weapons. This film deviates only slightly from the book by Tom Clancy.

Mad Max. Dir.: George Miller. Cast: Mel Gibson, Joanne Samuel, Hugh Keays-Byrne, Steve Bisley, Tim Burns, Roger Ward. 1979 Crossroads International Finance Co. (Vestron Video). Color. 90 min. R.

This, the first of the Mad Max movies (and the most successful Australian film of all time), introduces Max Rockatanski as a highway cop in a desolate future. Although not entirely clear until the third movie, the audience is witnessing the last vestiges of law and order after a nuclear apocalypse. This society in decline is plagued by "nomad trash from the wastelands" who Max ultimately overcomes after they have killed his son and maimed his wife. A good adventure story and an interesting if somewhat fanciful picture of life after a nuclear war. See: *Mad Max Beyond Thunderdome*.

Mad Max 2 (The Road Warrior). Dir.: George Miller. Cast: Mel Gibson, Bruce Spence, Vernon Wells, Mike Preston, Virginia Hey, Emil Minty, Kjell Nilson. 1981 Kennedy Miller Entertainment (Warner Bros.) Color. 94 min. R.

The saga of Mad Max continues in an even more desolate world where gasoline is now one of the most sought-after commodities. Major refineries were destroyed during the war and stockpiles, at least in Max's world, have essentially run out. In the middle of this future oil crisis, Max reluctantly befriends a community that has established a small oil refinery and produced enough oil to make their escape to the coast. Unfortunately, the warlord Humungus stands in their way until Max helps the community overcome him and his gang. The community is now safe and is last seen driving off to establish a new civilization. Like the other Mad Max movies, this is an absorbing adventure with elements of fantasy based on probability. It can also be viewed as a struggle of good against evil, civilization against barbarism, in a world devastated by nuclear war. This film was retitled *The Road Warrior* for American release. See: *Mad Max Beyond Thunderdome*.

Mad Max Beyond Thunderdome. Dir.: George Miller and George Ogilvie. Cast: Mel Gibson, Tina Turner, Helen Buday, Frank Thring, Bruce Spence, Angelo Rossitto. 1985 Kennedy Miller Productions (Warner Bros.). Color. 107 min. PG-13.

Finally, in this third movie in the series, it becomes irrefutable that Max and his world have survived a nuclear war. In this account of his travels he comes across Bartertown, which is administered by Auntie (Turner). Auntie's control over Bartertown is limited by Master (Rossitto), who controls the power source: methane produced by biomass. Max is hired by Auntie to overcome Master's bodyguard, Blaster. Eventually, Max is exiled to the desert, where he is rescued by a band of children who survive in a water-filled gorge in the middle of the desert. The children were stranded here when the plane ("sky raft") they were using to escape the war's devastation crashed nearby. Their leader, Captain Walker, later left them when he went looking for help and never returned. The children's society and development provide an interesting twist as their language uses unexpected idioms and their history has elevated technology to near-mythic status. Reluctantly, Max helps some of them on their way to the old cities where they begin civilization again with the help of Master. The Mad Max movies should be numbered among those movies that use nuclear destruction as a means to create a fictional, often barbaric and primitive, world for their characters to interact in; however, the Mad Max movies are among the best of this category. They are exciting if fanciful adventure stories that show aspects of a modern society blasted apart by war and trying to cope with bullies and shortages. These movies also contain elements of hope in characters who are willing to rebuild society and reject the chaos and barbarism that surrounds them. Max is the reluctant protector of these people and their future civilizations.

Missile. Dir.: Frederick Wiseman. Cast: Trainees and instructors at the 4315 Combat Crew Training Squad (SAC). Documentary. 1987 Frederick Wiseman (Zipporah Film). Color. 115 min. Not rated.
Land-based intercontinental ballistic missiles (ICBMs) form the bulk of the United States' nuclear deterrent force. Who controls these missiles and how they are trained is the subject of this documentary. A class of cadets and their fourteen weeks of training are the main focus of this documentary. First a seminar on personal responsibility is witnessed. As the instruction progresses, glimpses of the training sessions and instructors meetings are shown, along with the private lives of the cadets. As the film draws to a close, one team's final exam—a simulated launch—is documented, along with the graduation address by a general in the Strategic Air Command (SAC) who often mans the Airborne Command Center. A useful source of information that gives the military's point of view as well as an interesting contrast to movies such as *WarGames* and *Twilight's Last Gleaming*. This film is part of the MacArthur Library and has been given to many libraries throughout the United States along with supplementary materials for classroom use.

Missiles of October, The. Dir.: Anthony Page. Cast: William Devane, Ralph Bellamy, Martin Sheen, Howard Da Silva. 1974 MALJACK Productions, Inc. Color. 175 min. Not Rated (made for television).
This film dramatizes the Cuban missile crisis by taking the audience into advisory and private meetings of both President John F. Kennedy and Premier Nikita Khrushchev. Based on contemporary documents, the viewer is given insight into how and why each leader made the decisions he did and what options and opinions existed. Appropriate viewing for anyone interested in the crisis which brought the United States and the Soviet Union to the brink of nuclear war.

Nightline: "Chelyabinsk—Nuclear Nightmare." Dir.: None credited. Host: Ted Koppel. Documentary. Air date: Friday, January 31, 1992. ABC News. Color. 30 min. Not rated (television documentary).

This edition of ABC News's *Nightline* is a special report on the Soviet Union's nuclear weapons complex at Mayak, a secret city (also called Chelyabinsk-40) 75 miles north of Chelyabinsk. This is where the former Soviet Union made weapons-grade plutonium and were U.S. pilot Francis Gary Powers was spying in a U-2 plane when he was shot down. Since the beginning of the Soviet nuclear weapons program, radioactive wastes have been dumped into the lakes and rivers of the region. In 1957 a containment vessel exploded, spreading approximately 2 million curies of radiation over the countryside. This particular episode was detailed in Zhores A. Medvedev's book *Nuclear Disaster in the Urals*. Then, ten years after the explosion, in 1967, one of the dumping reservoirs dried up and the contaminated silt was spread over the region by wind. A *Nightline* crew visited these sites (the first U.S. news team to do so) and interviewed several victims, officials, and doctors, providing a chilling look at hidden side effects of the nuclear arms race.

Nova: "Einstein." Dir.: None credited. Writer-producer: Patrick Griffin. Cast: Albert Einstein. Documentary. 1979 WGBH Educational Foundation (Vestron Video). Color and black and white. 60 min. Not rated (made for television).
This documentary summarizes the role Albert Einstein played in the political and scientific developments during the first half of the twentieth century. Beginning in 1905, when he first became internationally famous in scientific circles, Einstein's career and humanitarian efforts are summarized up until just before his death in 1955. This film contains original footage of the times, including much of Einstein himself. The last 15 or 20 minutes of this 60-minute documentary deal almost exclusively with the development of nuclear weapons, which were based on Einstein's theories, and the subsequent Cold War. This film is recommended for its insights into Einstein's character and actions. and for its original footage of Einstein's dissertations on nuclear energy and weapons. See also *American Masters:* "A. Einstein."

Nova: "Nuclear Strategy for Beginners." Dir.: Robert Zalisk. Documentary. 1983 WGBH Educational Foundation. Color. 57 min. Not rated (made for television).
This documentary accomplishes the very difficult task of surveying U.S. nuclear policies from the Manhattan Project to the Reagan years. A number of noted experts are interviewed, and original footage of speeches, nuclear tests, and simulations are effectively used throughout. An excellent source of statistics and data as well. Highly recommended.

On the Beach. Dir.: Stanley Kramer. Cast: Gregory Peck, Ava Gardner, Fred Astaire, Anthony Perkins. 1959 Lomitas Productions, Inc. (United Artists; CBS/Fox Video). Black and white. 133 min. Not rated.
Set in Australia after an all-out nuclear war (which was speculated to occur in January 1964), the citizens and soldiers there are waiting for the winds to shift

with the seasons to bring nuclear fallout and death to what remains of humanity. In one last trip to the northern hemisphere, a submarine commanded by Peck explores uninhabited but intact land that was once the United States and returns to Australia without hope. Based on a Nevil Shute novel, this film is an indictment of the Mutual Assured Destruction policy and is a hopeless view of the results of an all-out nuclear war. It is also an interesting statement of the times that nuclear winter, fires, disease, and malnutrition, among other effects, are not mentioned as results of the war and that nuclear fallout was the only perceived threat.

Outer Limits, The: "Demon with a Glass Hand." Dir.: Byron Haskin. Cast: Robert Culp, Arline Martel, Abraham Sofaer. 1964 Daystar—Villa Di Stefano—U.A. Black and white. 52 minutes Not rated (made for television).
Earth of the future is invaded and conquered by aliens. As a last-ditch effort, humanity releases a radioactive plague that will destroy all intelligent life. To avoid their own destruction, a robot which is immune to the plague is constructed to carry the essence of the surviving human population. This Harlan Ellison story begins in current times, to which the robot Trent (Culp) has escaped, and is revealed piece by piece as Trent's glass hand is assembled. Considered one of the best of the *Outer Limits* television series, this story provides an interesting twist to total nuclear destruction and contrast to *Terminator 2.*

Sayer, Karen, and John Dowling, eds. *National Directory of Audiovisual Resources on Nuclear War and the Arms Race.* Ann Arbor: University of Michigan Media Resources Center, 1984.
An exhaustive listing of audiovisual resources prior to 1984. The listing is alphabetical, with a subject index in the front. The resources are rated by the editors for content, quality, violence and bias. Materials include films, videotapes, 35-millimeter slide shows, and filmstrips. The editors provide a listing of distributors, the dates of production, and the viewing times. This useful directory has not been updated since 1984, and unfortunately the Michigan Media Center has been dissolved.

Shaheen, Jack G., ed. *Nuclear War Films.* Carbondale: Southern Illinois University Press, 1978.
This compilation of twenty-five film reviews by twenty-one authors is divided into two categories: feature films, and documentaries or educational short films. Each review contains a plot summary and a critical appraisal of the film. Among the feature films are the following: *The Beginning or the End; Hiroshima, Mon Amor; On the Beach; Dr. Strangelove; Fail-Safe;* and *The Bedford Incident.* Documentaries include *The Decision to Drop the Bomb; Countdown to Zero; The War Game; Hiroshima: A Document of the Atomic Bombing;* and *Only the Strong.* A list of distributors and credits for each film are provided in the

appendix. A good source of information, giving the historical context and artistic evaluations of some important films about nuclear war.

TERMINATOR 2: Judgement Day. Dir.: James Cameron. Cast: Arnold Schwarzen-egger, Linda Hamilton, Robert Patrick, Joe Morton. 1991 Carolco (Tri-Star). Color. 135 min. R.
At the heart of this science-fiction thriller is a strong message against nuclear war. It is easy to get caught up in the action and special effects (which made this the most expensive motion picture ever produced up to that time). However, the motivation behind the characters the preservation of humanity and the prevention of Judgement Day—August 29, 1997. On that date, according to the plot, the computer which then controls all of the U.S. defense systems becomes self-aware and starts a nuclear war to destroy the humans which threaten it with shut-down. Sarah Connor's (Hamilton) dream depicts the destruction of Los Angeles. Like her, the audience is challenged to change the future and prevent Judgement Day.

Testament. Dir.: Lynne Littman. Cast: Jane Alexander, William Devane, Roxana Zal, Ross Harris, Lukas Haas, Philip Anglim, Lilia Skala, Leon Ames, Rebecca DeMornay, Mako, Lurene Tuttle, Kevin Costner. 1983 Paramount and American Playhouse. Color. 89 min. PG.
A touching and powerful portrayal of a how a family, spared the initial destruc-tion of an all-out nuclear war, might cope. The horror of nuclear war is brought out, not by direct horrific scenes, but by the slow deterioration of familiar things. Alexander gives a moving performance as a mother trying to keep her family together and their hopes up in spite of seemingly insurmountable difficulties and more and more deaths. Although sad, this film leaves one with a sense of human dignity, cooperation, and resourcefulness. Based on *The Last Testament* by Carol Amen. Highly recommended.

THEM! Dir.: Gordon Douglas. Cast: James Whitmore, Edmund Gwenn, Joan Weldon, James Arness, Onslow Stevens, Fess Parker. 1954 Warner Brothers. Black and white. 94 min. Not rated.
This well-respected science fiction film from the 1950's explores effects that radiation-induced mutations of ants might produce. Beginning near Alamogordo, New Mexico, it is discovered that the radiation from the first atomic bomb test has mutated ants to monstrous proportions. Seeking food, the ants have become carnivorous. Ultimately, the ants are destroyed in the sewers of Los Angeles. This film raises the awareness of the possible side effects caused by radiation and the use of nuclear weapons. Although not rated, this film contains little that would be considered objectionable and does discuss the habits of ants.

Threads. Dir.: Mick Jackson. Cast: Karen Meagher, Reece Dinsdale, David Brierley, Rita May, Paul Vaughan (narrator). 1984 BBC. Color. 110 min. Not rated.

This film is a serious attempt to portray the effects of nuclear war from the viewpoint of two families in Sheffield, England. Beginning a few months before the war, escalation of hostilities is all but unnoticed until it finally erupts into all-out war. Sheffield and its citizens are devastated in an attack that is realistically and horribly depicted. Of the two families at the center of the film, only one pregnant daughter survives. She gives birth to a daughter and they manage to survive the resulting hardships and nuclear winter for thirteen years. At the film's end, the daughter, who seems normal but uneducated, gives birth to a deformed child. Narration and captioning throughout indicate relevant points in this highly researched presentation. Highly recommended for the strong of heart, this film is part of the MacArthur Library and has been given to many libraries throughout the United States along with supplementary materials for classroom use.

Time Machine, The. Dir.: George Pal. Cast: Rod Taylor, Alan Young, Yvette Mimieux, Sebastian Cabot, Tom Helmore. 1960 MGM/UA. Color. 103 min. Not rated.

H. G. Wells explored the long-term results of global war in his story of a time traveler, and George Pal successfully adapted it to the screen. The traveler (Taylor) goes forward in time through nuclear wars that devastate the planet. Eventually, he emerges to find the earth inhabited by two types of people, the cannibalistic Morlocks and the cattlelike Eloi. The Morlocks are the descents of humanity that survived by living underground while the Eloi survived on the surface. Compare with *A Boy and His Dog*.

Triumph des Willens (Triumph of the Will). Dir.: Leni Riefenstahl. Documentary/Propaganda. 1935, 1975 Leni Riefenstahl Production (Embassy Home Entertainment). Black and white. 110 min. German with subtitles.

One of the most remarkable things about the construction of the first atomic bomb was that many of the men who built it were basically pacifists. For many of these men the fear of Hitler's Nazi Germany was the first and best reason for the construction of such a destructive and indiscriminate weapon. This documentary—actually a Nazi propaganda film—gives an unusual and chilling view of the organization and fanaticism that compelled these scientists in their efforts. Chronicling the Sixth National Socialists (Nazi) Party Congress in 1934, Riefenstahl puts the viewer at Hitler's elbow as he speaks at rallies and lets the viewer witness the total devotion of hundreds of thousands of people to Hitler's message and leadership. Although not directly linked to the atomic bomb, this is a contemporary record ("produced by order of the Fuehrer") of the political and social atmosphere in Germany before the outbreak of World War II—an atmosphere that compelled even Einstein to support bomb research.

Twilights's Last Gleaming. Dir.: Robert Aldrich. Cast: Burt Lancaster, Paul Winfield, Burt Young, William Smith, Charles Durning, Richard Widmark, Melvyn Douglas, Joseph Cotten. 1977 GERIA Film GMBH (Loriman-Bavaria). Color. 146 min. R.

An involving adventure story about a former Air Force General (Lancaster) who takes over a missile silo installation in Montana with the help of escaped convicts. The main purpose of the general's action is to force the disclosure of a document that outlines the futility of the Vietnam War and to establish a more open government. This film provides notable representations of Titan missile silos and command centers. The discussion among the president and his advisers concerning government policies involving nuclear weapons is interesting and could provide a beginning point for further discussion. Based on the novel *Viper Three* by Walter Wagner.

WarGames. Dir.: John Badham. Cast: Matthew Broderick, Dabney Coleman, John Wood, Ally Sheedy, Barry Corbin, Juanin Clay. 1983 MGM/UA. Color. 114 min. PG.

A strong antiwar message is contained in this entertaining adventure about a young computer hacker (Broderick) who nearly starts World War III by mistake. Broderick's character, David, begins to play "global thermonuclear war" with the War Operations Plan Response (WOPR) computer at the NORAD command headquarters in Cheyenne Mountain. David thinks he is trying out the latest offering from a computer game company, and WOPR, who thinks David is its creator, Dr. Falken, doesn't know the difference between reality and a game. In the final scenes, war is averted when WOPR finally learns that, regardless of strategy, no one wins a nuclear war. NORAD headquarters provides a notable backdrop for much of the action, and David's conversations with the despondent Falken (Wood) provide an interesting, if depressing, view of human fate.

Chapter 10
THE ATOMIC BOMB IN LITERATURE

Anderson, Kevin J., and Doug Beason. *The Trinity Paradox*. New York: Bantam Books, 1991.
This science fiction novel gives an alternative history of the Manhattan Project. During an anti-nuclear demonstration near Los Alamos, a young woman protestor is knocked unconscious and wakes up in 1943. She is hired to work on the bomb project under the supervision of mathematician John VonNeumann and physicist Richard Feynman. In one dramatic scene, she has the opportunity to change the course of history by shooting Oppenheimer, but she can not bring herself to pull the trigger. Some humorous contrasts in lifestyle since 1943 are noted, such as the lack of diet Cokes and the unacceptability for women to wear "dungarees" (jeans) to work. In this alternate version of history, the Trinity test explosion is sabotaged and the Germans bombard New York with radioactivity. An engrossing story.

Bartter, Martha A. *The Way to Ground Zero: The Atomic Bomb in American Science Fiction*. New York: Greenwood Press, 1988.
This review analyzes science fiction as a measure of the cultural climate and sociopolitical thinking, as affected by the atomic bomb. Part 1, "The Way to Hiroshima," deals with literature written before the atomic bomb. The author reveals "patterns that led us to create and use the atomic bomb." Part 2, "Circling Ground Zero," analyzes science fiction literature for its assumptions about human nature, individually and collectively, on which social and political systems are based. The final section, "Leaving Ground Zero," examines works which have created new societies based on different assumptions. An atomic bomb chronology and informative end notes for each chapter are provided. This book is a study about the interplay of technology, culture, and literature.

Blish, James. *The Day After Judgment*. Garden City, N.Y.: Doubleday, 1971.
A story of fantasy and bizarre imagination, giving a vision of the world after nuclear Armageddon. The devils of hell have erected a fortress named Dis in Death Valley, California. The Strategic Air Command in Colorado sends its remaining superweapons to attack the fortress, but the demons win. Satan himself has a meeting with four survivors: a priest who does white magic, a black magician, a weapons manufacturer, and his secretary. There seems to be a glimmer of hope because Satan admits that his power is limited, that evil can not exist apart from good. Allusions to the Book of Revelations and Dante's *Inferno* provide a context for the story.

Booth, Martin. *Hiroshima Joe*. Boston: Atlantic Monthly Press, 1985.
The story begins in Hong Kong in 1952, where Hiroshima Joe barely manages to survive by robbing hotel rooms, snatching a woman's purse, or smuggling opium. His past is gradually revealed through flashbacks. He was captured by Japanese troops in 1942. Scenes of bloody combat followed by inhumane cruelty in prisoner-of-war camps are depicted. At a prison camp near Hiroshima, Joe meets a Japanese laborer who speaks a little English. They enter the city together right after the bombing and both are overcome by the horrors of war. Eventually, Joe commits suicide, with the epithet on his grave: "He saw what no man should be made to see." A powerful antiwar novel.

Bradbury, Ray. *Twice Twenty-two*. Garden City, N.Y.: Doubleday, 1966.
A collection of short stories by an acknowledged master of science fiction, including a highly recommended story called "The Garbage Collector." The main character likes his work, picking up the trash and seeing how people live in different neighborhoods. One day he comes home and tells his wife that he is thinking of quitting his job. The garbage trucks have been assigned a new responsibility, to pick up the dead bodies in case of an atom bomb attack. In his simple way, the garbage collector cannot accept the idea of people as garbage. Effective protest literature, first published in 1951.

Brians, Paul. *Nuclear Holocausts: Atomic War in Fiction, 1895-1984*. Kent, Ohio: Kent State University Press, 1987.
An exhaustive survey of novels and short stories published before 1985 depicting nuclear war or its aftermath. The book contains more than 1,200 entries, with annotations describing the plot and context of each story. The author has written an informative introduction to give the reader a general overview. Since this compilation is limited to nuclear war, other kinds of fiction dealing with the Manhattan Project or Hiroshima survivors are not included. The appendix gives alphabetical listings by author, title, and subject, as well as a chronology telling which stories were published in each year since 1895. Clearly written, knowledgeable commentary; highly recommended for any library reference shelf.

Brinton, Henry. *Purple-6*. New York: Walker, 1962.
A Soviet missile approaches England, triggering off a purple alert that sends dozens of bombers with nuclear weapons flying toward Russia. The missile lands harmlessly and the planes are recalled, but some British leaders wonder if the Soviets were deliberately probing their defense system in preparation for a real strike. The fallen missile is found to contain a copy of a secret guidance system that had just been developed at the British military research center. The resulting espionage investigation forms the bulk of this novel, raising suspicions of disloyalty among scientific colleagues, longtime friends, and eventually between husband and wife. The growing lack of trust between people mirrors the break-

down of trust in international affairs. A well-written story, with good insight into the attitudes of scientists.

Buck, Pearl. *Command the Morning*. New York: John Day, 1959.
Pearl Buck won the Nobel Prize for Literature in 1938. The setting for this novel is the American atomic bomb project during World War II. The main character is a scientist whose marriage is severely strained because of his exclusive concentration on his work. A romantic interest develops between him and the only female scientist in this project. The background story includes appearances by actual historical figures such as Enrico Fermi, General Groves and a Hungarian refugee named Szigny (a pseudonym for Leo Szilard, no doubt). Conversations are used to reveal the qualms of scientists working on the atomic bomb, their last-minute attempts to prevent its use against Japan, and their shocked reaction to the massive destruction it caused.

Burdick, Eugene, and Harvey Wheeler. *Fail-Safe*. New York: McGraw-Hill, 1962.
A powerful novel showing how mechanical equipment failure could trigger a nuclear holocaust. The Positive Control Fail-Safe System malfunctions and orders six U.S. bombers to destroy Moscow with hydrogen bombs. The flight path of the planes is seen on radar screens by horrified observers at SAC headquarters in Omaha, at the Pentagon, in the president's underground shelter, and in Russia. Tension mounts as the president informs Premier Khrushchev that he cannot stop the destruction of Moscow. In order to avoid massive retaliation by Soviet nuclear missiles, the president offers to destroy New York City with hydrogen bombs, so Moscow and New York would be sacrificed to prevent total nuclear war. A frightening scenario with plausible technical details and realistic human reactions; highly recommended.

Caidin, Martin. *Operation Nuke*. New York: Arbor House, 1973.
An international organized crime group has acquired nuclear weapons. One of their hired jobs is to annihilate all the black nationalist leaders in Africa by exploding a small atom bomb during a meeting. Another job is to seize a jewelry shipment en route across the Atlantic, then make the ship disappear with a 20-kiloton blast. The superhero to stop these crimes is Steve Austin, a bionic man with artificial legs and arms that give him superhuman strength, and one eye socket that contains a tiny camera. The final showdown takes placed in Atlanta, where a hydrogen bomb is set to go off unless a ransom of $1 billion is paid. A wild adventure story, loosely based on the fear that criminals might obtain nuclear bombs.

Chevalier, Haakon. *The Man Who Would Be God*. New York: G. P. Putnam's Sons, 1959.
The author has a personal grievance against J. R. Oppenheimer, which was

described in another book, *Oppenheimer: The Story of a Friendship* (see chapter 2 of this bibliography). This historical novel focuses on the personality of Sebastian Bloch, a physicist at Berkeley who later becomes head of "Valhalla Laboratory." which develops an atom bomb. Bloch is portrayed as ambitious to the point of ruthlessness in personal relations with his scientific colleagues and family. During an interrogation by security officials looking for communist espionage, Bloch falsely accuses a close friend of a breach of security. There are interesting discussions about moral justification for the bomb project, objections to using the bomb against Japan, and the postwar controversy over building and testing ever-larger nuclear weapons.

Collins, Larry, and Dominique LaPierre. *The Fifth Horseman.* New York: Avon Books, 1980.
The villain of this story is Muammar Qaddafi of Libya, whose agents have secretly brought a hydrogen bomb into New York City. The president receives an ultimatum that the bomb is set to go off in three days unless Israel immediately returns its illegally occupied territories to the Palestinians. A 3-megaton demonstration explosion in the southern Libyan desert is preannounced and detonated as a warning that the threat is real. Several dramatic subplots are interwoven: how the Libyans got the bomb materials and design; an Israeli cabinet meeting; the useless and naïve civil defense preparations for evacuation of Manhattan; the search for the hidden bomb; the personal lives of three Palestinian terrorists. Combines fact and fiction in a climactic narrative; highly recommended.

Coppel, Alfred. *The Hastings Conspiracy.* New York: Holt, Rinehart and Winston, 1980.
Nuclear strategists in the Soviet Union, using computer simulations, have concluded that they cannot win a conflict in central Europe as long as NATO exists. They have a chance to destroy NATO when a CIA employee defects to the Soviet Union, bringing a copy of the ultrasecret "Hastings" plan with him. Hastings envisions a far-out contingency: The British pursue a neutralist policy and the United States responds by invading Great Britain. The KGB targets the British prime minister to be assassinated, using a hired killer who is none other than the prime minister's illegitimate son. A highly implausible plot, with scenes of violence, deviant sex, drugged confessions, and suicide.

Crosby, John. *Dear Judgment.* New York: Stein & Day, 1978.
The Mafia has stolen two F-22 Air Force fighter planes and is prepared to sell them to the highest bidder. Three potential customers are a foreign government, a reclusive billionaire (modeled after Howard Hughes), and the U.S. Air Force. Central characters in the story are a young lawyer and his recently married wife who are carrying the $10 million payoff money aboard a yacht in the Florida

keys. Gun battles, a hurricane, torture, and mob executions form the action. The final shootout takes place in a warehouse where the planes are hidden in packing crates. A far-fetched scenario of weapons theft, but it does raise questions about safeguards for nuclear bombs.

Drury, Allen. *The Hill of Summer: A Novel of the Soviet Conquest*. New York: Pinnacle Books, 1981.
A story of impending communist world domination, written by the author of an earlier bestseller, *Advise and Consent*. The Soviet premier is portrayed as a ruthless, deceitful, evil man, totally committed to the victory of communism. America is losing its influence in Africa, Latin America, and the Near East because of military weakness. The Soviets start large-scale troop maneuvers, including missile-carrying submarines sent to Cuba, all in the name of "preserving world peace." The embattled American president declares a national emergency but he has few supporters. United Nations representatives, NATO allies, and the American press are naïvely taken in by communist propaganda. The novel is a polemic calling on America to wake up and get tough before it is too late.

Elliot, George P. *David Knudsen*. New York: Random House, 1962.
The main character's father was one of the physicists who developed the atomic bomb. In the form of an autobiographical narrative, the son tells his story. He is drafted into the Army and becomes exposed to radioactive fallout from a bomb test in the Pacific. His Army buddy dies from the aftereffects of radiation sickness. The son's wife becomes pregnant and he is overcome with fear that the baby will be deformed, so he insists on an abortion. This traumatic event brings about the disintegration of his marriage and a mental breakdown. The embittered son writes to his father that the bomb was the "outcome of a copulation" between politics and physics. The author portrays the tragic effect of the bomb on personal lives.

Frank, Pat. *Alas, Babylon*. Philadelphia: J. P. Lippincott, 1959.
The title is a quotation from the Bible, when Babylon, a city of wickedness, was destroyed. The first several chapters of this story describe growing Soviet-U.S. military confrontations, culminating in nuclear war. Within one day, all major cities are annihilated. The effect of the war on survivors in a small town in Florida is effectively presented. Food supplies are hoarded, looters break into stores, electric power is gone (no cooking, refrigeration, or sanitation), fires break out with no water pressure to extinguish them, people need guns to protect their homes from marauders, and drug addicts attack the local doctor to seize his medical supplies. A grim depiction of lawlessness and human isolation as tragic aftermaths of the war. Worthwhile reading.

_____. *Mr. Adam*. Philadelphia: J. B. Lippincott, 1946.

A genuinely funny story in which all males in the world have become sterile except for one man, Homer Adam. He happened to be inspecting a lead mine in Colorado and was therefore shielded from the radiation that sterilized everybody else when a nuclear laboratory exploded. After his wife becomes pregnant, Mr. Adam gains sudden fame as a vital national resource because his sperm can be used for artificial insemination. A Congressman points out international implications, that keeping the sperm in America would wipe out communism in one generation. Another one wants to keep the sperm for whites only. A national lottery is set up, with numbers being drawn to determine which women will become mothers. Imaginative fiction, with a happy ending.

George, Peter. *Commander-1*. New York: Delacorte Press, 1965.

Communist China seeks to rule the world by deliberately triggering off a nuclear holocaust in which the Soviet Union and the United States will destroy each other. The plan succeeds, but China is also annihilated when both Soviet and U.S. bombs hit their country. The main action involves an American submarine that was submerged during the war. The captain decides to set up a new world order with himself as the commander. An island called Safe Base One has enough supplies stored for future use. Citizens are injected with a hypnotic drug and are indoctrinated as slaves. A somewhat disjointed narrative, which however focuses attention on the hazards of a military defense system that is always poised for immediate retaliation. Peter George coauthored the *Dr. Strangelove* story.

_____. *Dr. Strangelove: Or, How I Learned To Stop Worrying and Love the Bomb*. New York: Bantam Books, 1964.

In 1958, Peter George published a story entitled *Red Alert*, which was adapted as a script for the Dr. Strangelove movie by Stanley Kubrick and Terry Southern. The present version was rewritten from the screenplay by the original author. The story is a satire on the policy of mutually assured destruction (MAD) when human folly intervenes. General Jack D. Ripper launches an unauthorized preemptive nuclear strike against the Soviet Union. The Soviets, however, have a Doomsday Machine that will retaliate automatically against an attack, so the president desperately tries to recall the bombers. Unfortunately, one plane has lost radio contact and continues toward its target. Dr. Strangelove is the archetype mad scientist with a "strange love" for power and destruction. An effective, absurd comedy; highly recommended.

Gray, Anthony. *The Penetrators*. New York: G. P. Putnam's Sons, 1965.

In the 1960's, the United States was planning to phase out its bombers because they would presumably be obsolete in the missile age. In this story, a British liaison officer stationed in Omaha wrote an article strongly opposing this policy. He argued that the Soviets could launch a conventional air attack but the United

States would not dare to retaliate with missiles, because that would bring on nuclear annihilation. He presents his views at the Pentagon and to a Congressional committee, but the response is negative. Finally, he requisitions some British bombers to cross the Atlantic and makes a mock attack on Washington, to dramatize the weakness of U.S. air defenses. The case for maintaining and modernizing Air Force bombers is presented here in effective fictional form.

Hackett, General Sir John. *The Third World War: The Untold Story*. New York: MacMillan, 1982.
An imaginary scenario describing how a Soviet-U.S. war might be fought in the 1980's, written for a popular audience. The confrontation between NATO and Warsaw Pact forces starts in Germany. Battles involving ground troops, tanks, planes, submarines, and even earth satellites are described in great detail. Hypothetical political developments in the Middle East, Central America, the Far East, and elsewhere are discussed as part of the overall world conflict. Eventually, the Russian city of Minsk is destroyed by nuclear bombs, and the Soviet leaders give up without launching a nuclear counterattack. The book is an extended propaganda piece arguing in favor of a large military budget for conventional weapons, the assumption being that nuclear weapons would not play a major role in World War III.

Haldeman, Joe, ed. *Study War No More: A Selection of Alternatives*. New York: St. Martin's Press, 1977.
A collection of ten short stories by different authors, all on the general theme of the horrors of modern warfare. The editor provides an introduction and reprints one of his own stories, "To Howard Hughes, A Modest Proposal." A reclusive billionaire, living on an island off the coast of Florida, acquires enough plutonium to construct twenty-nine small atomic bombs. The bombs are hidden in all the major cities, set to go off within three days unless world leaders agree to give up their nuclear weapons. "Project Blackmail," as it is called, succeeds after one bomb is exploded as a warning. A rare example of a story with a happy ending.

Hardy, Ronald. *The Face of Jalanath*. New York: G. P. Putnam's Sons, 1973.
A mountaineering adventure story, set in the Himalayan Mountains between India and China. Six experienced climbers are brought to India to carry out a daring plan. They will try to destroy China's main nuclear weapons laboratory just across the border by attaching three hydrogen bombs to the face of Mt. Jalanath, which will start a huge rock slide and flood when the bombs are exploded. Each of the mountaineers has a personal grievance that is revealed through conversation and flashbacks. A well-written story that explores the contrasting personalities and viewpoints about this mission, with an ironic surprise ending.

Harris, Leonard. *The Masada Plan*. New York: Popular Library, 1976.
A war of annihilation against Israel has started with a coordinated attack by the neighboring Arab nations. The Israeli cabinet meets in emergency session and activates the "Masada Plan" as a last resort for survival. Masada was a historic battlefield in the year A.D. 73, when Jewish defenders committed mass suicide rather than surrendering to overwhelming Roman troops. The modern Masada plan involves nuclear bombs that have been set to destroy the world's major cities unless the Soviet Union and the United States together can convince the Arabs to halt their attack on Israel. A television newswoman in New York and her lover, the Israeli ambassador to the United Nations, are the main protagonists. Well-written suspense story with a plausible scenario.

Heinlein, Robert. "Solution Unsatisfactory," in *The Best of Science Fiction*, edited by Groff Conklin. New York: Crown, 1946.
Received high praise from Isaac Asimov as one of the most remarkable science fiction stories every written. First published in 1941, before the Manhattan Project was started, the story anticipated the creation of an atomic bomb, with radioactive dust (fallout) capable of killing all life over a large area. The bomb is used to end the war and then to impose world peace under a military dictatorship. Not only did the author accurately foresee the technological development of nuclear weapons, but he also predicted the unsatisfactory consequences of maintaining a fragile peace based on the fear of mutual annihilation.

Hoban, Russell. *Ridley Walker*. New York: Summit Books, 1980.
This story presumably takes place long after civilization was destroyed by nuclear war, depicting a very primitive kind of tribal society. Making a fire and hunting for food are vital skills for survival. The author has created a special phonetic language that is not easy to read. For example, a wild dog is described as follows: "Him what lookit like Death on 4 legs with his yeller eyes what dint even care if he livet or dyd." Ridley Walker, the main character, displays curiosity about his locality and kindness toward others, but his understanding of the world is very crude, perhaps like in medieval England.

Ibuse, Masuji. *Black Rain*. Translated by John Bester. Tokyo: Kodansha International, 1969.
The author, a native of Hiroshima, had already received public recognition before World War II for his writing excellence. This book has been called a "documentary novel" and describes the destructive effects of the atomic bomb. The stories of individual people are told with a delicate interweaving of horror and occasional humor. The black rain refers to the shower of dust that fell from the mushroom cloud, bringing radiation sickness to many. The overwhelmed medical facilities, the limited food supplies, the rumors about more

bombs—everything is described with an understatement of emotion. The grim events become comprehensible to the reader through this collection of human vignettes about survivors.

Jones, Dennis. *Barbarossa Red*. Boston, Mass.: Little, Brown, 1985.
A U.S.-Soviet arms limitation treaty calling for removal of nuclear weapons from central Europe is hailed as a great step toward peace. The chancellor of Germany strongly opposes the treaty because it would leave his country exposed to overwhelming Soviet conventional forces. When Soviet tanks cross the border into West Germany, the American president has to face an awesome decision whether to respond with nuclear weapons, risking escalation toward all-out war. Soviet infiltration at the highest level of the German government is part of a plot to surrender the country to the Russians. An action-packed story with well-drawn characters, representing plausible attitudes about military and political issues in Europe during the 1980's.

——————————. *Rubicon One*. New York: Beaufort Books, 1983.
A power struggle within the Soviet leadership between the Army and the KGB results in a military extremist seizing control. Meanwhile, Libya and Syria have acquired nuclear weapons, and an attack on Israel is imminent. Rubicon-One, the U.S. supercomputer that analyzes all available intelligence data, predicts all-out nuclear war. Since the time of Julius Caesar, to "cross the Rubicon" has meant that the point of no return has been passed. The only hope to avoid a holocaust is an unlikely plan in which the KGB and U.S. counterintelligence cooperate to oust the aggressive Soviet premier. The story of espionage, torture, and air battles with nuclear missiles leads to a dramatic climax.

——————————. *Russian Spring*. New York: Beaufort Books, 1984.
A young Russian Army officer stationed with the occupation troops in Afghanistan is shocked by the cruel slaughter of Afghan rebels and civilians. When he learns that the Army plans to use poison gas, he warns the rebels and informs an American intelligence officer. Meanwhile, in Moscow, the uncle of the officer has become the new premier. He wants to end the occupation of Afghanistan and allow more freedom of expression, against the vehement opposition of the head of the KGB. Civil war erupts as loyal Army units seize Leningrad. There is a battle for control of a nuclear weapons facility. The author shows remarkable insight into the power struggle between the Army, the KGB, and the Communist party. Good character development, highly recommended.

Kirst, Hans Hellmut. *The Seventh Day*. Translated from German by Richard Graves. Garden City, N.Y.: Doubleday, 1959.
The seven days of creation as described in the Bible happen in reverse here as humanity liquidates itself by nuclear war. An uprising by students and workers

in Poland against Soviet occupation forces triggers similar events in East Germany. Diplomatic tension quickly rises as U.S. and Soviet leaders make mutual accusations of aggression. By the fourth day, ground troops have been deployed and strategic forces (bombers and missiles) are on high alert. On the fifth day, atomic explosions kill several million people and all-out war ensues. There is no seventh day. The author tells a story of tragic individual lives and failed diplomatic maneuvering, all caught in a hopeless, overwhelming catastrophe.

Kornbluth, Cyril M. *Not This August*. Garden City, N.Y.: Doubleday, 1955.
Russian and Chinese Communist armies have invaded the United States and forced it to surrender. The president is executed, and occupation forces have set up a police state. The hero of this story is a dairy farmer in New England. He tries to organize an insurrection, but some neighbors are informers for the Communist overlords. One brutal scene describes the mass execution of townspeople in a football stadium, to make an example for others who may be disloyal. Finally, the good guys launch an earth satellite carrying hydrogen bombs that threaten to blow up Moscow and Peking unless the Communists withdraw. The attitude that Russians are barbarians and that superior technology can save us is presented here in a simplistic, comic-book version of good versus evil.

Kuttner, Henry. [Padgett, Lewis, pseudonym]. *Mutant*. New York: Gnome Press, 1953.
Through mutation, some people in this story are born with the power of mental telepathy. They are "Baldies," but they always wear wigs so people will not know who they are. Unfortunately, there is a group of evil telepaths who want to use their special power of mindreading to rule over the world. The good telepaths try to stop them, but the selfish ones seem to be winning the battle. Finally, a machine is invented that will make it possible for everyone to learn mental telepathy, thus taking away the advantage from the ones who abused it. A symbolic representation of how a superior force can be used for good or evil.

Lanham, Edwin. *The Clock at 8:16*. Garden City, N.Y.: Doubleday, 1970.
A compassionate love story between an American soldier on a one-week leave from Vietnam and a young woman from a traditional family in Japan. The year is 1965, twenty years after the bomb exploded over Hiroshima at 8:16 in the morning. The woman has written down her childhood memories of the great suffering from that event and eventually she allows the American to read them. In response, the soldier gradually reveals his intense opposition to the fighting in Vietnam. Contrasts between Japanese and Western customs of courtship and family relationships have to be overcome by the couple. Sensitive writing, with a delicate mixture of tragedy and joy.

Lenz, Millicent. *Nuclear Age Literature for Youth: The Quest for a Life-affirming Ethic.* Chicago: American Library Association, 1990.
A helpful guide for teachers, librarians, and parents who are concerned about selecting appropriate literature with a nuclear theme for young people through college age. The author provides a critical assessment of books, both fiction and nonfiction, categorized under nine major themes. Some chapter titles and examples are as follows: "Voices from Hiroshima and Nagasaki" (*Death in Life*, by Robert Lifton); "Scenarios of Endtime" (*On the Beach*); "Survivors in Atomized Eden" (*Alas, Babylon*, by Pat Frank); "The Peace Pilgrim" (*Protest and Survive*, by E.P. Thompson); "A Life-Affirming Ethic" (*Nuclear Fear: A History of Images*, by Spencer Weart). An extensive bibliography of primary and secondary sources, listing more than five hundred titles, is given in the appendix. Informative commentary on a wide selection of writings.

Lewin, Leonard C. *Report from Iron Mountain: On the Possibility and Desirability of Peace.* New York: Dial Press, 1967.
A humorous parody about an elite group of strategic governmental advisors, written in the style of Herman Kahn's *Thinking About the Unthinkable.* The unthinkable contingency to be considered here is the possibility of world peace. A fictional committee is assembled at Iron Mountain, a bombproof retreat center. Their final report concludes that the abolition of war would cause enormous changes that would undermine social stability. War production has been a vital necessity to stimulate the economy. Furthermore, maintaining political power depends on opposing a clearly defined external military threat. Also, an army provides an outlet for antisocial, aggressive elements and can be used to control a hostile minority. Weapons research gives opportunities for scientific creativity. Subtle allusions to current events; delightful reading.

Mason, Colin. *Hostage.* New York: Walker, 1973.
An Israeli general is assassinated and a fanatical military group in Israel seeks revenge against the Arabs. They seize several poorly guarded American nuclear bombs, transport them to Cairo by ship, and destroy the city. In the ensuing international crisis, the Soviet Union demands that the state of Israel must be dismantled immediately and the land given back to the Arabs. Sydney, Australia, comparable in size to Cairo, becomes a designated hostage city, which will be annihilated by the Soviets unless their demand is met. A Soviet submarine is prepared to fire on Sidney. The narrative is set against a credible background that describes radiation victims in Cairo, the intense emotions of the Arab-Israeli conflict, panic in Sydney, and human tension aboard the nuclear submarine.

Masters, Dexter. *The Accident.* New York: Alfred A. Knopf, 1955.
This novel is based on a real incident in 1946 at Los Alamos, New Mexico. A scientist named Louis Slotin was accidentally exposed to a lethal dose of radioac-

tivity while working on a bomb assembly experiment. This fictional story takes place during the days of radiation sickness following the accident. The various reactions of medical personnel, other scientists, an Army colonel, a Congressman, the victim's parents, and his girlfriend are explored through conversations. The morality of scientists working on nuclear weapons, the bomb tests at Bikini, and the controversy about developing a hydrogen bomb are discussed. The author dedicates this book "to the memory of Louis Slotin and more than one hundred thousand others," that is, the victims at Hiroshima and Nagasaki.

McMahon, Thomas. *Principles of American Nuclear Chemistry: A Novel.* Boston: Little, Brown, 1970.
The title makes it sound like a textbook, but this is really a story about the Los Alamos Laboratory, as seen through the eyes of a teenage boy whose father is a physicist. The boy's parents have just separated and the father arrives at Los Alamos with his son and a mistress. Symbolically, the author seems to suggest that the bomb project had a seductive attraction for the scientists, like a demanding mistress. The boy grows more resentful toward his father and has erotic fantasies. The director of the laboratory is portrayed as an Oppenheimer-like father figure. When the war ends, the mistress goes off with someone else, the parents are reunited, and the son tries to heal his psychological scars.

Merril, Judith. *Shadow on the Hearth.* Garden City, N.Y.: Doubleday, 1950.
Events are viewed through the eyes of a typical housewife. Her husband commutes to New York City and she has three children, a son in college, a daughter in high school, and a two-year-old at home. Nuclear disaster causes destruction in the city and lawlessness in the suburbs. The mother suddenly is forced to deal with unprecedented problems of radiation sickness and news broadcasts that are lies. Her whole social pattern is challenged as she becomes involved in helping a teacher and a physician who had opposed nuclear weapons production. Her small child sleeps with a favorite toy horse, but it is a Trojan horse, polluted with radiation. She asks, "Isn't anything safe?"

Miller, Walter M. *Canticle for Leibowitz.* Philadelphia: J. B. Lippincott, 1960.
One of the classics of postholocaust literature. Part 1 takes place some six hundred years after a nuclear war. A novice at a monastery accidentally finds an ancient fallout shelter, recovers some artifacts, and adds them to the memorabilia at the abbey. Society is in the Dark Ages. Part 2 is several centuries later, when a renaissance of learning has started, with the abbey acting as a sanctuary from local warloads. Part 3 is another leap through time into a world of modern technology. A nuclear war has started and the abbey is being evacuated by means of a spaceship departing for the stars. A depressing story, skillfully written.

Morris, Edita. *The Flowers of Hiroshima*. New York: Viking Press, 1959.
A young American goes to Hiroshima on business and becomes a lodger with a Japanese family. The host family has the Japanese cultural trait of displaying a facade of happiness to outsiders, even though they are suffering inside as atom bomb survivors. Gradually, the visitor becomes aware of the tragic legacy of the bomb: people with scarred skin who cannot go to public baths; a man who always wears a cap because his ears were burned off; the young woman who is rejected for marriage because she may bear deformed children. The symbolism of flowers set afloat to drift down the river is sensitively explained by the author. This well-written story creates a deeper awareness of how the bomb continues to affect the private lives of survivors.

Pollard, Ernest C. *The Cataclysm*. Lemont, Penn.: Woodburn Press, 1988.
The author was a biophysicist with a life-long concern about issues relating to science and society, especially the nuclear arms race. In this novel, a group of fundamentalist religious fanatics in New Mexico steal the components for a single 1-megaton hydrogen bomb. They believe that it is their God-given duty to eradicate New York City because of its sinfulness. Using a small private plane to carry the bomb, they destroy the city in a suicide mission. Three million people are killed, three million more burned and injured, while panic spreads to other cities. The disastrous consequences eventually cause a cataclysm of political changes, including the drastic reduction of the U.S. nuclear stockpile down to ten bombs. This story gives a dramatic warning mixed with hope.

Prochnau, William. *Trinity's Child*. New York: G. P. Putnam's Sons, 1983.
The Soviets launch a BOOB ("Bolt Out Of the Blue") preemptive nuclear attack against selected military targets in the United States. The Soviet premier warns the American president not to retaliate, because U.S. cities would then become the next targets. When the president's helicopter crashes, confusion develops about who is in charge. A major theme of this story is the danger of destroying the enemy's command and control structure, because no one in authority is available to end the fighting. An all-out holocaust is narrowly averted when crew members of a B-52 bomber headed for Russia disobey their orders to attack. The author writes authoritatively about military strategy and weapons technology. A frightening portrayal of the chaos in communication and leadership once a war has started.

Rascovich, Mark. *The Bedford Incident*. New York: Atheneum, 1963.
The destroyer-escort USS *Bedford* is on patrol searching for Russian submarine activity in the Arctic Ocean. An American journalist is on board, with camera and tape recorder, to document everyday activities of the crew. The ship's commanding officer is eager to engage in pursuit when an enemy sub is discovered off the coast of Greenland. The chase and ensuing battle make an exciting

adventure story. The personality of the captain is compared to Ahab chasing Moby-Dick. In the background is the fear that the maneuverings of these two ships could quickly escalate into full-fledged nuclear war. The author is clearly knowledgeable about the technology of naval warfare and the tense situation aboard ship during a sea battle.

Shute, Nevil. *On the Beach*. New York: William Morrow, 1957.
The setting for this story is Australia in 1963, two years after a devastating nuclear war in the Northern hemisphere. It is not clear who started the war, in which all major cities were destroyed within a few days and radioactive fallout killed everyone else. A nuclear submarine goes on a reconnaissance mission from Australia to the U.S. West Coast but finds no survivors. Eventually, the radioactivity is spread to the Southern hemisphere by atmospheric circulation. Suicide pills are distributed to people when radiation sickness strikes and death is inevitable. A highly dramatic and widely read novel, leaving no shred of hope for escape from the spreading radiation. (See Films listing.)

Simpson, George E., and Neal R. Burger. *Fair Warning*. New York: Delacorte Press, 1980.
It is the summer of 1945. Germany has surrendered to the Allies, and the invasion of Japan is imminent. If the atomic test in New Mexico is successful, President Truman intends to use the bomb to end the war quickly. In this story, a team of U.S. scientists is assembled in great secrecy to warn the Japanese of their impending annihilation by showing them photographs of the test explosion. The Soviets infiltrate the secret mission and try to stop it, because Stalin does not want Japan to surrender solely to the United States. The presentation of real, historical events is overshadowed by the authors' fictional depiction of brutal murders, sexual liaisons, and a final manhunt on the coast of Japan.

Snow, C. P. *The New Men*. New York: Charles Scribner's Sons, 1955.
The author was a notable British novelist whose essay on the cultural gap between scientific and literary education received wide publicity. In this World War II story, two brothers play key roles; one is a physicist and the other one a government official in London. When a uranium chain reaction experiment is set up, the tension of the scientists hoping for its success is dramatically described. Two people develop radiation sickness as a result of an accidental overexposure. One physicist goes to America and later turns out to have been a Soviet spy. The scientists are shocked when they hear that the atomic bomb was used at Hiroshima without any warning. A mixture of historical fact and fiction is used to explore conflicting viewpoints about the bomb project from a British perspective.

Szilard, Leo. *The Voice of the Dolphins and Other Stories*. New York: Simon & Schuster, 1961.

Humorous political satire about the U.S.-Soviet arms race, written by the well-known physicist who had tried to mobilize scientists from the Manhattan Project against using the bomb in Japan. In this imaginative story, biologists at a research institute in Austria learn to communicate with five dolphins. The dolphins make remarkable progress in understanding modern technology and human nature. Eventually, the dolphins become involved with political issues. Their solution to an escalating international crisis is to designate a list of twelve U.S. and Soviet cities, of which one on each side would be annihilated after allowing time for evacuation. Lobbyists for the twelve cities soon force the politicians to settle the supposedly insoluble crisis. Sophisticated insights in fictional form; enjoyable reading.

Terman, Douglas. *First Strike*. New York: Charles Scribner's Sons, 1978.

A story of espionage and intrigue, in which the Soviet KGB has devised an elaborate scheme to promote the election of a U.S. president who would carry out a policy of unilateral disarmament. A nuclear bomb is to be detonated in Seattle harbor just when a U.S. submarine is coming into port. If people believed that one of the sub's own missiles had exploded accidentally, a national outcry against nuclear weapons would result. After the United States disarms itself, the Soviets would rule the world. The plot is gradually uncovered and eventually foiled by a Vietnam veteran and his girlfriend. A clearly delineated battle between good and evil, with some exciting escapades to maintain interest.

_____. *Free Flight*. New York: Charles Scribner's Sons, 1980.

A seven-hour nuclear war has devastated the world, leaving as survivors only those who were in underground shelters or in remote rural areas. A rigidly controlled police state now keeps order. People have to spy on their neighbors in order to accumulate points for obtaining food, clothing, and medicine. The principal character is a man who survived the war in a cabin in Vermont. The authorities hunt him down with armed helicopters while he and a friend try to escape to Canada. It is an adventure story of two men against an evil and authoritarian regime, reminiscent of the "better dead than Red" anticommunist hysteria of the 1950's.

_____. *Shell Game*. New York: Poseidon Press, 1985.

The setting for this novel is Cuba during the autumn of 1962, when the Soviets were secretly installing nuclear missiles that could be launched against targets in the United States. Two half-brothers who were comrades in the Cuban revolution against Battista have now become enemies. One brother is Castro's top intelligence man and a double agent for the Soviet KGB. The other one is on a mission to Cuba for the CIA to gather information about the missile installations. The KGB plan is nothing less than to make an overwhelming first strike against the United States. The story features intrigue and betrayal, violence and sex. In the final showdown, the missile base is destroyed by sabotage, but the Soviets start rebuilding.

THE ATOMIC BOMB

INDEX

Ackland, Len, and Steven McGuire, eds. 63
Adams, Ruth, and Susan Cullen, eds. 111
After the Fall of New York 128
Ahrens, John, Ellen Frankel Paul, Fred D.
  Miller, Jr., Jeffrey Paul, eds. 99
Aizenstat, A. J. 111
Akira Kurosawa's Dreams 128
Alas, Babylon 152
Aldridge, Robert C. 63
Allardice, Corbin, and Edward R. Trapnell 55
Allison, Graham T., Albert Carnesale, and
  Joseph S. Nye, Jr., eds. 64
Allison, Graham T., Joseph S. Nye, and Albert
  Carnesale, eds. 98
Alperovitz, Gar 64
Alsop, Joseph, and Stewart Alsop 14
Alsop, Stewart, and Joseph Alsop 14
Amazing Grace and Chuck 128
*American Masters: "Einstein—The World as I
  See It."* 128
Amrine, Michael 34
Anders, Günther 35
Anderson, David L., and Hans G. Graetzer 10
Anderson, Kevin J., and Doug Beason 142
Anderson, Oscar E., Jr., and Richard G.
  Hewlett 26
Arbatov, George 76
Arkin, William M., Milton M. Hoenig, and
  Thomas B. Cochran 73
Arkin, William M., Robert S. Norris, Jeffrey I.
  Sands, and Thomas B. Cochran 74
Arnow, Saul, Frank R. Ervin, and Victor W.
  Sidel, eds. 111
Aron, Raymond 42
Atomic Cafe 129
Atomic Energy Commission (AEC) 55-57, 72,
  82, 86
Avogadro, Amadeo 15

Bader, William B. 42
Bailey, Charles W., and Fletcher Knebel 27
Baker, Paul R., ed. 34
Ball, Desmond 64
Ball, Howard 55
Bar-Joseph, Uri, Amos Perlmutter, and Michael
  Handel 51
Barash, David P. 65
Barash, David P., and Judith Eve Lipton 112
Barnaby, Frank, and Ronald Huiskens 65
Bartter, Martha A. 142
Baruch Plan, the 67, 102
Baylis, John, Gerald Segal, Edwina Moreton,

and Lawrence Freedman 105
Beason, Doug, and Kevin J. Anderson 142
Beaton, Leonard 42
Becquerel, Antoine-Henri 1, 15
Bedford Incident, The 138
Beginning or the End, The 138
Beilenson, Laurence W. 65
Bennett, John C., ed. 112
Beres, Louis René 66, 75
Berlin blockade, the 66, 101
Bernstein, Barton J., ed. 34
Bernstein, Jeremy 14
Bethe, Hans 14, 15, 28, 66, 120
Betts, Richard K. 66
Beyerchen, Alan D. 43
Bhatia, Shyam 43
Bidwell, Shelford, ed. 66
Bigelow, Albert 113
Blackett, Patrick M. S. 67
Blish, James 142
Blow, Michael 25
Blumberg, Stanley A., and Louis G. Panos 14
Bohr, Niels 10, 15, 20, 21, 120
Boorse, Henry A., Lloyd Motz and Jefferson H.
  Weaver 15
Booth, Martin 143
Born, Max 84
Boskey, Bennett, and Mason Willrich, eds. 43
Boston Study Group 67
Boy and His Dog, A 129
Boyer, Paul 67
Bradbury, Ray 143
Bradley, David 55
Brembeck, Howard S. 112
Brians, Paul 143
Brinton, Henry 143
Brodie, Bernard 68
Brown, Allen, and Edward Teller 61
Brown, Anthony Cave, ed. 68
Brown, Anthony Cave, and Charles B.
  MacDonald, eds. 25
Brown, Neville 69
Brown, Thomas A., Gregory Jones, David C.
  McGarvey, Henry Rowen, Vince Taylor,
  Roberta Wohlstetter, and Albert Wohlstetter
  109
Brues, Austin M., ed. 56
Buchan, Alastair, ed. 43
Buck, Pearl 144
Burdick, Eugene, and Harvey Wheeler 144
Burger, Neal R., and George E. Simpson 155
Burns, E. L. M. 69

161

Burns, Grant 9
By Dawn's Early Light 130
Byers, R. R., ed. 69

Cahn, Anne C., Bernard T. Feld, Kosta Tsipis, eds. 107
Caidin, Martin 144
Calder, Nigel 70
Calder, Ritchie 9
Caldicott, Helen 111, 113
Campbell, Christopher 70
Campbell, John W. 9
Cantelon, Philip, Richard G. Hewlett, and Robert C. Williams, eds. 10
Carlton, David, and Carlo Schaerf, eds. 70
Carlton, David, and Herbert M. Levine, eds. 70
Carnesale, Albert, Graham T. Allison, and Joseph S. Nye, Jr., eds. 64, 98
Carnesale, Albert, Paul Doty, Stanley Hoffmann, Samuel P. Huntington, Joseph S. Nye, Jr., and Scott D. Sagan 71
Chalfont, Alun 71
Chayes, Antonia H., and Paul Doty, eds. 71
Chelyabinsk 137
Chernobyl 4, 12
Chernoff, Fred, and Bruce Russett, eds. 102
Chevalier, Haakon 15, 144
Childs, Herbert 15
Chinnock, Frank W. 34
Church, Peggy Pond 25
Cimbala, Stephen J. 72
City of Corpses 39
Clarfield, Gerard H., and William M. Wiecek 72
Clark, Ian 72
Clark, Ronald W. 73
Coale, Ansley J. 73
Cochran, Thomas B., William M. Arkin, and Milton M. Hoenig 73
Cochran, Thomas B., William M. Arkin, Robert S. Norris, and Jefrey I. Sands 74
Codevilla, Angelo 74
Cohen, Avner, and Steven Lee, eds. 74
Collins, Larry, and Dominique LaPierre 145
Compton, Arthur H. 26
Cook, Fred J. 75
Coppel, Alfred 145
Cottrell, Leonard S., and Sylvia Eberhart 75
Countdown to Zero 138
Cousins, Norman 114
Cox, Arthur Macy 75
Cox, Donald W. 114
Cox, John 115
Craig, Paul P., and John A. Jungerman 76

Craig, William 35
Crosby, John 145
Cuban Missile Crisis, the 66, 90, 101
Cullen, Susan, and Ruth Adams, eds. 111
Cunningham, Ann Marie, and Mariana Fitzpatrick 76
Curie, Irene 10
Curie, Marie 1, 11, 15

Dahl, Robert 76
Dalton, John 15
Daniel 130
Davis, Nuell Pharr 15
Day After Trinity, The 130, 133
Day the Earth Stood Still, The 131
Day, Samuel H., ed. 115
. . DEADLINE 131
Death in Life 152
Decision to Drop the Bomb, The 138
Dellums, Ronald V., with R. H. (Max) Miller, H. Lee Halterman, and Patrick O'Heffernam, eds. 115
Dr. Strangelove 131, 138
Dolan, Philip J., and Samuel Glasstone, eds. 11
Dotto, Lydia 77
Doty, Paul, and Antonia H. Chayes, eds. 71
Doty, Paul, Stanley Hoffmann, Samuel P. Huntington, Joseph S. Nye, Jr., Scott D. Sagan, and Albert Carnesale 71
Douglass, Joseph D., and Amoretta M. Hoeber 77
Dowling, John, and Karen Sayer, eds. 138
Drell, Sidney, et al. 16
Drinan, Robert F. 116
Drury, Allen 146
Duncan, Francis, and Richard G. Hewlett 86
Dunn, Lewis A. 44
Dworkin, Gerald, Robert E. Goodwin, Russell Hardin, John J. Mearsheimer, eds. 85
Dyson, Freeman 77

Eatherly, Claude 35, 37
Eberhart, Sylvia, and Leonard S. Cottrell 75
Ehrlich, Paul and Anne Ehrlich 74
Ehrlich, Paul, Carl Sagan, Donald Kennedy, and Walter Orr Roberts 78
Einstein, Albert 15, 16, 22, 84, 120, 122, 128, 137
Elephant Parts 132
Elliot, George P. 146
Ellsberg, Daniel 117
Enola Gay 41
Enola Gay: The Men, the Mission, the Atomic Bomb 132
Ensign, Tod, and Michael Uhl 62

INDEX

Enthoven, Alain C., and K. Wayne Smith 78
Ervin, Frank R., Victor W. Sidel, and Saul
   Arnow, eds. 111
Evans, Medford 78

Fail-Safe 132, 138
Falk, Richard, and Robert Jay Lifton 119
Fallout shelters 59, 84, 90, 108, 111
Fallows, James 79
Fat Man and Little Boy 133
Feis, Herbert 34, 35, 79
Feiverson, Harold A., Ted Greenwood, and
   Theodore B. Taylor 44
Feld, Bernard T., Kosta Tsipis, and Anne C.
   Cahn, eds. 107
Fermi, Enrico 1, 2, 10, 15, 16, 18, 19, 22, 23
Fermi, Laura 16
Final Chapter?, The 133
Fineberg, S. Andhil 30
Fisher, R., and W. Ury 116
Fitzpatrick, Mariana, and Ann Marie
   Cunningham 76
Fleming, D. F. 79
Fogelman, Edwin 36
Ford, Daniel 80
Ford, Daniel, Henry Kendall, and Steven Nadis
   116
Forsberg, Randall 67, 81, 116
Forsee, Aylesa 16
Fourth Protocol, The 133
Fowler, John M., ed. 56
Fradkin, Philip L. 56
Frank, Pat 146, 147
Freed, Fred, and Len Giovannitti 36
Freedman, Lawrence, John Baylis, Gerald
   Segal, and Edwina More 105
Fryklund, Richard 80
Fuchs, Klaus 27, 28, 31-33
Fuller, John D. 56

Galbraith, John Kenneth 111
Gallagher, Thomas 44
Gallois, Pierre 80
Garfinkel, Adam M. 81
Garthoff, Raymond L. 81
Gay, William, and Michael Pearson 81
General Advisory Committee of the Atomic
   Energy Commission (GAC) 106
George, Peter 147
Gerson, Joseph, ed. 116
Gilpin, Robert 82
Giovannitti, Len, and Fred Freed 36
Glasstone, Samuel 10
Glasstone, Samuel, and Philip J. Dolan, eds. 11
Golden Rule 113

Goldstein, Alvin H. 30
Goodchild, Peter 17
Goodwin, Robert E., Russell Hardin, John J.
   Mearsheimer, and Gerald Dworkin, eds. 85
Gouzenko, Igor 30, 31
Gowing, Margaret 44
Graetzer, Hans G., and David L. Anderson 10
Gray, Anthony 147
Green, Harold P., and Alan Rosenthal 82
Green, Philip 82
Greene, Owen, Ian Percival, and Irene Ridge
   83
Greenwood, Ted, Harold A. Feiverson, and
   Theodore B. Taylor 44
Griffiths, Franklyn, and John C. Polanyi, eds.
   83
Grinspoon, Lester, ed. 83
Grodzins, Morton, and Eugene Rabinowitch,
   eds. 83
Groves, General Leslie R. 2, 26, 27, 28
Guillain, Robert 36

Ha, Young-Sun 45
Hachiya, Michihiko 37
Hackett, General Sir John 148
Hafemeister, David, ed. 84
Hahn, Otto 1, 10, 17
Haldeman, Joe, ed. 148
Halliday, Fred 84
Halperin, Morton H. 45, 84
Halterman, H. Lee, Patrick O' Heffernam,
   Ronald V. Dellums, and R. H. (Max) Miller,
   eds.
Handel, Michael, Amos Permutter, and Uri
   Bar-Joseph 51
Hardin, Russell, John J. Mearsheimer, Gerald
   Dworkin, and Robert E. Goodwin, eds. 85
Hardy, Ronald 148
Harkavy, Robert E. 45
Harris, Leonard 149
Hart, David 46
Harwell, Mark A. 85
Hawkins, David 26
Hecht, Selig 11
Heims, Steve J. 17
Heinlein, Robert 149
Heisenberg, Werner 15, 18, 19
Herken, Gregg 85, 86
Hersey, John 37
Hewlett, Richard G. and Oscar E. Anderson, Jr.
   26
Hewlett, Richard G., and Francis Duncan 86
Hewlett, Richard G., Philip Cantelon, and
   Robert C. Williams, eds. 10
Hibakusha 2, 40

Hines, Neal O. 57
Hirohito, Emperor 27, 39
Hiroshima: A Document of the Atomic Bombing 138
Hiroshima and Nagasaki 2, 9, 12, 27-29, 34, 64, 93, 134
Hiroshima Maiden 134
Hiroshima, Mon Amour 134, 138
Hirsch, Richard 30
Hoban, Russell 149
Hoeber, Amoretta M., and Joseph D. Douglass 77
Hoenig, Milton M., Thomas B. Cochran, and William M. Arkin 73
Hoffmann, Stanley, Samuel P. Huntington, Joseph S. Nye, Jr., Scott D. Sagan, Albert Carnesale, and Paul Doty, eds. 71
Huie, William Bradford 37
Huiskens, Ronald, and Frank Barnaby 65
Hunt for Red October, The 134
Huntington, Samuel P., Joseph S. Nye, Jr., Scott D. Sagan, Albert Carnesale, Paul Doty, and Stanley Hoffman 71
Hutchins, Robert M. 117
Hyde, H. Montgomery 31

Ibuse, Masuji 149
Iklé, Fred Charles 87
Imai, Ryukichi, and Henry S. Rowen 46
Irving, David 46

Jabber, Fuad 47
Jastrow, Robert 87
Joint Committee on Atomic Energy (JCAE) 82
Jones, Dennis 150
Jones, Gregory, David C. McGarvey, Henry Rowen, Vince Taylor, Roberta Wohlstetter, Albert Wohlstetter, and Thomas A. Brown 109
Jungk, Robert 18, 37

Kahn, Herman 82, 87, 88, 96
Kapur, Ashok 47
Katz, Arthur M. 89
Katz, Milton S. 117
Kegley, Charles W., and Eugene R. Wittkopf, eds. 89
Kelly, Orville E., and Thomas A. Saffer 61
Kemp, Geoffrey, Robert L. Pfaltzgraff, Jr., and Uri Ra'anan, eds. 48
Kendall, Henry, Daniel Ford, and Steven Nadis 116
Kennan, George F. 89
Kennedy, Donald, Walter Orr Roberts, Paul Ehrlich, and Carl Sagan 78

Kenny, Anthony J. 117
Ketchum, Linda E., and Henry H. Wagner 12
Keyes, Ken 118
Keyes, Langley, and Jennifer Learning, eds. 119
Keys, Donald, ed. 118
Kirst, Hans Hellmut 150
Kissinger, Henry A. 90
Kiste, Robert C. 57
Kistiakowsky, George B. 111
Knebel, Fletcher, and Charles W. Bailey 27
Kornbluth, Cyril M. 151
Kothari, D. S. 57
Kramish, Arnold 48
Krosney, Herbert, and Steve Weissman 53
Kunetka, James W. 18
Kurzman, Dan 27
Kuttner, Henry 151

Lamont, Lansing 27
Lang, Daniel 58
Lanham, Edwin 151
Lapp, Ralph E. 11, 58, 84, 90, 118
Larson, Jeanne, and Madge Micheels-Cyrus 119
Larus, Joel 91
Latil, Pierre de 18
Laurence, William L. 11, 28, 91
Lawrence, Ernest Orlando 1, 11, 15, 23
Learning, Jennifer, and Langley Keyes, eds. 119
Lebedinsky, A. V. 59
Lee, Steven, and Avner Cohen, eds. 74
Lehman, John F., and Seymour Weiss 91
Lens, Sidney 92
Lenz, Millicent 152
Levine, Herbert M., and David Carlton, eds. 70
Lewin, Leonard C. 152
Lewis, Flora 92
Lewis, John Wilson, and Xue Litai 48
Lewis, Richard S., Jane Wilson, and Eugene Rabinowitch, eds. 28
Libby, Leona Marshall 19
Lieberman, Joseph I. 93
Lifton, Betty Jean, with photographs by Eikoh Hosoe 38
Lifton, Robert Jay 38
Lifton, Robert Jay, and Richard Falk 119
Lilienthal, David E. 119
Lipton, Judith Eve, and David P. Barash 112
Litai, Xue, and John Wilson Lewis 48
Loeb, Paul Roget 120
London, Julius, and Gilbert F. White, eds. 93

INDEX

Lovins, Amory B., Patrick O'Heffernam, and L. Hunter Lovins 50
Lovins, L. Hunter, Amory B. Lovins, and Patrick O'Heffernam 50
Lucky Dragon 3, 57, 58, 113, 115

MacArthur Library, the 5
McBride, James Hubert 95
MacDonald, Charles B., and Anthony Cave Brown, eds. 25
McGarvey, David C., Henry Rowen, Vince Taylor, Roberta Wohlstetter, Albert Wohlstetter, Thomas A. Brown, and Gregory Jones 109
McGuire, Steven, and Len Ackland, eds. 63
McMahon, Thomas 153
McNamara, Robert S. 95
MacPherson, Malcolm C. 19
Mad Max 135
Mad Max 2 135
Mad Max Beyond Thunderdome 135
Major, John 19
Mandelbaum, Michael 93, 94
Manhattan Project, the 2, 19, 25, 55, 58, 61, 81, 93, 97, 100, 130, 133
Markey, Edward J. 49
Markusen, Ann, and Joel Yudken 94
Maruki, Toshi 38
Marx, Joseph L. 39
Mason, Colin 152
Masters, Dexter 152
Masters, Dexter, and Katherine Way, eds. 120
Mastny, Vojtech, ed. 94
Mawrence, Mel, with John Clark Kimball 59
Maxwell, James 15
Mearsheimer, John J., Gerald Dworkin, Robert E. Goodwin, and Russell Hardin 85
Medvedev, Zhores A. 137
Meitner, Lise 15
Melman, Seymour, ed. 59
Mendeleev, Dmitri 15
Mendl, Wolf 49
Merril, Judith 153
Merton, Thomas 120
Metz, William D., Richard A. Scribner, and Theodore J. Ralston 104
Micheels-Cyrus, Madge, and Jeanne Larson 119
Miller, Fred D., Jr., Jeffrey Paul, John Ahrens, Ellen Frankel Paul, eds. 99
Miller, R. H. (Max), H. Lee Halterman, Patrick O'Heffernam, and Ronald V. Dellums 115
Miller, Walter M. 153
Milton, Joyce, and Ronald Radosh 32
Minear, Richard H., ed. 39

Missile 136
Missiles of October, The 136
Moore, Ruth 20
Moreton, Edwina, Lawrence Freedman, John Baylis, and Gerald Segal 105
Morimoto, Junko 39
Morland, Howard 121
Morris, Edita 154
Moss, Norman 96
Motz, Lloyd, Henry A. Boorse, and Jefferson H. Weaver 15
Moulton, Harland B. 96
Murray, Thomas E. 96
Muste, Abraham J. 121
Myrdal, Alva 121

Nacht, Michael 96
Nagasaki. See Hiroshima and Nagasaki.
Namboodiri, P. K. S., and D. K. Palit 50
Nathan, Otto, and Heinz Norden, eds. 122
Nevada test site 55-58, 60-62
Newby-Fraser, A. R. 49
Newhouse, John 97
Newman, James R. 122
Nichols, K. D. 97
Nightline: "Chelyabinsk—Nuclear Nightmare." 136
Nizer, Louis 31
Nogee, Joseph L. 98
Nolan, Janne E. 98
Non-proliferation Treaty, the 102
Norden, Heinz, and Otto Nathan, eds. 122
Norris, Robert S., Jeffrey I. Sands, Thomas B. Cochran, and William M. Arkin 74
North Atlantic Treaty Organization (NATO) 69, 79
Nova: "Einstein." 137
Nova: "Nuclear Strategy for Beginners." 137
Nuclear Age Literature for Youth 152

Nuclear Fear: A History of Images 152
Nuclear Freeze movement, the 4, 67, 81, 100, 116
Nuclear navy 86
Nuclear Test Ban Treaty, the 95, 96
Nuclear winter 77, 78, 83, 85, 89, 93, 103
Nye, Joseph S., Jr., Graham T. Allison, and Albert Carnesale, eds. 64, 98

O'Connel, Pat 96
O'Heffernam, Patrick, Ronald V. Dellums, R. H. (Max) Miller, and H. Lee Halterman 115
O'Heffernam, Patrick, Amory B. Lovins, and L. Hunter Lovins 50
O'Keefe, Bernard J. 60

On the Beach 3, 137, 138, 152
Only the Strong 138
Operation Castle 57
Operation Crossroads 57
Operation Greenhouse 57
Operation Hardtack 57
Operation Ivy 57
Operation Sandstone 57
Oppenheimer, J. Robert 2, 14, 15, 17, 18, 19, 20, 22, 24, 27, 66, 120, 130, 144
Osada, Arata, ed. 39
Oughterson, Ashley W., and Shields Warren, eds. 40
Outer Limits, The: "Demon with a Glass Hand." 138
Overholt, William H., ed. 50

Padgett, Lewis. *See* Kuttner, Henry.
Pais, Abraham, Glenn T. Seaborg, Isidor I. Rabi, Robert Serber, and Victor F. Weisskopf 20
Palit, D. K., and P. K. S. Namboodiri 50
Palomares, Spain 91, 92, 106
Panofsky, W. K. H. 99
Panos, Louis G., and Stanley A. Blumberg 14
Paul, Ellen Frankel, Fred D. Miller, Jr., Jeffrey Paul, and John Ahrens 99
Paul, Jeffrey, John Ahrens, Ellen Frankel Paul, and Fred D. Miller 99
Pauling, Linus 3, 82, 123
Paulson, Dennis, ed. 123
Pearson, Michael, and William Gay 81
Percival, Ian, Owen Greene, and Irene Ridge 83
Perlmutter, Amos, Michael Handel, and Uri Bar-Joseph 51
Pfaltzgraff, Robert L., Jr., Geoffrey Kemp, and Uri Ra'anan, eds. 48
Pfau, Richard 20
Philby, Kim 31
Pierre, Andrew J. 51
Pilat, Oliver 31
Plate, Thomas Gordon 99
Pogodzinsky, Michael 100
Polanyi, John C., and Franklyn Griffiths, eds. 83
Pollard, Ernest C. 154
Pontecorvo, Bruno 31, 32
Potsdam Conference, the 35, 64, 93, 105
Powaski, Ronald E. 100
Pranger, Robert J., and Dale R. Tahtinen 51
Pressler, Larry 100
Pringle, Peter, and James Spigelman 51
Prins, Gwyn, ed. 101
Prochnau, William 154

Protest and Survive 152

Quester, George H. 101

Ra'anan, Uri, Geoffrey Kemp, and Robert L. Pfaltzgraff, Jr., eds. 48
Rabi, Isidor I. 15, 21
Rabi, Isidor I., Robert Serber, Victor F. Weisskopf, Abraham Pais, and Glenn T. Seaborg 20
Rabinowitch, Eugene, and Morton Grodzins, eds. 83
Rabinowitch, Eugene, Richard S. Lewis, and Jane Wilson, eds. 28
Radiation sickness 37, 39, 40, 56, 111, 133
Radosh, Ronald, and Joyce Milton 32
Ralston, Theodore J., Richard A. Scribner, and William D. Metz 104
Rapoport, Roger 60
Rascovich, Mark 154
Reiss, Mitchell 52
Reynolds, Earle 60
Rigden, John S. 21
Riordan, Michael 101
Roberts, Chalmers M. 101
Roberts, Walter Orr, Paul Ehrlich, Carl Sagan, and Donald Kennedy 78
Root, Jonathan 32
Rosenberg, Howard L. 60
Rosenberg, Julius and Ethel 30-32, 130
Rosenthal, Alan, and Harold P. Green 82
Rosenthal, Debra 123
Rowen, Henry S., and Ryukichi Imai 46
Rowen, Henry, Vince Taylor, Roberta Wohlstetter, Albert Wohlstetter, Thomas A. Brown, Gregory Jones, and David C. McGarvey 109
Rozental, Stefan, ed. 21
Russett, Bruce 102
Russett, Bruce, and Fred Chernoff, eds. 102
Rutherford, Ernest 1, 11, 15

Saffer, Thomas A., and Orville E. Kelly 61
Sagan, Carl 4
Sagan, Carl, and Richard Turco 102
Sagan, Carl, Donald Kennedy, Walter Orr Roberts, and Paul Ehrlich 78
Sagan, Scott D., Albert Carnesale, Paul Doty, Stanley Hoffmann, Samuel P. Huntington, and Joseph S. Nye, Jr. 71
Sakharov, Andrei 16, 21, 84
Sands, Jeffrey I, Thomas B. Cochran, William M. Arkin, and Robert S. Norris 74
Sankichi, Toge 39
Sayen, Jamie 22

Sayer, Karen, and John Dowling, eds. 138
Schaerf, Carlo, and David Carlton, eds. 70
Scheer, Robert, with Narda Zacchino and
Constance Matthiessen 103
Scheinman, Lawrence 52
Schell, Jonathan 124
Schelling, Thomas C. 82, 103
Schloming, Gordon C. 103
Schweitzer, Albert 3, 124
Scoville, Herbert 104
Scribner, Richard A., Theodore J. Ralston, and
William D. Metz 104
SDI. *See* Strategic Defense Initiative.
Segal, Gerald, Edwina Moreton, Lawrence
Freedman, and John Baylis 105
Segre, Emilio 22
Selden, Kyoko, and Mark Selden, eds. 40
Selden, Mark, and Kyoko Selden, eds. 40
Serber, Robert, Victor F. Weisskopf, Abraham
Pais, Glenn T. Seaborg, and Isidor I. Rabi
20
Shaheen, Jack G., ed. 138
Sharp, Malcolm P. 32
Sherwin, Martin J. 105
Shute, Nevil 3, 155
Sidel, Victor W., Saul Arnow, and Frank R.
Ervin, eds. 111
Simpson, George E., and Neal R. Burger 155
Smith, Alice Kimball, and Charles Weiner, eds.
22
Smith, Gerard 105
Smith, K. Wayne, and Alain C. Enthoven 78
Smith, Ralph Carlisle, and Edith C. Truslow 29
Smyth, Henry D. 28
Snow, C. P. 155
Spector, Leonard S. 52
Spigelman, James, and Peter Pringle 51
Star Wars. *See* Strategic Defense Initiative (SDI)
Steinberg, Rafael 40
Sterba, James P., ed. 125
Stimson, Henry L. 34
Strategic Arms Limitation Talks (SALT I,
SALT II) 3, 12, 91, 99, 104, 105
Strategic Defense Initiative (SDI) 4, 70-72, 74,
81, 87, 99, 100, 107
Strauss, Lewis L. 20, 106
Strout, Cushing, ed. 22
Summer Flowers 39
Sylves, Richard T. 106
Szasz, Ferenc M. 29
Szilard, Gertrude Weiss, and Spencer R. Weart,
eds. 23
Szilard, Leo 23, 27, 84, 120, 156

Tahtinen, Dale R., and Robert J. Pranger 51

Talbott, Strobe 107
Tamiki, Hara 39
Taylor, Theodore B., and Mason Willrich 108
Taylor, Theodore B., Ted Greenwood, and
Harold A. Feiverson 44
Taylor, Vince, Roberta Wohlstetter, Albert
Wohlstetter, Thomas A. Brown, Gregory
Jones, David C. McGarvey, and Henry
Rowen 109
Teller, Edward 14, 82, 84, 96
Teller, Edward, with Allen Brown 61
Terman, Douglas 156
TERMINATOR 2: Judgement Day 139
Testament 139
THEM! 139
Thomas, Gordon, and Max Morgan Witts 41
Thompson, Edward P. 125
Thompson, James 125
Threads 140
Three Mile Island 12
Tibbets, Colonel Paul 41, 132
Time Machine, The 140
Tirman, John, ed. 107
Titus, A. Constadina 61
Trapnell, Edward R., and Corbin Allardice 55
Trinity test, the 2, 10, 12, 24, 28, 29, 100
Triumph des Willens (Triumph of the Will) 140
Trumbull, Robert 41
Truslow, Edith C., and Ralph Carlisle Smith 29
Tsipis, Kosta, Anne C. Cahn, and Bernard T.
Feld, eds. 107
Turco, Richard, and Carl Sagan 102
Twilight's Last Gleaming 141

Uhl, Michael, and Tod Ensign 62
Ury, W., and R. Fisher 116

Van de Graaff, Robert 15
Van Ornum, William, and Mary Wicker Van
Ornum 126
Von Neumann, John 17

Wade, Nicholas 108
Wagner, Henry N., and Linda E. Ketchum 12
War Game, The 24 138
WarGames 141
Warner, Edith 25
Warren, Shields, and Ashley W. Oughterson,
eds. 40
Way, Katherine, and Dexter Masters, eds. 120
Weart, Spencer R. 12
Weart, Spencer R., and Gertrude Weiss Szilard,
eds. 23
Weaver, Jefferson H., Henry A. Boorse, and
Lloyd Motz 15

Weiner, Charles, and Alice Kimball Smith, eds. 22

Weiss, Seymour, and John F. Lehman 91

Weisskopf, Victor 23

Weisskopf, Victor F., Abraham Pais, Glenn T. Seaborg, Isidor I. Rabi, and Robert Serber 20

Weissman, Steve, and Herbert Krosney 53

Weston, Burns H., ed. 108

Wheeler, Harvey, and Eugene Burdick 144

Wheeler, Keith 41

White, Gilbert F., and Julius London, eds. 93

Wiener, Norbert 17

Wigner, Eugene P., ed. 108

Wilcox, Robert K. 53

Willens, Harold 127

Williams, Robert C., Philip Cantelon, and Richard G. Hewlett, eds. 10

Williams, Robert Chadwell 33

Williams, Shelton L. 53

Willrich, Mason, and Bennett Boskey, eds. 43

Willrich, Mason, and Theodore B. Taylor 108

Wilson, Jane, ed. 23

Wilson, Jane, Richard S. Lewis, and Eugene Rabinowitch, eds. 28

Wittkopf, Eugene R., and Charles W. Kegley, eds. 89

Witts, Max Morgan, and Gordon Thomas 41

Wohlstetter, Albert, Thomas A. Brown, Gregory Jones, David C. McGarvey, Henry Rowen, Vince Taylor, and Roberta Wohlstetter 109

Wohlstetter, Roberta, Albert Wohlstetter, Thomas A. Brown, Gregory Jones, David C, McGarvey, Henry Rowen, and Vince Taylor 109

Wolfson, Richard 13

Woodworth, Elizabeth M. 126

Wyden, Peter 29

Yoko, Ota 39

York, Herbert 24, 109

Yucca Flats, Nevada. *See* Nevada test site.

Yudken, Joel, and Ann Markusen 94

Zuckerman, Edward 127

Zuckerman, Solly 110